ATLA Monograph Series
edited by Dr. Kenneth E. Rowe

1. Ronald L. Grimes. *The Divine Imagination: William Blake's Major Prophetic Visions.* 1972.

2. George D. Kelsey. *Social Ethics Among Southern Baptists, 1917-1969.* 1973.

3. Hilda Adam Kring. *The Harmonists: A Folk-Cultural Approach.* 1973.

4. J. Steven O'Malley. *Pilgrimage of Faith: The Legacy of the Otterbeins.* 1973.

THE HARMONISTS
A Folk-Cultural Approach

by

HILDA ADAM KRING

ATLA Monograph Series No. 3

The Scarecrow Press, Inc., Metuchen, N. J.
and
The American Theological Library Association
1973

335.974815
K92h
1973

Library of Congress Cataloging in Publication Data

Kring, Hilda Adam.
  The Harmonists.

  (ATLA monograph series, no. 3)
  Originally presented as the author's thesis,
University of Pennsylvania.
  Bibliography: p.
  1. Harmony Society. I. Title. II. Series:
American Theological Library Association. ATLA
monograph series, no. 3
HX656.H2K74 1973   335'.9'74815   73-2571
ISBN 0-8108-0603-7

ACKNOWLEDGMENTS

One who researches never does it alone. Professors, scholars, librarians, friends, and strangers come to one's assistance; so where acknowledgments start and stop one never knows. My indebtedness should begin with my father and late mother, Mr. and Mrs. Alfons Adam, who had the foresight to start my education in Germany although they lived in New York City. There I received the thorough training in German scriptwriting without which I would not have been able to translate the personal letters so pertinent for any thorough study of the Harmonists.

It was Dr. George Swetnam, author of <u>Pittsylvania Country</u> and numerous other books and pamphlets about the Pittsburgh area, who encouraged my interest in Old Economy Village.

I am especially indebted to Dr. Don Yoder of the University of Pennsylvania who was enthusiastic about this proposed folk-cultural study and whose support and criticisms were invaluable. Also, most helpful was the encouragement and assistance of Dr. Kenneth Goldstein of the University of Pennsylvania. And Mrs. Hilda Rifkin was a splendid "liaison officer."

My research in the Old Economy Village archives would have been impossible had it not been for the cordial and able assistance of its curator, Dan Reibel. His entire staff, especially Mrs. Evelyn Matter and Mrs. Betty Post, were more than kind. In this Ambridge area, Miss Christiana Knoedler, Mrs. Margaret Rupp, Mrs. E. A. May and Max Henrici were links to the past.

When I visited New Harmony, Indiana, I became indebted to Mrs. Frances Lewis, Mrs. Josephine Elliott, and Don Blair who shared their knowledge, the Workingmen's Institute Library, and their friends. In Harmony, Pennsylvania, Dr. Arthur Stewart was of great help.

Being an amateur photographer, I leaned heavily on

Mrs. Eugene Liggitt for all special pictures used to depict the Harmonist material culture.

When difficult questions arose, authorities Dr. Karl J. R. Arndt and Dr. William E. Wilson graciously answered inquiries. Mrs. Rae Korson of the Library of Congress answered all S. O. S. calls with her famed efficiency and genuine concern.

I wish to pay tribute to my husband, Dr. Frederick S. Kring, for his criticisms and, above all, his patience. It was his Geduld that kept the harmonious spirit alive when the Harmonist problems became my "dragon."

Hilda Adam Kring

TABLE OF CONTENTS

EDITOR'S FOREWORD

At a time when much of Europe was torn by religious controversey, America offered refuge to many religious groups persecuted in their homelands. Not only was the religious climate milder here than in Europe, but the country had available land aplenty upon which to establish new versions of religious communities. The resultant communal societies, some short-lived, others still flourishing, form a unique part of American social history.

The Harmony Community was founded in 1805 by George Rapp, a Separatist from Württemberg, Germany. The first settlement in Pennsylvania was later relocated in Indiana and then in Economy, Pennsylvania. Their celibate, communitarian way of life lasted for a century, until 1905.

Today, under stress of urban life or dissatisfaction with the larger socio-political context, many Americans again consider communalism to be a social and personal ideal. Thus a study of one of the pioneer "communes" of the 19th century offers more than just insight into our history. These communities form the basis of an ongoing American social phenomenon.

Mrs. Kring's sympathetic study makes a timely contribution to a topic of current interest which extends to sociologists and anthropologists as well as to historians and theologians.

Although most American and Canadian doctoral dissertations in religion are available to scholars on microfilm or expensive xerographic copies, distribution and scholarly use is limited. A number of studies are submitted each year which deserve a better fate than to remain in the drawers of library microfilm cabinets.

The American Theological Library Association has undertaken responsibility for a modest dissertation publishing program in the field of religious studies. Our aim in this monograph series is to publish in serviceable format and at reasonable cost two dissertations of quality in the field of religious studies each year. Titles are selected by the Committee on Publication from titles nominated by Graduate School Deans or Directors of Graduate Studies in Religion.

Professor Kring, a native of Germany, has studied at Millersville State College and the University of Pennsylvania and received the doctorate from the University of Pennsylvania. She is the author of several articles in English literature and American folklore studies and currently serves as Associate Professor of English at Grove City College, Grove City, Pa. We are pleased to publish her study as number three in our series.

Kenneth E. Rowe, Editor

Drew University Library
Madison, New Jersey

PREFACE

On June 22, 1677 William Penn wrote from Frankfurt "An Epistle to the Churches of Jesus Christ throughout the world" in which he said:

> I dearly embrace and salute you all, in this day of the glorious fulfilling of His promises to His Church in the wilderness. For, He hath reached unto us, and brought salvation near us! For, He hath found us out, and hath heard our solitary cries, the deep mournful supplications of our bound spirits when we were as the dove without its mate, and the lonely pelican in the wilderness, when we were ready to cry out, Is there none to save, is there none to help?

> ... Friends and Brethren who have been visited with the fatherly visitation from on high, and have received God's eternal Word and Testament in your hearts, by which you have been gathered home to Christ Jesus, the true Shepherd, from all the idol-shepherds and their barren mountains and unprofitable hills, where you have been scattered in the dark and gloomy days of apostasy....

> Friends! The Lord of heaven and earth hath heard our cries, and the full time is come, yea, the appointed time is come, and the voice of the eternal Spirit in our hearts hath been heard on this wise many a time--Awake, thou that sleepest, and I will give thee life. [1]

Many German Pietists answered Penn's call, and came to eastern Pennsylvania. One hundred and twenty-seven years later George Rapp and his adherents followed, settling in western Pennsylvania. They, like the Pietists and Mystics before them, abhorred what they called the general deplorable state of religion in Germany. They wanted an inward and living faith; one based on simplest Christianity which entertained the hope of the immediate second coming of Jesus. They acknowledged no written creed. The Bible, especially Acts 2:44, 45, Acts 4:32, and Revelation, regulated their lives. Added to their communal living inspired by Acts, and their belief in chiliasm inspired by Revelation, were mysticism and celibacy so that they would be pure enough to be among the chosen ones for the New Jerusalem. This way of life, lasting for one hundred years, the Harmonists established in western Pennsylvania, later in Indiana, and again in western Pennsylvania.

Like other social and religious experiments of the 19th century, the Harmonists were copy for the travelers of the day who were recording the development of the young America. The Duke of Saxe-Weimar, Morris Birkbeck, J. S. Buckingham, William Cobbett, William Faux, E. P. Fordham, Henry Heald, William Hebert, Harriet Martineau, John Melish, H. R. Schoolcraft and others had their say. But their writings were only vignettes.

It was not until the Harmonists were scurrilously and anonymously attacked in the May 1866 issue of The Atlantic Monthly that a complete and objective account of their sect was written and published by Aaron Williams in answer to The Atlantic Monthly. Williams's The Harmony Society was the main source for Nordhoff's thirty-two page account of the Harmonists in The Communistic Societies of the United States. Of course, Nordhoff visited Economy in 1874, and was thus able to give a personal account of the sect in its later stage. However, Nordhoff's interest was not with the Harmonists per se, but with the labor question. Because of this he visited the Harmonists and ten other communal societies in the United States. He studied the existing literature about the sects, added his observations, and classified his findings re their respective religious practices, their mores and customs, industries, businesses, governments, and histories.

John A. Bole, publishing The Harmony Society in 1904, one year before the Society was dissolved, is the first scholar who was able to use the German documents and, thus, produce a significant work. His work, however, has been out of print for a long time. It was not until 1965, when Dr. Karl J. R. Arndt published his comprehensive George Rapp's Harmony Society, 1785-1847, that German scholarship was again in evidence. Dr. Arndt has just published his second volume, George Rapp's Successors and Material Heirs. He now has an "encyclopaedia" of Rappania. John S. Duss, one of the last trustees of the Society, and Christiana Knoedler, a daughter of one of the Harmonist employees, published memoirs in 1943 and 1954, respectively. Dr. William E. Wilson devoted 113 pages to the Harmonists in his The Angel and the Serpent, published in 1964.

Added to these non-fiction accounts is Marguerite Young's very inaccurate conception of the Harmonists in her 1945 novel, Angel in The Forest. Unfortunately, this fantastic novel was republished in 1966. It shows no understanding of Father Rapp or of his followers and the communitarian sects.

With the opening of the museum at Harmony, Pennsylvania, the restoration work at New Harmony, Indiana, and the restoring of Old Economy Village at Ambridge, Pennsylvania, brochures are readily available telling historians, folklorists and tourists about the Harmonists. But with this surge of interest comes the danger of losing the moving spirit behind the Harmonists. This spirit is found in their religion, a communitarian sect, which gave them an actual way of life--a harmonious way as they chose to call it. One could not exist without the other. But people, failing to see the Harmonists in volkskundlicher Sicht, see instead "Red Communism" when they hear communal living; fanatics, when they hear celibacy.

Arthur E. Bestor Jr., in his Backwoods Utopias, calls the experimental communities of the past century communitarian movements because the community was the central point. He says about communitarianism: "It is collectivistic not individualistic, it is resolutely opposed to revolution, and it is impatient with gradualism. "2

He further explains that "for the first century and a half of its history in America, the communitarian point of view was peculiarly associated with religion. "3 Bestor also found that the communitarian ideal as it developed in America was involved with the specific religious ideology "of the radical Protestant sects that arose in the Reformation. "4 Bryan R. Wilson, in his Sects and Society, sees the sect as a social unit when he says:

> The sect is not only an ideological unit, it is, to
> a greater or lesser degree, a social unit, seeking
> to enforce behaviour on those who accept belief,
> and seeking every occasion to draw the faithful

apart from the rest of the society and into the company of each other.... The essential difference, however, is that the sect, as a protest group, has always developed its own distinctive ethic, belief and practices, against the background of the wider society; its own protest is conditioned by the economic, social, ideological and religious circumstances prevailing at the time of its emergence and development. [5]

Wilson's statement is the basis for the study of sects in volkskundlicher Sicht--a folk-cultural approach. Irmgard Simon pioneered such a study in 1965 with her study of the Seventh-Day Adventists in her Die Gemeinschaft der Siebenten-Tags-Adventisten in volkundlicher Sicht (Münster: Aschendorffsche Buchdruckerei, 1965). She wrote not only about the theology and worship of the Seventh-Day-Adventists, but also about how these factors influenced their complete way of life.

Dr. Don Yoder, chairman of the Department of Folklore-Folklife of the University of Pennsylvania, teaches Religious Thought 525, Sects and Cults in American Religion. Here he proposes the thesis that in many cases it is paramount to connect religion and folk-cultural studies in order to understand fully their personal meaning and social significance, and to see a given body functioning in its entirety. He says that we have studied the organized bodies from the standpoint of theology and worship, but need with many of them to study their complete way of life, as the folklife scholar or cultural anthropologist studies other forms of community.

The thesis of this book is to show how a simple, devout people followed their "drummer" to the kingdom of God, not with lip-service but with action found in the Bible, music, rites of passage, calendric customs, home patterns, work, and community relations. Their religion was a complete way of life. It was an integral part of their daily living which put them at odds with the general society. Were it not for this, they would not have answered Penn's call made 127 years earlier to other sects. There would not have been a Harmonie named for their harmonious state, nor an Economy, which had nothing to do with economics but with a divine Economy about which George Rapp said:

This divine Economy, which has been so long

xiv

neglected is now coming to light, in its true and nobel characters, exhibiting the image of God in man, and because it was once implanted in man, he must infallibly arrive at the point of his original destination. And therefore, all good men, however few in number, must unite together to obtain this arm and withdraw from the degraded scenes of life, and associate for nobler purposes. [6]

Notes

1. <u>Journal of William Penn while visiting Holland and Germany in 1677</u>, Philadelphia, 1874, pp. 50-51. Quoted in John Joseph Stoudt, Pennsylvania Folk-Art (Allentown: Schlechter's, 1948), pp. 60-61.

2. Arthur E. Bestor Jr., <u>Backwoods Utopias</u> (Philadelphia: University of Pennsylvania Press, 1950), p. 4.

3. <u>Ibid.</u>, p. 4.

4. <u>Ibid.</u>, p. 5.

5. Bryan R. Wilson, <u>Sects and Society</u> (Berkeley: University of California Press, 1961), p. 1.

6. [George Rapp], <u>Thoughts on the Destiny of Man</u> (Indiana: Harmony Society, 1824), p. 31.

Chapter I

THE HARMONISTS

The beginning of Pietism, Separatism, Mysticism, and Dissent in Württemberg did not start with George Rapp and his followers, nor did it end with them. For almost three hundred years there had been religious disputes which often were more terrible than the hell they sought to avoid. Enthusiasms ran high. The layman, caught in the whirlwind, often looked for escape from the furor and the trappings of official churches in the Bible per se. Here, more often than not, he found solace and an answer which at first seemed simple. However, as this seeker for an inward light became involved in interpretation, he, too, had to seek for help, which more than likely he found in mystics like Johann Arndt, Johann Herder and Jakob Böhme. The latter carried "the mood into a mystical union of the individual soul with a God conceived as the Universal Well and Ground of all things, containing all contradictions, all 'evil' as well as 'good.'"[1] And Rufus M. Jones says:

> One idea underlies everything which Bohme [sic]
> has written, namely that nobody can successfully
> 'search into visible Nature,' or can say anything
> true about man or about the problem of good and
> evil, until he has 'apprehended the whole Nature
> out of which all things were made.' [sic]2

That George Rapp was influenced by Böhme is clearly seen in the following passage from Thoughts on the Destiny of Man, Rapp's only work other than his hymns:

> In how many thousand different schems [sic] have
> mankind already been engaged! All of which fell
> sacrifices to corruption; from their fragments,
> others came forth, and disappeared again. Should
> there be no need then for something permanent,
> to fill the vacuum of man's expanded heart? It
> is unity of well combined strength, towards pro-
> moting a united Whole both for spiritual and tem-

1

poral happiness, and whoever has this problem at
heart, and who has lost a relish for the orthodox
doctrine of man, will find it.
. . . .

It is our destination to get clear of all bad habits,
and then we will have more extensive and precise
views, to immolate our best thoughts and sentiments, into the sanctuary of a more exalted friendship, and live in the intimate circle of brothers.
This is heaven, sought for by so many people,
taking the bypath, because in their imagination,
they create for themselves a heaven, either too
sensual or too spiritual, according to their notions,
which however exists no where except in their
ideas.   Whatever you look for, lays [sic] before
your feet to stumple [sic] over it every day. [3]

But such simplicity of heart was not for the sophisticated clergy and upper classes, especially in Württemberg
which was continually plagued by Enthusiasts of various
degrees.   However, Aaron Williams does not consider this
an endurance test for them.   He says:

It has been usually found that in a period of religious deterioration, the clergy and men of higher
classes are among the first to go astray, while
true religion still lingers in the homes and hearts
of the middle and lower classes of people.   It
was so in Germany, and especially in Württemberg.[4]

Not that the middle and lower classes did not also
have their struggles and doubts, even after they aligned
themselves to a charismatic leader like Rapp.   Man consists of contraries spoken of by Böhme and which Rapp knew
only too well.   The following letter shows Rapp's handling
of a problem:

Johan Christoph,
     Instead of receiving a letter from you we
heard a rumor; we love you even though you are
leaving because we know truth (now hidden) has
been revealed to you.   Go far and amuse yourself on the broad forest-path; don't miss the May-
flowers, but you know the southern path has passion (Feuer-brod); none of this shall keep you
from our friendship.   Indirectness is bound to the

direct, therefore bring your exuberant companions.
Everything has shape and form.   Because of this
the outer substance cannot exist without the inner
substance.   Everything hangs together and seeks
form, and everything will become visible through
Christ, but our soul has a long way to go.   Because of this there is no union with the spirit.
And as long as it is like this, there will be sorrow and crippling effects.   Nor should brothers
be separated for too long a time.   Implore God
that it won't happen.

Further, I am convinced that if you had followed your inclination you would have come, for
I was ill for three weeks and was close to the
last hour.   It would have been pleasant to see you.
Now that I have recovered, we can get together
and show you ways of the spirit and if they are
united with Jesus.   Fare well, and I hope for a
visit soon.

                            Cordially,
              (signed) Johann Georg Rapp[5]

But Rapp's own problems with the Lutheran Church
grew.   Since it was the state church it naturally followed
that the civil authorities also became uneasy about Rapp and
his followers.   They did not fear an actual rebellion, but
neither were they pleased with Rapp's refusal to baptize
children, to attend church, and to take communion.   Finally,
in the early spring of 1798, the Rapp group was annoying
enough to attract the attention of the Württemberg legislature
and was asked to submit a statement about its belief.   Briefly
it consisted of seven points:

1.   The Church. --They believed in a Christian
Church based on the plan of the Apostles and where, according to 1 Cor. 14:27-32, the spirit is allowed to move
one to speak.

2.   Baptism. --They found no real evidence in the
Bible for child baptism.   There is mention of it in Rom.
6:3, 4 and 1 Cor. 7:14, but they said it is not for all men.
Children, however, according to Mark 10:13-16, should be
blessed by tried men.

3.   Holy Communion. --It is in the nature of an agape
before which there is confession, secret and public according to circumstances.   Each brings a gift from which a

a meal is prepared. After the meal, a short address is
given, bread and wine are brought in and blessed and dis-
tributed by a brother with the statement: "Mark well, and
do this in memory of me."

     4. School. --The Separatists do their own teaching be-
cause they do not want the children tainted by others.   After
they are grown up, they make their own choice of religion.

     5. Confirmation. --They do not allow the children to
take part in the ceremonies because the children are more
concerned with clothing than the vow.

     6. Government and Taking an Oath. --They thought
government is good and that one cannot do without it; therefore they supported it.   "Yea," "Yea," and "Nay," "Nay,"
was substituted for an oath.

     7. The Military Order. --They will not serve because
their frame of mind, like the minds of all men who have
"practiced sanctification," is not good for it.   However, in
lieu of service they will submit to payment of taxes. [6]

     These points were adhered to in America.   But three
of their most important tenets are missing from this statement: the idea of holding all property in common, the idea
of celibacy, and the belief in the second coming of Christ.
This indicates cautiousness, a wait-and-see attitude.   They
did not have to wait long, for the general tension caused by
religious unrest was heightened by Napoleon's knocking on
the door.   Before long, Rapp again was considered a threat
to the authorities, and he in turn, feeling stronger, gave way
to his thoughts on emigration.   Arndt says that "France and
even Louisiana had been considered at one time," but Louisiana was sold by the time plans were made. [7] But, the die
was cast and Rapp, with his son John and friends Dr. P.F.C.
Haller and Dr. Christoph Müller, set out for America.   In
Germany they left Frederick Reichert in charge; he later became Rapp's adopted son, and the great businessman of the
Harmonists.

     The foursome sailed from Amsterdam on the ship
"Canton" and arrived in Baltimore on October 7, 1803. [8] Although Rapp was delighted with the freedom of faith and the
plentiful land, he also knew that building a new community
would be a great deal of work, and so advised Frederick not
to persuade anyone to come. [9] At the same time Frederick

was having considerable trouble with Amsterdam and the cap-
tain who was to take them at the beginning of April, 1804,
and was also having great difficulty in raising money for the
journey. In his despair he wrote about their finances and
conditions in general:

> I wish that we did not have anything if it was the
> will of God; we could surely depart or get away
> more easily, for nothing is nearer to God than ab-
> solute poverty.
> . . . .
> Conditions are such that all want to go. Almost a
> third of the population wants to leave--some to
> Russia, some to Austria, and some to America.
> It looks like total ruin.[10]

On July 4, 1804 the "Aurora" arrived in Baltimore
with 300 future Harmonists; on September 15, 1804, 269 arrived on the "Atlantic" in Philadelphia; and on September 19,
1804 the "Margaret" brought 80 more for Butler County
where they had assembled to lead a harmonious life, and so
called the town Harmony and took the name Harmonists, although some outsiders called them Rappites after their
leader.

It should be noted here that Dr. P. F. C. Haller did
not stay with George Rapp. With a group of Württembergers,
who had arrived with the "Margaret" on September 18, 1804,
and had spent the winter of 1804-05 in Germantown, he settled in Lycoming County, Pennsylvania. Russell Wieder Gilbert gives May 20, 1805 as the date for their settlement which
they chose to call Blooming Grove, possibly because of the
dogwood and laurel in bloom at that time.[11] This separation, however, does not mean that they had broken relationships with each other. Relatives lived in both places and
visited back and forth.[12] If one judges from the wills, the
matter of private ownership would appear to be one of the
points of their dissent. Gilbert cites two examples. Chris-
topher Rall wrote in 1833:

> If there is any more property left, my Son Martin
> shall be the heir for it with this condition: If he
> moves from Economie and begins house keeping
> for himself (for I am not willing to have been
> Rapps Negro), but, should he or none of his
> children move out of Economie within the space of
> ten years from this date and begin house keeping

for himself, he hath no right of heritage any more.
But if he still remain in Economie where he is now,
he shall receive hereditary five dollars. [13]

John Stump revealed the same feeling toward Economy in 1834
when he wrote:

> ... my Son John shall receive one hundred and fif-
> ty Dollars, [sic] upon this Condition, [sic] if he or
> his Son Jacob will move out of Economy and stays
> out, for in Economy shall come nothing.... [14]

The Blooming Grove group was not celibate; and, as
their name "Dunkers" denotes, they accepted baptism by im-
mersion.

Dr. David Gloss, another early follower of George
Rapp, also came to a different way of thinking when he was
on American soil. He and his followers, disturbed by Rapp's
growing asceticism, settled in 1805 in Salem Township,
Columbia County, Ohio, the place first chosen by Rapp for
his people. [15]

So it is evident that the first years brought dissension
and difficulties to the Harmonists. The following undated,
unsigned document eloquently tells of these early struggles.
It appears to have been written for a Harmonifest celebration,
February 15. The handwriting would indicate it to be
Frederick Rapp's.

> One says in the maxim: All the beginning is dif-
> ficult, and this The Harmony Society experienced
> in full measure. If we think in toto about the dif-
> ficulties, anxiety, care and work brought on by
> our emigration from Germany and immigration to
> America and the founding of our society we would
> be amazed to think that we were able to accom-
> plish so much. The emigration from Württemberg
> and crossing the ocean was something to consider,
> but the society's spirit, which already then guided
> them in everything, gave them courage to carry on
> regardless of the cost. The faithful achieved their
> goal and what they wanted stands fulfilled after a
> slow beginning. It is something to consider that
> since the time our society made possible the de-
> parture en masse, many thousands of people from
> all parts of Germany yearly followed our example,

and many clever American statesmen today honor
George Rapp and his society as pioneers of German
immigration in the United States who through diligence and saving soon achieved wealth. This also
amazed many people about us that we were able to
hold together so many people, especially since we
had so little capital. For even after the brothers
pooled their money it came to only $23,000. It is
well known that this occurred first on February 15,
1805. However, already in the fall of the previous
year some came together and made small beginning, but there were poor among them who couldn't
even pay their trip, but Father [Rapp] added the
gift money he received in Baltimore and Philadelphia. With this he also had to buy food for all.
Everything was scarce and expensive in this new
area; few Americans had anything to offer. For a
whole year they had to get flour from the Beaver
mills until they were able to harvest rye, potatoes
and turnips the first year.

It must be remembered that with that $23,000 not
only was the land to be paid, but also the food for
450-500 persons, the cattle, horses, tools, machinery and clothing had to be bought.

During the first year there also were people who
withdrew and wanted their money, who made difficulties for the society, reported us, and demand-
ed their money on the spot. But already at that
time our credit was established and the court ruled
that all those who withdrew had to adhere to the
contract, wait the allotted time and be satisfied with
the three yearly installments. For after the society had put the money to use it was impossible to
do it any other way.

These dissenters spread all type of calumny and
reported that we could not last a year. Americans
not sympathetic to our cause listened to this and
didn't even want to establish a post office which
first was placed in Zelienople, but soon thereafter
was brought to Harmony. The doubt and mistrust
of our plan even reached the people in Pittsburgh
so that where at one time we could get a load of
salt, iron and other necessary articles on credit
we could get nothing. [Paper is torn here.] But

someone whom we did not know offered us credit
and thereby we were able to stave off trouble for
awhile.

Just think what concerns, troubles and countless
cares were on the shoulders of the leaders surrounded by a strange language, strange customs, without
money, without friends, in a strange land with an
uncultured people many of whom were dissatisfied
and false. Those of the society here today who personally know about the beginnings, who experienced
the birth-pangs know the importance of uniting the
community spirit. The king of a country protects
himself through power; the general of an army,
through military law; the state-church, through
government protection. But, Society, where was
your strength and your protection? First, in the
word of the Scripture through the leader who with
the inner Word united in enlightenment through
which the spirit of the society took form and tied
the knot of brotherhood; secondly, in the endurance,
care and patience of the leader awaiting the development through light and darkness of each member
so each one could be taken up in brotherhood.

One shudders when one thinks of all the difficulties
at the beginning. For right at the start many showed
their colors. The weak ones wanted to cast doubt
on the leader. They complained about everything--
nothing was right: the work was too difficult; living too unpleasant; obedience too burdensome;
[paper torn.] And what have they achieved?
Those who were unfaithful and left the society?

In contrast, what have we who endured the days of
the beginning, the poverty, the cares? They are
gone, those days without houses and huts when
goods were unloaded under the trees. When this
family and that during the first winter suffered
privations; the days of doubt about our plan which
had to be started from the beginning; when much
had to be done by hand; where the leader because
of lack of cloth had his first coat in Harmony
made from two old German coats; when many a
mother made children's clothing from bed-ticking;
up to the time when some income was realized
from the harvest of rye; when it was carried for a

mile in large baskets on the head. We were delighted when we completed the first small cloth because we knew little about factory-work since we
were mostly farmers and vine-tenders and had to
start at the beginning with factory technique. All
this together is something to ponder and consider. [16]

Notes

1. Will and Ariel Durant, The Age of Reason Begins (New
   York: Simon and Schuster, 1961), p. 553.

2. Rufus M. Jones, Spiritual Reformers in the 16th and
   17th Centuries (Boston: The Macmillan Company,
   1914), p. 172, quoting Böhme's Aurora.

3. [George Rapp], Thoughts on the Destiny of Man
   (Indiana: Harmony Society, 1824), p. 23.

4. Aaron Williams, The Harmony Society (Pittsburgh:
   W. S. Haven, 1866), p. 14.

5. Letter, Johann George Rapp to Johann Christoph,
   Feb. 10, 1801, Old Economy, Archives, Series 2.

6. Karl J. R. Arndt, George Rapp's Harmony Society
   1785-1847 (Philadelphia: University of Pennsylvania
   Press, 1965), pp. 36-39.

7. Ibid., p. 49.

8. Williams, Society, p. 39. [Arndt, 1785-1847, p. 61,
   says they landed in Philadelphia.]

9. Arndt, 1785-1847, p. 62.

10. Letter, Frederick Reichert Rapp to George Rapp,
    March 27, 1804, Old Economy, Archives, Series 2.

11. Russell Wieder Gilbert, "Blooming Grove, The Dunker
    Settlement of Central Pennsylvania," Pennsylvania
    History, January, 1953, pp. 22-39.

12. Ibid., p. 28.

13. Ibid., p. 29, quoting the Lycoming County Will Book

A, p. 264.

14. Ibid., p. 29, quoting the Lycoming County Will Book A, p. 276.

15. Arndt, 1785-1847, p. 99.

16. Document, n.d., Old Economy, Archives, Box 7.

Chapter II

THE CREDO

The Harmonists acknowledged no written creed. The
Bible, especially the 1534 Luther translation which is still
in the Old Economy archives, and the Berleburger Bible, no
longer in these archives, served as the guide of this communitarian sect. Separated from the world and the "church,"
they found in Acts and Revelation a way of life. All of the
beliefs were not expressed; some were implied. But it mattered not into which category the beliefs fell; they were of
equal importance to the Harmonist way of life.

A. Expressed Beliefs

1. Communal living. --This way of life is first and
foremost governed by Acts 4:32--Acts 2:44, 45:

> And the multitude of them that believed were of
> one heart and of one soul: neither said any of
> them that ought of the things which he possessed
> was his own; but they had all things common.

> All that believed were together, and had all
> things common;
> And sold their possessions and goods, and
> parted them to all men, as every man had need.

It is this firm belief that prompted Rapp in 1818 to
burn the record showing how much each member had contributed to the common coffer. It prevented discontent.
Even Romelius Baker as a child had asked how much his
family had contributed.[1] If any were like Ananias and Sapphira, they would not meet death as Ananias and Sapphira did
but they would meet hostility and would have to leave. With
each withdrawal Rapp, by this time called "Father" even
though he was only 47, thought the fold grew stronger, because he firmly believed "that many are called, but few are
chosen."

2. Chosen people. --That they considered themselves
the Chosen People is evident from their hymns, in which
they frequently call themselves "du auserwählte Schar."

3. The dual Adam. --The Harmonist views on the
original character of Adam are like the Shakers', with whom
they also shared the persuasions of communitarian and celibate life. Nordhoff states that the Shakers hold "that God
is a dual person, male and female; that Adam was a dual
person, being created in God's image."[2] And it was so with
the Harmonists, who thought of Adam as a dual being, having
both sexual elements, taking Gen. 1:26, 27 literally:

> And God said, Let us make men in our image,
> after our likeness, and let them have dominion
> And so God created man in his own image; in
> the image of God created he him; male and female
> created he them.

They understood the word "them" in both these verses
as applying to the dual Adam, before the separation of Eve
from him.[3] With this separation came the downfall of man,
and until this state of unity is again obtained there will be
sorrows.

4. Celibacy. --Because of this bi-unc Adam, they
have a somewhat mystical basis for their idea of celibacy
which they introduced in 1807, and all those who were married were to live as brother and sister. In addition to point-
ing to the Old Testament, they have the exemplification of
Jesus Himself and the writings of St. Paul and Matthew respectively:

> 1 Cor. 7:1, 7, 8, 32
> ... It is good for a man not to touch a woman.
> ....
> For I would that all men were even as I am
> myself ....
> I say therefore to the unmarried and widows,
> It is good for them if they abide even as I.
> ....
> ... He that is unmarried careth for the things
> that belong to the Lord, how he may please the
> Lord.

> Matthew 19:12
> ... and there be eunuchs, which have made them-
> selves eunuchs for the kingdom of heaven's sake.

5. Chiliasm. --Their denial of the flesh was to prepare them for the great second coming, which they connect
with Acts 1:11:

> ... Ye men of Galilee, why stand ye gazing up into
> heaven? this same Jesus which is taken up from
> you into heaven, shall so come in like manner as ye
> have seen him go into heaven.

And with Acts 3:20, 21:

> And he shall send Jesus Christ, which before
> was preached unto you:
> Whom the heaven must receive until the times
> of restitution of all things, which God hath spoken
> by the mouth of all his holy prophets since the
> world began.

And Romans 8:19-23:

> For the earnest expectation of the creature
> waiteth for the manifestation of the sons of God.
> For the creature was made subject to vanity,
> not willingly, but by reason of him who hath sub-
> jected the same in hope,
> Because the creature itself also shall be de-
> livered from the bondage of corruption into the
> glorious liberty of the children of God.
> For we know that the whole creation groaneth
> and travaileth in pain together until now.
> And not only they, but ourselves also, which
> have the firstfruits of the Spirit, even we ourselves
> waiting for the adoption, to wit, the redemption of
> our body.

All this, Williams says:

> They expect to take place, not as perhaps most
> Christians do, at the final winding up of this
> world's affairs, before the great day of judgment,
> but at the beginning of the 'thousand years, ' during
> which the saints are to live and reign with Christ,
> according to Rev. 20:4, 5 etc. This is that 'first
> resurrection' in which they expect the risen and
> transfigured saints to be fully restored to the
> image of God by being clothed in bodies like unto
> Christ's glorious body, and like the dual organiza-
> tion of Adam, when he first left the Creator's hand.

> They believe also, that under the glorious king-
> dom of the Messiah, then to be set up, there will
> still be a race of men in the flesh, as at present,
> but who will 'be all righteous,' the kingdoms of
> the world having become the kingdoms of the Lord. [4]

There will be a Jerusalem above and one below. The
relation of one to the other may be like the Sanctuary to the
Holy of Holies, but both will belong to one. As Dr. Joseph
Seiss, the Lutheran pastor and author who lived from 1823-
1904, said: " ... both belong to the one sublime and wonderful economy which is to encompass this planet, when once
its redemption is complete. "[5]

Although they constantly were expecting this glorious
event, they never gave an actual date. However, Rapp was
so convinced of this event in his lifetime that even on his
deathbed he could not believe that death was near. He ended
his life saying: "If I did not so fully believe, that the Lord
has designed me to place our Society before his presence in
the land of Canaan, I would consider this my last. "[6]

6. "Church Fund" for the new Jerusalem. --George
Rapp taught that with the second coming of Christ and a
heavenly kingdom there would also be an earthly Jerusalem
where the temple had to be rebuilt. With this in view he began in 1834 to gather money; by 1846 he had $510,000.
Romelius Baker testified to the following during the Nachtrieb
Lawsuit (Nachtrieb having withdrawn from the society de-
manded a share of the society's wealth. He lost.):

> ... Mr. George Rapp, who was then the General
> Agent, directed that I should bring some specie
> home from Pittsburgh. I think it was ten thousand
> dollars I brought home first, and more at sundry
> other times afterwards. I also brought home from
> Philadelphia at three different times--one time,
> 110,000 dollars--the other two times I do not dis-
> tinctly recollect the amount --but continued to
> gather, up to the period of 1846, in all five hundred
> and ten thousand dollars. Since that period we did
> not gather any more. [7]

When asked why no more money was gathered, Baker
answered:

> I don't know any particular object, except that he
> didn't want any more specie; and the sum on hand

should be considered as a reserve, or church fund,
spoken of in the Old Testament, where it is stated
'that the children of Israel, for the purpose of re-
building and repairing the temple at Jerusalem,
contributions should be gathered, and those contributions placed under the hands of trustees, and
no account to be kept of them.' Moreover they
reckoned not with the men into whose hands they
delivered the money to be bestowed on workmen,
for they dealt faithfully, 2 Kings, 12:15. Also,
how be it there was no reckoning made with them
of the money that was delivered into their hands,
because they dealt faithfully, 2 Kings, 22:7. [8]

Baker was further questioned as to why the accounts
were burned and why only Rapp and Fleckhammer (Rapp's
steward and apparently close to him) knew of the location of
the vault in the Great House. Baker was asked, "What
were you not to set your hearts on, and what were you to
forget?" He replied:

The money and the amount; on the same principle
upon which the fathers would not tell their sons
the amount of the original contributions, [communal
contributions of the members at the beginning] and
upon the same principle upon which the book containing the original contributions was burned in
1818, and on the expression of the New Testament,
where it is stated that the followers of Christ
should possess their goods as though they possessed
them not. [9]

And so it was with the Harmonists. They firmly believed in this new Jerusalem and that money would be needed.
Actually how much, they as individuals did not know, nor
did they concern themselves about the matter. In fact,
Elijah Lemmix, under cross-examination in a suit he brought
against the Harmonists, said that this information was not
known among the members. [10] What mattered was that they
knew it would be taken care of; for them it became a closed
book, " ... until the words of God shall be fulfilled."[11]

B. Implied Beliefs

While the implied beliefs may be found in the Bible,
they are not as clear-cut as were the expressed beliefs. The

implied beliefs may be compared to folk-art because they,
like folk-art, derive from and involve community conception.
"Folk-art holds to, derives from and manifests a common
fund of ideas and images by which it is spiritually energized
and in which it finds its full meaning."[12] This is a comparison only in the abstract sense, for folk-art as it is generally
understood had very little representation in the Harmonist
community. Even though many hymns were written to Sophia,
only once was a sculpture made of "her." The rose fared
better, appearing above a church doorway in New Harmony,
Indiana; on the newel posts of the Great House at Economy;
on the ceiling of the Economy grotto; in the Harmonist silk
designs, and on the only Harmonist tombstone found in their
Harmony, Pennsylvania cemetery. Their manner of life did
not require certificates of the usual kind--marriage, birth,
death. It was with these that the Pennsylvania Dutch showed
"folk-art" ingenuity.

    1. Virgin Sophia.--As stated above, Jacob Böhme
had a great influence on the Harmonists. It was only natural
then that the Virgin Sophia would appear, for Böhme's
"world of idea is a personalized, intriguing figure, the Virgin
Sophia."[13] She is the personification of wisdom. Such spiritual wisdom was the all-consuming passion of the Harmonists,
for it was their way to harmony. This concept came from
the ancient philosophers and St. Paul, who divided men into
"psychical men" and "pneumatical men"--men who live according to nature, and men who live by the life of the
spirit.[14] In the second century the Gnostic sects proposed
a "way" by which the trapped soul was freed and then became
spiritual. The Gnostics thought of man as consisting of
two "halves"--one half, the visible body as Adam was before
his fall; the other half, the invisible body consisting of lower
and higher stories. The latter contained a spiritual seed
which eventually destroys evil and elevates the person into
spiritual life. At the same time the Montanists started a
movement for only "spiritual" persons. This meant that one
had to be a participator in the life of God. Furthermore,
the Spirit was thought of as "coming" in sporadic visitations
to whomever it chose.[15]

    Spiritual religion continued to appear even though the
Catholic hierarchy was taking form. Nor was the Reformation able to stop it. Mystics like Böhme continued to question and search and transcend the status quo. He found inspiration in the Montanists, who believed in chiliasm and
descendance to earth of the heavenly Jerusalem, and in the

Gnostics, who laid much emphasis on the dualism of nature
and on the wisdom of the Virgin Sophia. Interestingly enough,
wisdom's personification may take on a warmth and ardor
that becomes a lover. It is so in the numerous hymns the
Harmonists wrote in her honor (see Chapter VIII), and it was
so with Böhme, as his following dialogue between man and
man's soul shows.

The soul further speaks to her noble Virgin Sophia,
who has returned her to grace:

> O, my noble pearl, and awakened flames of my
> light, in my fearsome life of fire, how you change
> me in your joy! O beautiful love, I became sinful
> through my Father Adam, and through fiery temp-
> tation turned to the outer world of indulgence and
> idleness and strange companions; and I would have
> been doomed to eternally wander in the dark valley
> among strangers if you in your great faithfulness
> had not interceded to soften the Lord's anger and
> thus restored gentleness and love to my troubled
> life.

Thereupon the noble Sophia answers the soul:

> My dear love, my faithful treasure, you make me
> most happy with your approach; for you I broke
> through the gates of God, through God's anger,
> through hell and death and came to your house of
> misery. I gave you my love through grace and re-
> leased you from chains of bondage; I remained
> true. But now you ask me a difficult thing, one
> which I do not willingly barter with you. You want
> my pearl for yourself. Remember, my beloved
> bridegroom, how you wasted it before with Adam.
> Because of this you still are in grave danger, and
> are wandering in two dangerous kingdoms--you
> wander in the country in your primitive fiery-state
> that a strong jealous God calls a consuming fire;
> in the other kingdom you wander in the outer-world
> in dissipation where the world's pleasure and the
> devil have a hold on you. In your joy you would
> again tarnish my pearl. Also you would become
> proud as Lucifer was when he had my pearl; and if
> you would turn from God's harmony I would lose
> my love forever.

Envelope yourself with patience; avoid carnal pleasure, and I will give you my kiss of love, and a
garland from Paradise as a token of my love
. . . .
But the crown of pearls which I am laying by, you
may not wear until you stand cleansed before me. [16]

This same reverence for Sophia, without the sensuous-
ness, is formed in the Medieval Morality play Everyman when
Everyman is called to his death and finds that no one will
accompany him.   It is Wisdom who advises him to become
cleansed, to return to a state of grace.

The Hirten-Brief, thought perhaps to have been written by Böhme, or at least by someone with Böhme's convictions, had long been a guide for George Rapp. In 1855 the
trustees placed a copy of it in each household. [17] It is a
retelling of the creation of man, his purpose, downfall, and
redemption. Wisdom plays a most important role in this
pastoral letter. It emphasizes the original dual-Adam who
was not of the flesh but of wisdom, and who was to propagate
his kind in, through, and from God. He was like the angels
and blessed spirits, who neither marry nor are given in
marriage for the propagation of their kind; but who, in the
chaste embrace of Sophia, the great mother above, will
propagate themselves in a magical, super-sensual way.
(Er war überhaupt wie die Engel und seligen Geister, welche
weder freyen, noch um der Fortpflanzung willen zur Ehe
ausgegehen werden, sondern in Sophiens, dieser allgemein-
en Mutter, die droben ist, keuscher Umarmung fruchtbar
sind, und sich auf eine magische, übersinnliche Weise fortf-
flanzen.) But after the fall, man lost this heavenly indwelling
of Sophia. [18] Without her he was vulnerable; he had fallen into
the outer world and lost the perfect harmony he had enjoyed. [19]
It should be man's aim to regain this wisdom and restore
harmony.

When pictured, Sophia was usually shown with a head
and wings. Frederick Rapp sculptured her in this manner for
a doorway in Harmony, Pennsylvania. She may also be
shown as a heart with head and wings, and sometimes only
as a heart.

In 1807 Frederick Rapp appeared as zealous about
chiliasm as the elder Rapp. In a Frederick Rapp letter quoted
by Arndt, one finds Frederick convinced that Jesus will soon
come and that everything will be made anew, for "The man

child which the woman has born will bring it all to pass, the
woman actually is in the desert, but soon her time there will
be over. Happy is he who knows her and happier still is he who
is associated with her.'' Arndt says Rapp was writing in
terms of Böhme and the Berleburger Bible and that:

> The last remark referred to the woman in Rev.
> 12:1, who brought forth a man child, who was to
> rule the world, but who for a time was forced to
> flee into the wilderness 'where she hath a place
> prepared of God, that they should feed her there
> a thousand two hundred and three-score days....'
> This woman was another symbol of the Harmony
> Society, which had fled to America and which,
> like the woman of Revelation, would have to flee
> again. [20]

2. The golden rose. --Luther's translation of Micah
4:8, "Unto you will come the golden rose," has a special
place in the hearts of the Harmonists, for to them it is the
fulfillment of their harmonious state, their brotherly love.
It is a tradition that has taken on new meaning.

3. The lily. --The lily, like the rose, appears in
Harmonist hymns and they appear to be used interchangeably,
as in the Song of Solomon 2:1:

> I am the rose of Sharon, and the lily of the valleys.

They are used allegorically--they are Christ; He is the golden
rose; He is the lily of the valley who will come to see the
chosen ones.   This is especially evident in their hymns,
and again Böhme is in evidence.   Stoudt, the authority on
Pennsylvania Folk-Art, states that:

> Boehme [sic] elevated the Lily and the Rose into
> metaphysical and historical categories, and he
> frequently speaks of the 'time of the lily' for this
> is the Lily which shall bring man full knowledge;
> and the lily-rose which originates in Gods own
> tree.   With Boehme the Lily and Rose were inter-
> changeable.
> ....
> In Boehme the Lily-Rose image symbolizes the pure
> devine principle which both dwells within and
> transcends substantial reality, being the dialectical
> counterpart of what he calls the magna turba, or

the principle of radical evil which inhabits all
reality. In this sense also the Lily is apocalyptic
in that the 'time of the Lily, ' as Joachim of Flora
predicted, is that glorious age at the end of time
when all evil shall have been overcome in the final
victory of God:

> Let it remain hidden until the time
> of the Lily; there it stands all open;
> and the tincture is then the light
> of the world.
> or
> Truly the time of the Rose brings it
> forth, and it is high time to awake,
> for the sleep is at an end, there shall
> be a great rent before the Lily; there-
> fore let everyone take heed of his ways. [21]

4. The Philosopher's Stone. --The jasper stone of
Rev. 21:11 is really the philosophical stone, for philosophy
is truly likened to a magic jewel whose touch transmutes base
substances into priceless gems like itself. Wisdom is the
alchemist's powder of projection which transforms many
thousand times its own weight of gross ignorance into the precious substance of enlightenment. [22] We must go on to say:

> The Philosopher's Stone is an ancient symbol of the
> perfected and regenerated man whose divine nature
> shines forth through a chain of purified and unfolded
> vehicles. As the rough diamond is dull and lifeless
> when first removed from the black carbon, so the
> spiritual nature of man in its 'fallen' state reveals
> little, if any, of its inherent luminosity. Just as
> in the hands of the skillful lapidary the shapeless
> stone is transformed into a scintillating gem from
> whose facets pour streams of varicolored fire, so
> upon the lathe of the Divine Lapidary the soul of man
> is ground and polished until it reflects the glory of
> its Creator from every atom. [23]

The language of the alchemist also is strong in the
Hirten-Brief. The author speaks of Universal-Lebens-Tink-
tur (universal-life-tincture) in reference to Christ's passion
for us which was highlighted by the bread and wine of the
"Last Supper. " It is "Christ's glorified flesh and blood that
is the universal-life-tincture of all humanity which has exist-
ed, exists, and will exist. "[24] The tincture mentioned above

was a certain powder or tincture used by alchemists. This
was poured into the aludel or alembic full of some prepared
metal which is to be transmuted into gold or some special
medicine which is to be transmuted into a panacea. In the
case of the wine and bread of the "Last Supper," the change,
as already mentioned, becomes the life-giving substance for
man.

The Hirten-Brief goes on to say that souls in the process of regeneration have advanced to a stage where they have
received this tincture in a special measure-medium-tinc-
tures or real projection channels, whereby Christ will gradually extend the reign of the spirit all over the world.[25]

This philosophy cut deeply into Rapp's heart as he
tried to perfect his Society. The enthusiasm and determination
spilled over to his alchemist-mind, which was feverishly
working with the idea that a perfect man could make gold.
Nor was Rapp alone. Frederick also was interested in this,
and it was this belief that caused some of the Harmonists to
follow Count Leon.

5. The Woman in the Wilderness. --Arndt says Rapp
considered the Harmony Society to be the Sun Woman described in Revelation 12:1.[26] Revelation 12:6, 13, 14, 15, 16,
besides allegorically telling the story of the Harmonists,
also demonstrates the power of three, for three times did the
Harmonists have to move. At the beginning the Harmonists
were in Germany producing their own teachings when "the
great red dragon" came to devour them, and they fled into
the wildenness which they called Harmony to exemplify their
unity. But soon problems beset them, and once more they
fled into the wilderness again calling their settlement
Harmony. For a time all went well; however, troubles
arose and once more they fled, this time naming "the earth"
Economy which "... is the true end, where each effort finds
its reward. The seed which has originally been planted in
the heart of man, has come up, sprouted and grown to a
considerable plant, appearing in a true godlike human form,
whose beauty surpasses every terrestrial idea."[27]

Notes

1.   Joshua Nachtrieb vs Romulus L. Baker, et al.,
        Circuit Court of the United States, Western District
        of Pennsylvania, Pittsburgh, 1849, p. 8.

2. Charles Nordhoff, The Communistic Societies of the
    United States (New York: Schocken Books, 1965), p.
    132.

3. Aaron Williams, The Harmony Society (Pittsburgh:
    W. S. Haven, 1866), p. 99.

4. Ibid., pp. 107-108.

5. Dr. Seiss's Last Times, p. 207, quoted in Aaron
    Williams, The Harmony Society (Pittsburgh: W. S.
    Haven, 1866), p. 110.

6. Williams, Society, p. 182.

7. Nachtrieb vs Baker, et als., 1849, p. 14.

8. Ibid., p. 42.

9. Ibid., p. 15.

10. Elijah Lemmix vs Romulus L. Baker, et al., Circuit
    Court of the United States, Western District of
    Pennsylvania, Pittsburgh, 1854, p. 57.

11. Rev. 17:17.

12. John Joseph Stoudt, Pennsylvania Folk-Art (Allentown:
    Schlechter's, 1948), p. 5.

13. Ibid., p. 44.

14. Rufus M. Jones, Spiritual Reformers in the 16th and
    17th Centuries (Boston: Beacon Press, 1914), p. xi.

15. Ibid., p. xiii-xiv.

16. Jacob Böhme, De Poenitentia Vera or Von Wahrer
    Busse (n.p., 1730), [pp. 32-35.]

17. Williams, Society, p. 137.

18. Hirten-Brief (Pittsburgh: L. and W. Neeb (1855), p.
    137.

19. Ibid., p. 82.

20. Arndt, 1785-1847, p. 101.

21. Stoudt, Folk-Art, pp. 44-46.

22. Manly P. Hall, The Secret Teachings of All Ages
(California: The Philosophical Research Society,
Inc., 1959), p. xcviii.

23. Ibid., p. xcvii.

24. Hirten-Brief, p. 125.

25. Ibid., p. 125.

26. Arndt, 1785-1847, p. 95.

27. [Rapp,] Man, p. 31.

Chapter III

THE SOCIETY

A. The Organization

When one speaks of the Harmonists one always speaks
of the group of dissenters from the Lutheran Church, led by
George Rapp from Germany to Pennsylvania to Indiana and
back to Pennsylvania. During these moves there were a
number of withdrawals, the largest in 1832 (see Chapter XI),
but these dissenters did not form otner Harmonists groups.
So there was only one congregation. The actual dating of
the society does not begin in December, 1804 when the articles of purchase were formally signed, but with the signing
of The Articles of Association on February 15, 1805. Also,
from this time on, the name Harmonists, though not officially
stated, was understood. Since these articles are basic to
their communal spirit, and since in these they call themselves a church or congregation (a name denied them by
some materialists), they are included here:

> Be it hereby known to all who need to know it, that
> the following agreement has this day been made
> and concluded between us, the subscribers of the
> one part, and George Rapp and his Society of the
> other part. Firstly. We, the subscribers, on our
> part and on the part of our heirs and descendants,
> deliver up, renounce, and transfer all our estate
> and property consisting of cash, land, cattle, or
> whatever else it may be, to George Rapp and his
> Society in Harmony, Butler County, Pennsylvania,
> as a free gift or donation, for the benefit and use
> of the congregation there, and bind ourselves on
> our part, as well as on the part of our heirs and
> descendants, to make free renunciation thereof,
> and to leave the same at the disposal of the super-
> intendents of the congregation, as if we never had
> nor possessed same.

Secondly. We do pledge ourselves jointly and
severally to submit to the laws and regulations of
the congregation, and to show due and ready obedience toward those who are appointed and chosen by
the congregation as superintendents in such a manner that not only we ourselves endeavor, by the
work of our hands, to promote the good and interest
of the congregation, but also to hold our children
and families to do the same.

Thirdly. If, contrary to our expectation, the case
should happen that we jointly or severally could not
endure in the congregation and would within a few
years or more abstain from our promises and withdraw from the community, for whatever cause it
may be, we will never demand any reward, either
for ourselves or our children or those belonging
to us, for work or services rendered, but whatever
we jointly and severally have done or shall do, we
will have done as a voluntary service for our
brethren.

On the other hand, George Rapp and his Society
adopt the subscribers jointly and severally as members of the congregation whereby each of them
obtains the privilege to attend all religious meetings,
not only they themselves, but also their children
and families, shall and will receive the necessary
instruction in church and school which is needed and
requisite for temporal and eternal felicity.

Secondly, George Rapp and his Society promise to
supply the subscribers jointly and severally with
all the necessaries of life, as lodging, meat,
drink, and clothing, etc., and not only during their
healthful days, but also when one or several of
them should become sick or otherwise unfit for
labor, they shall have and enjoy the same care and
maintenance as before; and if, after a short or long
period, the father or mother of a family should die,
or be otherwise separated from the community and
leave a family behind, none of those left behind
shall be left widows or orphans, but receive and
enjoy the same rights and care as long as they
live or remain in the congregation, as well in sick
as healthful days, the same as before, or as their
circumstances or needs may require.

Thirdly. And if, as stated above, the case should
happen that one of several of the subscribers after
a short or long period should abstain from their
promise and could or would not submit to the laws
and regulations of the church or congregation, and
for this or another cause would leave the Harmonie,
George Rapp and his Society promise to refund him
or them, the property brought into the Harmonie
without interest, and that in one, two or three
annual installments, as the sum may be, large or
small; and if one or more of them was poor and
brought nothing into the congregation, they shall,
provided they depart openly and orderly, receive
a donation in cash, according to their conduct
while here, or as their circumstances and needs
may require, which George Rapp and his Society
shall determine at his or their departure.

In confirmation whereof, both parties have signed
their names.
So done, Harmonie, February 15, 1805. [1]

While today's scholarship may call the Harmonists a
communitarian sect under the charismatic leadership of
George Rapp, after having discussed the matter with Jacob
Henrici and R. L. Baker, the spiritual heirs of Father Rapp,
Aaron Williams wrote:

They do not regard themselves as a distinct religious sect, and they have no ecclesiastical organization apart from the civil community. In this respect their system is strictly patriarchal,
while, at the same time, they constitute a voluntary
association, in which all who are permitted to sub-
scribe to their articles of agreement become entitled
alike to all the civil and all the religious privileges of
the Society. [2]

After Father Rapp's death, the Society elected nine
elders, two of whom were made trustees. These trustees
became the executive heads and spiritual leaders, but they did
not possess the charisma of George Rapp.

Charisma, that elusive quality, sets certain individuals
apart as having exceptional powers or qualities. Max Weber
says, "These powers are such as are not accessible to the
ordinary person, but are regarded as of divine origin or as

exemplary, and on the basis of them the individual concerned
is treated as a leader. " And "what alone is important is how
the individual is actually regarded by those subject to charismatic authority by his 'followers' or disciples. "[3] The followers ascribe this quality of charisma to a given leader because
they are emotionally involved and think the leader has con-
nections with "the ultimate, fundamental, vital, 'order-
determining powers'. "[4] However, this is strongest at the
beginning. Weber says that "it cannot remain stable, but becomes either traditionalized or rationalized, or a combination
of both. "[5] With the Harmonists it became a combination of
both.

B. The "Father"

"Father" Rapp had no formal training. George Rapp,
both the religious and civil head, was a "self-made man. "
He dictated all the rules and regulations and was the supreme
arbiter in all disputes. He divided the community into class-
es--old men, old women, young men, young women, the
youth--biweekly meetings "for social intercourse and mutual
improvement. "[6] Rapp met with them as often as possible.

After Rapp's death, the society elected from among
themselves a board of nine elders who divided the assignments
previously taken care of by Rapp. Two of these elders became trustees.

Although the trustees who followed Father Rapp were
able, noble, and spiritual men, they could not replace him.
Regardless of what Rapp's detractors called him--fanatic,
dictator, egomaniac, tyrant, slave-driver--it had to be
admitted that he was of superior mettle and a "prophet"
who had led his people. Hinds sums him up the following
way:

> George Rapp, their founder, had great strength
> of character, and maintained his position until his
> decease at four-score and ten, preaching only two
> weeks before his death. He is represented as of
> commanding appearance, being six feet high, and
> well proportioned; very industrious, spending his
> leisure hours in study of the natural sciences;
> easy of approach, and even witty in conversation;
> eloquent in his sermons; deeply religious--'a man
> before whom no evil could stand'; and very simple
> in his habits. [7]

When Nordhoff visited Economy he asked, "Is there
any monument to Father Rapp?" The old man to whom he put
the question said quietly, "Yes, all that you see here, around
us." From other persons Nordhoff heard:

> He was nearly if not quite six feet high; well-built,
> with blue eyes, a somewhat stately walk, and a full
> beard, which he was the first in the society to wear.
> He was extremely industrious, and never wasted
> even a minute; knew admirably how to use every
> spare moment. [In his spring 1823 letters he com-
> ments about his nonpreaching activities of cutting
> seed, working in the wheat field, making hay,
> planting rice, and corn.[8]] He was cheerful, kind-
> ly, talkative; plain-spoken when he had to find fault;
> not very enthusiastic, but somewhat dry and very
> practical. In his earlier years in Germany, he
> was witty; and to the last he was ready and apt in
> speech. His conversation centered always upon re-
> ligion and the conduct of life; and no matter with
> whom he was speaking, or what was the character
> of the person, Rapp knew very well how to lead
> the talk of these topics.

> The young were very fond of him. 'He was a man
> before whom no evil could stand.' 'When I met him
> in the street, if I had a bad thought in my head, it
> flew away.' He was constantly in the fields or in
> the factories, cheering, encouraging, or advising
> people. 'He knew everything--how to do it, what
> was the best way.' 'Ah, he was a man; he told
> us what to do, and how to be good.' In his spare
> moments he studied botany, geology, astronomy,
> mechanics. 'He was never idle, not even a quarter
> of an hour.' He believed much in work; thought
> hard field-work a good cure for spiritual as well
> as bodily diseases. He was an 'extraordinarily elo-
> quent preacher'; and it is a singular fact that, dying
> at the great age of ninety, he preached in the church
> twice but two Sundays before his death; and on the
> Sunday before he died addressed his people from
> the window of his sick-room. He was 'a good man,
> with true, honest eyes.' He 'always labored
> against selfishness, and to serve the brethren and
> the Lord.'[9]

From such accounts one can see an apotheosis taking
place, and while this naturally comes to a great man in time,

it is not all just a hazy memory of a grand old man. There
are kernels of truth grown into myth. In the Rapp letters
one always finds concern for the people, one always finds
business matters, and one always finds God, just as Nordhoff's interviewees remembered it up to sixty years later.
One such letter taken at random follows:

From George Rapp to Frederick Rapp, February 24,
1813:

It will not be unpleasant for you to receive another
letter from me which is to let you know that we
are well except for the children who have come
down with red spots [measles?]. Most have recovered; none have died and Gertrude is still in
good health. She will not leave the house in order
to keep well. Up to now nothing particularly
dangerous or interesting has happened. The
weather is still robust and the ground is still
frozen. This week I made a trip to Beaver because
the road is in good condition, the water of the
Beaver is low and the ice has been removed. Old
Foller is home sick; however we can get by because
little country-cloth is coming in. With our carders
[of wool] we also have some trouble. Be that as
it may. The well is finished; in four days six feet
of water! Given time, we think it will rise to the
rock. Dr. Basse called on me today and asked for
twenty tubs of pork for someone who wants to pick
it up in May. He wants an answer so that he can
write to the man. I have promised him nothing but
placed the matter in your hands so write to him
about it. Aldwek wants to see 100 bushels of
[not clear] for cash. I bought fifty and am leaving
the rest to you.

I have not received a letter from you; tomorrow I
shall send Gottlieb to Pittsburgh to see about letters; he can mail this one.

Perhaps time passes more quickly for you than it
does for me. I often do not know what I am doing
in this world. It takes much effort for me to practice patience and overcome my defects. However,
on the other hand, I view with impatience the grand
plans and destinies of the world and hope that
something splendid be behind it all. May time,

therefore, as the day and the night, pass hurriedly
by revealing the design of God, in which we certainly will not be forgotten. Half of your absence
from us is now over. I long to hear how things
stand for you and with you. You may not be able to
change the inner sentiment, and if the outward functions do not develop as to our wishes, don't be concerned. It is all of short duration and transitory.
Therefore keep your mind at peace.

Just now on the 24th at five o'clock in the evening
I received your letter from Washington. It is
wonderful how Providence works. I rejoice as I
read the good news. In respect to the post, I shall
attend to everything. Our enemies have received a
severe blow. I am most pleased that you had the
pleasure of speaking with the President [Madison].
Your journey was quite worthwhile. I hope that the
rest will turn out as well for there will remain
enough bitterness.

I greet you with affection.
                              George Rapp[10]

As can be seen, it is not a profound letter, but it is
sincere, concerned, religious. These are the qualities of
the Harmonists who found the world selfish, unconcerned,
irreligious. George Rapp exemplified their hopes and religion, and thus had absolute power over them. Many times
it took wing into mystic areas which perhaps most of the
members did not understand, but this does not make them
unique in religious circles. Gnothiseauton Society of Sewickly,
Pennsylvania took note of Rapp's spiritual search, and on
September 12, 1839 elected him an honorary member.
Gnothiseauton--Know Thyself--was inscribed upon the ancient
temple of Apollo at Delphi.[11]

C. The Role of Frederick Rapp

Elders, as such, actually did not exist while George
Rapp was the head of the Society. However, he had a "co-
manager," Frederick Reichert Rapp, his adopted son. This
extraordinary man was a stone cutter and architect by trade.
In his travels in Germany he heard about the preachings of
George Rapp. Since he, too, was disturbed with the affairs
of church, he soon became a serious disciple of Rapp's.

Apparently, Rapp recognized the young man's ability and
earnestness and so he was taken into the Rapp household,
which he managed when George left for America. Frederick
also enrolled all those planning to emigrate and made all the
necessary preparations for America. Once in Pennsylvania,
the division of management was no problem. George had the
spiritual and home functions, and Frederick the affairs of the
"outside world." And as the society's faith and work prospered
beyond anyone's imagination, they needed a business manager
for all their production. Frederick conducted all negotiations
of purchase and sale, traveling to Pittsburgh, Philadelphia,
New York, Indiana, and down the Mississippi to New Orleans.
He carried on in his name all the external business of the
society, but under a solemn contract for the society he had
declared that everything held in his name was the sole property of the Society. In addition to being the financial head,
Frederick also was an assistant religious leader and the
"culture bearer." When the elder Rapp was absent, Frederick
preached. He also wrote hymns. It was he, with Dr. Müller,
who was interested in the architecture, music, library and
art of Economy. Correspondence files show that he was a
welcome guest in many cultured homes in the cities he fre-
quented. [12] Without Frederick the George Rapp dream would
have been short lived, for all dreams need a foundation if they
are to be fulfilled.

D. Elders

        After George Rapp's death in 1847 a re-organization
of the Society was necessary. In Article I they reaffirmed the
Articles of 1827 and 1836 except insofar as they were rendered
void because of Rapp's death.

        In Article 2 they established a council of elders to con-
sist of nine members of the Society. They named: Johannes
Stahl, Johannes Schnabel, Adam Nachtrieb, Matthäus Scholle,
Joseph Hornle, Johannes Eberle, Romelius L. Baker, Jacob
Henrici, and Jonathan Lenz.

        Article 3 defined their duties:

        a) To manage the internal temporal affairs of
        the Society, and to appoint and depose foremen for
        the various branches of business, and to see that
        the members of the Society perform the duties
        assigned them.

b) To decide disputes between the members; to
give advice, and to give reproof when necessary.

c) To receive new members into the Society and
to expel members. New members are to sign the
articles of association as a proof of their membership.

d) To care for the improvement of morals and
instruction of the members.

e) To appoint one or more of the members of
religious teachers and leaders.

f) To depose a member of the council of
elders of one of the trustees and to appoint another
instead.

g) To fill all vacancies in the council of elders
and in the office of trustee.

h) The agreement of six members of the council
shall be regarded as the legal action of the whole
council.

i) To keep a record in a record book of all
important proceedings. [13]

E. Trustees

Article 4 provided for a creation of a council of
trustees or agents for the exclusive management of the external business and affairs of the society. This council was
to consist of two persons who must be members of the council of elders.

Article 5 defined their powers:

a) To manage all the business of the Society.

b) To make donations to withdrawing and ex-
pelled members, and for such charitable and
philanthropic purposes as they may think proper.

c) To have joint power to buy and sell real
estate and to execute deeds.

d) To represent the Society in all legal
matters.

e) To have authority over all property of the
Society. [14]

1. Romelius Baker and Jacob Henrici. --These two
men were the first trustees. With Frederick's early death
in June, 1834, the first link in the Harmonist chain was
broken. George Rapp readily saw that he needed help,

although he knew Frederick could not be replaced. He appointed Romelius L. Baker and Jacob Henrici to attend to the outside business. Baker, luckily, had been trained by Frederick and, since he too was a very able man, business matters remained on an even keel. Baker was also a very religious man. He never wrote a business letter home without spiritual involvement. At the same time he remained realistic. On the other hand, Jacob Henrici took more spiritual flights, like Father Rapp. Although Henrici was an excellent teacher and cultured gentlemen in every respect, his business head was not like Frederick's or Baker's. With George Rapp's death in 1847, Baker and Henrici became titular heads.

2. Jonathan Lenz. --After Baker's death, Henrici was joined by Jonathan Lenz as the junior trustee. Lenz had been born in the first Harmony in 1807, so he was the first "American" to be a trustee in this Society. He was a fine man with a lot of Harmony experience but he did not have the business acumen of Frederick and Baker. Christiana Knoedler recounts that he was a great story-teller.[15]

3. Ernest Woelfel and John Duss. --When Lenz died in January, 1890, Ernest Woelfel was appointed junior trustee. He died in July, 1890, and John Duss was then appointed co-trustee with Henrici. Duss had come to the Society with his mother in 1862 because of the Civil War. Since his mother was widowed soon thereafter, they stayed at Economy on and off for the rest of their lives (see Chapter XI). Like all the trustees, Duss had special talents, ability and leadership, and they were all tested during the very trying declining years.

4. Samuel Sieber and Gottlieb Riethmüller. --Henrici died on December 25, 1892. On December 27, Samuel Sieber was appointed, but he withdrew from the Society the following July, whereupon Gottlieb Riethmüller became a junior trustee. He died in 1897.

5. Susanna Duss. --By an agreement made on February 13, 1897, Duss was made sole trustee endowed with all the powers previously conferred on the Board of Trustees. Then, on May 2, 1903, he resigned his position, and on the same day his wife Susanna was chosen sole trustee until the Society dissolved in 1905.[16]

F. The Members

      The Harmonists represented a totalitarian Christianity
which was their way of life; they were "one," and one could
not be without the other. At the beginning there were between
450-500 members. The records are not accurate, but
Romelius Baker gives this number. The number rose to
about 1200. With withdrawals and deaths the number had
dwindled to 327 by 1847, the year of Rapp's death. They
never were concerned with numbers; they wanted truly
dedicated people who did not come because bed and board
would be assured in this uncertain world. As stated above,
George Rapp had warned Frederick Rapp not to urge the
would-be emigrants. They did not proselytize and severely
questioned anyone who came asking for membership, because
they strongly felt that "many are called, but few are chosen"
to a life integrated with religion and work which had spiritual
and harmonious values as its reward.

      In a letter to Frederick Rapp, dated May, 1823,
George Rapp gives a good glimpse of the admission pro-
cedure:

> Day before yesterday the stranger was examined.
> After the council of seven brethren had met
> several suggestions were made as to how this and
> that was to be done and to be improved, also
> several discussions were held about the stranger's
> circumstances and experiences. Then he was
> called in and asked: What is your name? Answer:
> 'Trogle.' 'From which land and place?' Answer:
> 'From Schorndorf in the land of Württemberg.'
> 'For what reason did you come here?' Answer:
> 'I should like to be taken into the congregation.'
> 'Well, that isn't done so easily. Why would you
> like that?' Answer: 'Because in Germany I al-
> ready know of you and finally found an opportunity
> to make the long trip.' 'How long have you been
> in this country?' Answer: 'Four years.' 'Why
> did you not come to us the first year? You are
> probably a swindler, a good-for-nothing who does
> not do well anywhere.' Answer: 'Oh no, I have
> had misfortune and in Holland was cheated out of
> my money, so I had to serve for my passage in
> Maryland.' 'Well, good, but what good do you plan
> to do here?' Answer: 'I am a farmer and a
> viniculturist and can do all sorts of work.' 'Do you

> have a family in Europe or here?' Answer: 'No,
> I am a single man.'   'Have you contracted any
> debts which would have to be paid?'   Answer:
> 'No.'   'How did you get here?   Did you have travel
> money?   and how much?'   Answer: '$2.00.'   'And
> when they were gone?'   Answer: 'Then I worked
> again four or five weeks until I had enough money
> to travel on.'   The President said: 'So you seem
> to be an honest man, but to see whether according
> to your inner worth and inclination you are capable
> of fulfilling the word of Jesus: 'Deny thyself,'
> without which practice no one can remain here,
> you must be tested to determine what lies in your
> heart.   So go into the home of this family.   They
> will give you all you need, then in six or nine
> months it will be revealed how you like it or how
> we like it.'   But he wept and said, 'May the Lord
> guide me by His good spirit that I may be happy
> and may stay with you.'   And we wished him well
> for this.[17]

This clearly shows that no one was coerced into membership.   The young people who grew up in the society, either those born of "the backsliding" Harmonists or those born
of hireling-parents or taken in as orphans, on reaching the age
of 21 were allowed a choice of becoming members.   While
from all indications there was freedom to decide whether to
join or not, there was undoubtedly some "family" pressure.
When Elijah Lemmix was asked in court why he joined the
Society if he didn't want to, he said: "Because there was
more coaxing than free will.   The coaxing was by my
brothers, sisters, and relatives."[18]   Many stayed on as
hirelings or left the society.[19]

The members in general could not have been dullards.
To create three thriving villages in the wilderness of south-
western Indiana and western Pennsylvania in the span of twenty
years takes clever heads as well as clever hands.   Besides,
a dullard would have been a great drawback, just as having
all leaders would have been.   Someone had to follow; but
this does not make them stupid.   William Wilson notes that of
the five hundred who signed Harmonie, Indiana over to Robert
Owen, only thirty-nine were unable to write their names.[20]

The mood of anti-intellectualism that prevailed among
many of the members was really an enlargement of the spirit,
a naiveté compared to sophistication.   Furthermore, they had

the Bible as an anchor. Acts 4:13 observes:

> Now when they saw the boldness of Peter and John,
> and perceived that they were unlearned and ignorant
> men, they marvelled; and they took knowledge of
> them, that they had been with Jesus.

Of the members, special mention must be made of
Gertrude Rapp, the granddaughter of George, the daughter of
his only son John. Born in 1807 in Harmony, Butler
County, she grew up in the household of the patriarchal Rapp.
Travelers mention and letters reveal her grace and charm
and abilities in music, art, and languages. She often accompanied Frederick Rapp on his business trips. At such
times she attended plays and concerts. Gertrude was considered the first lady of the society until the evening of
December 29, 1889. At choir practice that evening, director
George Kirschbaum announced, "die Gertrud ist soeben heim-
gegangen."[21]

The members themselves left no written records as
such. However, their communal spirit of brotherly love and
firm hope in heavenly guidance can be ascertained from the
chalk scrawling under the stairway in No. 2, New Harmony,
Indiana:

> den 24 Mai sind wir abegereisst, 1824 Herr,
> Deine grosse Hülfe und Gut im Leib und Seel uns
> all behüt.

> We departed on May 24. Lord, with your great
> help and goodness protect us all in body and soul.

Notes

1.   John S. Duss, The Harmonists (Harrisburg, The
     Telegraph Press, 1943), pp. 419-420.

2.   Aaron Williams, The Harmony Society (Pittsburgh:
     W. S. Haven, 1866), p. 97.

3.   Max Weber, The Theory of Social and Economic Organ-
     ization, trans. by A. M. Henderson and Talcott
     Parsons (New York: Oxford University Press, 1947),
     pp. 358-59.

4.   "Charisma," International Encyclopedia of the Social

Sciences, 1968, II, 386.

5. Weber, Economic Organization, p. 364.

6. Williams, Society, p. 41.

7. William Alfred Hinds, American Communities (New
    York: Corinth Books Inc., 1961), p. 11.

8. Karl J. R. Arndt, George Rapp's Harmony Society
    1785-1847 (Philadelphia: University of Pennsylvania
    Press, 1965), pp. 246-247.

9. Charles Nordhoff, The Communistic Societies of the
    United States (New York: Schocken Books, 1965)
    [first published in 1875], p. 91.

10. Letter, George Rapp to Frederick Rapp, Feb. 24,
    1813 Old Economy, Archives, Series 2.

11. Letter, R. T. Nevin to George Rapp, Sept. 12, 1839
    Old Economy, Archives, Box 48.

12. Williams, Society, pp. 45-46.

13. Vereinigungs--Artikel der Harmonie--Gesellschaft
    (Pittsburgh: Ernst Luft, n.d.), pp. 10-11.

14. Ibid., pp. 12-13.

15. Christiana Knoedler, The Harmony Society (New York:
    Vantage Press, Inc., 1954), p. 37.

16. Ibid., pp. 46-47.

17. Karl J. R. Arndt, George Rapp's Harmony Society
    1785-1847 (Philadelphia: University of Pennsylvania
    Press, 1965), p. 247.

18. Elijah Lemmix vs Romulus L. Baker, et al., Circuit
    Court of the United States, Western District of
    Pennsylvania, Pittsburgh, 1854, p. 79.

19. Hinds, Communities, p. 19.

20. William E. Wilson, The Angel and the Serpent (Bloom-
    ington: University of Indiana Press, 1964), p. 86.

21.   Knoedler, Society, p. 44.

Chapter IV

PLACE OF WORSHIP

A. The Churches

The first church was built in 1808 in Harmony, Pennsylvania. This church, greatly altered, is still standing.
There is a sketch of the original church on an 1837 map in
the possession of Old Economy Village. The best descrip-
tion of the original church comes from an address by John H.
Wilson on January 26, 1937 at Harmony, later published in
pamphlet form. He received his information from an article
furnished by an unidentified traveler who had spent some
time with the Harmonists. He wrote:

> Near the centre of the town is a brick church
> erected with a small cupola; the ringing of its
> bell regulates the movements of the whole town.
> The church is 75 feet by 45, and very strongly
> built. The desk of the minister is elevated about
> two feet, and the benches are plain and regular,
> capable of accommodating 6 or 700 persons.
> Instrumental music is performed therein, and
> the Rev. John George Rapp, their much respected
> and venerable minister, preaches twice on the
> Sabbath, and on two evenings in the week.... The
> upper story of the church is supported by eight
> strong pillars, and is a granary large enough to
> contain several thousand bushels of grain.[1]

The second church was finished in 1815 in Harmony,
Indiana.

> ... it was a frame construction, two-storied with
> six arched windows on each side and two at the
> ends, which also had rounded windows in the gables.
> A twenty-by-twenty-foot belfry twenty feet tall
> crowned the east end of the church above the
> entrance, and above this belfry was a hexagonal

clockroom with two clockfaces eight feet in
diameter, one on the northeast side and one on the
southeast.   The clock struck the hours on a large
bell and the quarter hours on a smaller bell, and
the bell tones, it was said, could be heard at a
distance of seven miles in the surrounding woods. [2]

When William Hebert, one of the many visitors, de-
scended from the steeple of the old church he noticed that the
upper compartment of the building was used for storage--
grain, cotton, and so forth.   He also noted that the 1822 church
had vaults for storage.   (Owen states in his diary: "We
visited cellars under the new church and under Mr. Rapp's
house, well filled with wine, cider, etc. ")[3]   Of this new
church, Hebert writes:

They are erecting a noble church, the roof of
which is supported in the interior by a great number of stately columns [twenty-eight Doric columns],
which have been turned from trees of their own
forests.   The kinds of wood made use of for this
purpose are, I am informed, black walnut, cherry,
and sassafras.   Nothing I think can exceed the
grandeur of the joinery, and the masonry and
brickwork seem to be of the first order.   The form
of this church is that of a cross [Maltese Cross],
the limbs being short and equal; and as the doors,
of which there are four, are placed at the ends of
the limbs, the interior of the building as seen from
the entrances, has a most ample and spacious
effect.   A quadrangular story or compartment containing several rooms, is raised on the body of the
church, the sides of which inclining towards the top,
are terminated by a square gallery, in the centre
of which is a small circular tower of about ten feet
in height, which is surmounted with a silvered
globe.   The reason assigned by our guide for the
erection of this fine edifice was, that the first
church being built wholly of wood, is found to be so
hot during the summer, when the whole of the society are assembled within it, as to be scarcely
supportable, in consequence of which it was resolved
to delay the building of their houses for a time, and
raise a more spacious and substantial place of
worship, and the one they are employed upon bids
fairly to do them honor, both in the design and
execution. [4]

William A. Wilson says that each column was made
"from a single stick of timber about six feet in diameter."[5]

Victor Duclos, in his diary and recollections up to
1834, had some additional comments about this ambitious
building:

> The place of worship during the last few years of
> their residence here was a building constructed
> from plans of George Rapp and conceived by him
> in a dream. [Many of the accounts state this.
> William E. Wilson adds the variant that Rapp sup-
> posedly told his people that the plan was revealed
> to him by an angel.] This was a two story brick
> building constructed in the year 1822, but the
> internal arrangement was never carried out. . . .
> It was planned so that the interior at the pulpit
> represented a large cross. . . . The centre of the
> roof was supported by four columns about eighteen
> inches in diameter and twenty-five feet in height
> [really two feet in diameter], each turned by hand
> from one stick of timber, of cherry, poplar, or
> walnut. These columns stood on a large dome, en-
> circling which was a balcony at times used as a
> band stand. The entrances to each wing were large
> stone foundations with the semi-circular stone steps.
> The second and third steps were moulded on the
> edge. The north door, which was the principal
> entrance, was of cherry. The doorway was of
> carved stone capped by a cornice terminating in
> a gable in the panel of which was carved a rose,
> gilded, with a reference to it taken from the Bible,
> carved in stone. The other doorways were also of
> stone, but more simply finished.[6]

The golden rose referred to by Duclos was carved by
Frederick Rapp, and was graced with a Luther translation of
Micah 4:8: "Unto thee shall come the golden rose, the first
dominion." The golden rose and all its symbolism became
an identifying mark of the Harmonists. The window above
the door may be the unfolding of the emergence of the golden
rose. This symbol and others will be discussed below. It
should be noted that this celebrated north door of the 1822
church is now the door of the New Harmony public school.

The fourth church was built in Economy, Pennsylvania.
It was an undistinguished frame building, 45 feet by 40 feet,

built as their final settlement began. It is now used as a
duplex.

        The fifth church, a red brick building designed by
Frederick Rapp, still stands, calling Ambridge Lutherans to
worship. Its white steeple, surmounted by a cross topped by
a copper rooster, is one hundred feet from the ground. The
tower has a balcony from which many visitors were greeted
by hornists as they came to observe the communal group
where religion was a way of life. Today, as then, one can
get a lovely view of the area.

        In 1839 Buckingham described the church as follows:

> The interior of the building was perfectly plain,
> but lofty and spacious, well lighted and ventilated,
> and beautifully clean. There were neither pews,
> pulpit, altar, or other furniture; in which respect
> it resembled the simple interior of a Quaker
> meeting-house. The seats were substantial forms,
> or benches, with a broad flat rail at the back, of
> unpainted wood, and without cushions. The plat-
> form for the preacher, was a single elevation, of
> about 3 feet, enclosed on each side with a wooden
> railing, open in front where the ascent was by a
> few steps; and on this platform, about 12 feet by 8,
> was a table and chair for the preacher. [7]

        Christiana Knoedler added a "sinner's bench" for those
guilty of misbehavior. They would have to confess to the
group. [8]

        Today the interior of the church is essentially the
same. Three stained-glass windows and a baptismal font have
been added; and an altar with cross and candles were substituted for the table when the church officially became Lutheran
in 1909. The story of the Harmonists had gone full circle.

        These churches were not meant for socializing. Buck-
ingham reports that at the sound of the bell the people rushed
forth, and in less than five minutes the church was filled.
At the end of the service the same was true, with "the females rising and retiring first, and the males remaining seated, until every female had passed over the threshold, when
they rose and followed. "[9]

        In 1819 William Faux commented about the hastily
filled church:

> At the moment the bells began chiming, the people,
> one and all, from every quarter, hurry into their
> church like frightened doves to their windows; the
> street leading to the temple seems filled in a
> minute, and in less than ten minutes, all his large
> congregation, 1,000 men, women, and children all
> who can walk or ride [over two hundred too many]
> are in the church, the males entering in at the
> side, the females at the tower, and separately
> seated.[10]

These descriptions of the quickness with which the
church filled for the services reminds one of the scurrying
through the cloister halls of European Monasteries to the
"monastic hour" services.   The European cloister walks and
garden chapels also come to mind when one looks at the Harmonist labyrinth and grotto.

B. Outdoors

It has been noted that the Harmonists built five churches: one in Harmony, Pennsylvania; two in Harmony, Indiana;
and two in Economy, Pennsylvania.   However, their Würt-
temberger practice of meeting in each other's homes for
religious worship (because there the churches were controlled
by the established church) impressed upon them the idea that
church and worship are not synonymous.   Had it been, they
would not have waited until 1808 to build a church in Harmony,
Pennsylvania, having first built houses, barns, a gristmill,
an oilmill, a tannery, a blue-dyer's shop, a storehouse, a
sawmill, a brewery, and an inn.[11]   In Harmony, Indiana the
church was their first public structure built in 1815.[12]
There they also built a second one in 1822.[13]   Although they
built a community-house in 1825 at Economy, they did not
finish the church there until 1831.   It would seem that before
the churches were built, they may have met in their homes
as they had done in Germany or, in favorable weather,
in the great outdoors, as may be noted in Owen's diary:

Sunday, February 27, 1825 (Harmony, Indiana)

> Very delightful day. After dinner the Harmonians
> assembled to the call of the bugle and at Mr.
> Rapp's invitation we joined them. We walked pre-
> ceeded [sic] by music and occasionally singing to the
> vineyards, into one of which we entered. In the
> center of one is an open space, from which leads

an alley overhung by vines. Here we remained for
some time listening to the Harmonians band. We
then proceeded to a hill whence we had a fine view
of the town, which appeared to be situated in a fine
valley between two hills. We here seated ourselves
in a ring and Mr. Rapp seated on an old stump,
read for an hour an account of the Moravians. After
some music and singing we proceeded on our return.
We reached the top of the hill which overlooks the
road, here Mr. Rapp stopped and said, "Follow me
ye young and you old can go round." With that he
began running down the hill and all followed him.
Some came more leisurely. Afterwards we returned
with music as we had come. It was very pleasant,
and the whole population appeared to enjoy the walk.
He took occasion to remark they should beware of
luxury.[14]

Sunday, March 13, 1825

The Harmonians walked to the river and Mr. Rapp
read to them. We walked to the hill, walked into
the orchard and discovered for the first time what we
supposed was the burying ground for the Harmonians.[15]

This meditation in the out-of-doors can also be seen
in a letter from Romelius Baker to Frederick Rapp:

New Harmony--Easter Sunday
Evening April 11, 1830

Frederick!
On the evening of the 9th I arrived well after
spending my Good Friday in a small wagon from
Princeton. Yesterday and today I spent in the country and just now returned from our cemetery where
I at sunset spent an hour of Easter-celebration.
The young grass on the green sod of the graves of
our friends swaying in the cool breeze, the festive
solitude, the thoughts about death and decay over
which my feet trod, the bodily resurrection of
Christ and my loneliness affected me so strongly
that in quiet wonder about the great plan for salvation I returned to my room a poor, poor man, yet
not without comfort....[16]

Such communion with nature and God does not need a
church.

C. Labyrinth

In addition to the formal places of worship, Father
Rapp's mysticism inspired the building of a labyrinth in all
three towns. For meditation, these circular mazes had in
the center a grotto, rustic on the outside, high-style on the
inside. The labyrinth's tortuous paths pointed to the uneven
road of life, and yet exemplified a reward for those who did
not despair along the wayside. As a final lesson for the pilgrim, the grotto's decoration was to remind him that one
does not judge from outside appearances. Here, he also
could move into the mystical world of Rapp where he could
observe and ponder the duality of man--the loathly and the
lovely; the light and the dark; the sin and the redemption. Of
all the travelers who came to visit the Harmonist towns,
there was only one who seemed to lack all understanding of
this ancient symbol that had been involved in Egyptian, Cre-
tan, Etruscan, English, and medieval church history, myth,
literature and art. Henry Heald wrote to his brother, after
he visited the deserted Butler-County Harmony on May 28,
1819:

> ... but the most profound piece of childish folly
> amongst these religious Babies is their Labyrinth:
> it is an enclosure of about a half or so [sic] three-
> fourths of an acre of ground, a short distance
> from the road and outside of the town. In this they
> have a crooked winding pathway, formed by plant-
> ing trees and shrubbery in such a manner that peo-
> ple unacquainted with it find it difficult either to
> enter or return without a guide. This puzzle gar-
> den has afforded ample diversion for these grown
> up children![17]

The other observers were more worldly, wise or
tolerant; at least they just commented on the flowers and
shrubbery. William Hebert spoke of currant and hazel bushes, an illustration of Rapp's utilitarian bend even when pursuing the device of the mystics. Said Hebert:

> I must mention, that in addition to their vineyards
> Harmonians have formed an extensive garden in
> the form of a labyrinth, having a pretty rustic
> building in the centre. The mazy walks toward this

hermitage are formed by espalier fruit trees and
currant and hazel bushes in almost interminable
rounds.[18]

The best reference to the labyrinth comes from Robert
Dale Owen:

> When my father first reached the place, he found
> among the Germans--its sole inhabitants--indica-
> tions of plenty and material comfort, but with
> scarcely a touch of fancy or ornament; the only ex-
> ceptions being a few flowers in the gardens, and
> what was called 'The Labyrinth, ' a pleasure-ground
> laid out near the village with some taste, and in-
> tended--so my father was told--as an emblematic
> representation of the life these colonists had chosen.
> It contained small groves and gardens, with numer-
> ous circuitous walks enclosed by high beech hedges
> and bordered with such intricacy, that, without
> some Daedalus to furnish a clue, one might wander
> for hours and fail to reach a building erected in
> the centre. This was a temple of rude material, but
> covered with vines of the grape and convulvulus,
> and its interior neatly fitted up and prettily fur-
> nished. Thus George Rapp had sought to shadow
> forth to his followers the difficulties of attaining a
> state of peace and social harmony. The perplexing
> approach, the rough exterior of the shrine, and the
> elegance displayed within, were to serve as types
> of toil and suffering, succeeded by happy repose.[19]

   1. The Grotto. --When the New Harmony Commission
restored the grotto at New Harmony they made studies of
labyrinths and visited the only remaining Harmonist-built
grotto at Old Economy. Since they did not know what inscriptions the original Indiana grotto had, they inscribed that
which was typical of the Harmonists:

                   The Grotto - New Harmony

> The Creator of the universe has always in view
> the happiness of all the human race
> God requires no more of any human being than
> one man of honor and reputation requires of an-
> other.
> Under the serene sky and friendly clime will
> the fruits of noble achievement and wholesome

constitutions come to greater maturity.
We endure and suffer, labor and toil, sow and
reap with and for each other.
A harmonious and united society of men, may
be said to be a kingdom of God.
Love to God above all, and to thy neighbor as
thyself.
Let not the sun go down upon your wrath. (Paul
to Eph. iv. 26)
Again a day is passed and a step made nearer
the end. Our time runs away and the joys of
heaven are our reward.
The day of the Lord is drawing near, and will
dominate over all that is high, and humiliate all
which is lofty.
The golden treasure of this world to those who
know how to preserve it is Friendship.

Bottom row
The true principles of religion and the prudent
regulations of industry and economy by their united
influence produce a heaven upon earth, a true
harmony.
And the multitude of them that believed were of
one heart and one soul: Neither said any of them
that aught of the things which he possessed was his
own but they had all things in common. Acts IV:32
What a harmonious people! The safety man
reachest the lofty summit, where few can travel, and
from which many fall, or become lost and be-
wildered in the labyrinth of the artificial philosophy
of the world.
                                George Rapp
                                Founder of
                                The Harmony Society
Born - 1757-1847
Harmony, Pa. - 1804
Harmony, Ind. - 1814
Economy, Pa. -1824

Aaron Williams, considered the 19th-century "outside"
authority of the Harmonists, found "the Chinese principle of
pleasing by contrast" in the grotto of Economy. He wrote:

You approach, by a narrow tangled path, a small
rude structure, of the roughest stone, overgrown
with wild vines, and with a door apparently of

rough oak bark. You enter--and you stand in the
midst of a beautiful miniature Grecian temple, with
a life-sized piece of emblematic statuary before
you, and the dates of the great events in the Society's history conspicuously engraved in niches
around you. [20]

2. The canonical S. --The S form was used by the
Harmonists extensively in designs for braces, pottery, furniture and silk ribbons. The "S" signifies the serpent; the
seven deadly sins; the seven penitential psalms (6, 32, 38, 51,
102, 130, 143); the seven virtues and the seven works of
mercy, spiritual and corporal. In the world of numbers,
seven is symbolic of perfect order, a complete period or
cycle.

Much symbolism can also be found in the Economy grotto restored by John Hornstein Yelland during the summer of
1958. The full-blown Harmony rose in the ceiling is certainly its most dominant symbol. In his dedication speech, Yelland
said that the grotto was "the soul" of the Harmony Society,
for here "Father Rapp put his faith into physical expression."
He pointed to the three-part panel construction representing
the Trinity and the ivory frames forming the "A" of Alpha,
while the Roman ring around the building formed the "O" of
Omega. This ring has one hundred and forty-four blocks in
honor of the one hundred and forty-four thousand chosen ones
described in Revelation. [21]

The most puzzling aspect of the grotto is the inscription, "The Traveler's Disappointment," found on a tablet between the south and west windows. It completes the points of
a cross. No record has been found to explain it. J. S.
Buckingham, when describing the grotto, added his interpretation:

> ... On entering the interior, however, the visitor
> is pleasingly surprised to find an ornamented cir-
> cular-room, with wrought ceiling, and ornamented
> panels; and in the centre of the whole, a well-
> executed female statue, meant as the personification
> of Harmony, holding a lyre, and presiding as the
> genius of the place. Around the walls of the in-
> terior were several inscriptions; one of which was,
> "The Traveller's 'Disappointment,' " meaning to
> express the surprise intended to be occasioned by
> the finding this statute and those ornaments within
> so rough an exterior, ... [22]

There is no record of George Rapp's reaction to
Buckingham's interpretation.   But might George Rapp not have
had a nuance of reproof here?   There is a world that raises
expectations, only to disappoint the pilgrim.   It implies that
there is a search for purity which in actuality is not possible
here, and there is a redemption only in heaven.   However,
in spite of it all there will come an inner completeness if one
continues to strive for harmony.   If bitterness returns and
defiance momentarily takes over, there always comes the
sobering thought, "This too shall pass," and the golden rose
will come.

3.   The golden rose. --The golden rose, referred to
above in relation to the Harmony, Indiana church and now
found in the ceiling of the grotto, is also a question: Why
did the rose mean so much to the Harmonists?   And why did
Rapp use the Luther translation of Micah 4:8: "Unto thee
shall come the golden rose, the first dominion?"   All other
translations have: "... unto thee shall it come, even the
first dominion."   We first should ask why Luther chose the
golden rose as a substitute for "it" and a synonym for kingdom.   Although the word "rose" does not appear in the
Hebrew Micah 4:8, the word for ornament does (עֹפֶל).[23]
Traditional and liturgical-minded Luther readily substituted
golden rose, which had a legendary background and was
firmly fixed in Rose Sunday (Laetare Sunday, the 4th Sunday
of Lent), at which time a presentation of a golden rose was
given to an illustrious person or a group of people conspicu-
ous for loyalty to the Holy See.   This had been instituted in
1049 by Pope Leo IX.[24]   It may have been a variant of the
familiar feudal custom of the presentation by serfs to their
lords and masters of a real rose as a symbol of their
fealty or as a token of payment of annual rent to the land-
owners.[25]

That Martin Luther was greatly influenced by the rose
is further seen by his coat of arms.   Said Luther:

... But this heart is fixed upon the centre of a
white rose...
....
And around this ground base is a golden ring, to
signify that such bliss in heaven is endless, and
more previous than all joys and treasures, since
gold is the best and most precious metal.[26]

Besides his Lutheran heritage, Rapp had the Bible and

his mysticism to guide him. In hymn and prayer the rose is
the Divine Word made Incarnate; it is the Messianic Rose.
The Rose of Sharon from Song of Solomon became a symbol
of Christ when allegorically considered;[27] and the simile of
Isaiah, where the age of the spirit is the time when Israel
shall rejoice and "blossom as the rose," gives added significance to this image.[28]

The rose in outline resembles a wheel, a circle, a
unity, a perfection. So, in a true religious spirit and tradition, one finds the golden rose as a trademark of the Harmonists in Harmony, Indiana; on some of their flat-irons; on
the newel posts of the Great House in Economy; on the one
and only tombstone of the society found in Harmony, Pennsylvania, and in the Grotto at Economy. No matter where they
sang--outdoors, in the church, in the labyrinth, they believed,
"Unto you will come the golden rose."

Notes

1. John H. Wilson, The Historic Town of Harmony, Butler
      Co., Pa., 1937.

2. Wilson, Serpent, p. 47.

3. Owen, Diary, p. 77.

4. William Hebert, A Visit to the Colony of Harmony,
      in Indiana in the United States of America (London:
      George Mann, 1825), pp. 334-5.

5. Wilson, Serpent, p. 48.

6. Victor Colin Duclos, From the Diary and Recollections
      of Victor Colin Duclos. Copies from the original
      manuscript by Mrs. Nora C. Fretageot (Indianapolis:
      Indiana Historical Collections, III, 1916), p. 541.

7. James Silk Buckingham, The Eastern and Western States
      of America, II (London: Fisher, Son & Co., 1842), p.
      221.

8. Christiana F. Knoedler, The Harmony Society (New
      York: Vantage Press, Inc., 1954), p. 89.

9. Buckingham, America, p. 223.

10. William Faux, Memorable Days in America, Being a
     Journal of a Tour to the United States (London:
     W. Simpkin and R. Marshall, 1823), p. 265.

11. Karl J. R. Arndt, George Rapp's Harmony Society,
     1785-1847 (Philadelphia: University of Pennsylvania
     Press, 1965), p. 106.

12. William E. Wilson, The Angel and the Serpent (Bloom-
     ington: Indiana University Press, 1964), p. 47.

13. Ibid., p. 47.

14. William Owen, Diary of William Owen from November
     10, 1824, to April 20, 1825, ed. Joel W. Hiatt
     (Indianapolis: Indiana Historical Society Publica-
     tions, 4, No. 1, 1906), p. 107.

15. Ibid., p. 126.

16. Letter, Romelius Baker to Frederick Rapp, April 11,
     1830, Old Economy, Archives, Box 27.

17. Henry Heald, A Western Tour (Wilmington: J. Wilson,
     Printer, No. 105, Market St., [1819]), p. 151.

18. Hebert, America, p. 336.

19. Robert Dale Owen, Threading My Way: Twenty-Seven
     Years of Autobiography (London: Trübner, 1874),
     pp. 212-213.

20. Aaron Williams, The Harmony Society (Pittsburgh:
     W. S. Haven, 1866), pp. 66-67.

21. John Hornstein Yelland, "The Garden Grotto at Old
     Economy," Old Economy Village, 1959. (Mimeo-
     graphed.)

22. Buckingham, America, p. 227.

23. Rud, Kittel, Biblia Hebraica (Leipzig: J. C. Hin-
     richssche Buchhandlung, 1912), p. 869.

24. "The Golden Rose," The Catholic Encyclopedia, 1912,
     VI, 629.

25. Jean Gordon, Pageant of the Rose (Woodstock: Record
     Press, 1961), p. 101.

26. Martin Luther, "Martin Luther's Seal," (Minneapolis:
     Lutheran Brotherhood, 1956).

27. Song of Solomon 2:1.

28. Isaiah 35:1.

Chapter V

THE SABBATH

A. The Sabbath in General

The Harmonists kept the Sabbath (Sunday) by abstaining from ordinary and unnecessary labor and by assembling twice for public worship which was conducted in the usual non-liturgical Protestant manner: a hymn, a prayer, a sermon, another hymn. Sunday School had not come to the Harmonists because it was not in the German tradition. Religious instructions were included in their formal education which was completed at age fourteen. Interestingly, the Old Economy library houses at least one hundred 1866-booklets used by Lutherans for catechetical instruction.[1] It would appear that under Baker and Henrici these had been used during the regular school. However, according to Elijah Lemmix, they had regular school on Sunday for those young people beyond age fourteen, which was a German education custom. Asked whether he attended regular school at Economy, Lemmix replied, "No, only Sunday School at which was taught reading and writing."[2]

Aaron Williams noted that the Harmonists were like the Germans generally in enjoying Sunday evening as a social time:

... their band of music in years past was often heard sending forth its soft strains from some secluded spot, as the sun went down.[3]

Apparently it did not matter if one did not attend services, providing there was a good reason for not going. In 1839 Buckingham observed, on a Sunday:

The church was filled in less than five minutes, the whole number being about 450, out of a community of 500; the remainder being left at home to prepare the food, and take care of the very few

53

young children, and the dwellings.[4]

B. The Sermon

Non-Harmonists and travelers always were eager to attend a Harmonist service to see what the sermon was like. The language, of course, was German; so, a non-German-speaking guest had to sense the spiritual experience of these people. More than likely, many had failed to see that religion was a way of life for these dissenters from the established church. Because of this, many a would-be-guest was rebuffed by the reticent German who was not willing to bare his innermost convictions to a sneering, mocking stranger. A good example of this was recorded by Sandor Farkas, who came to America as a companion to Count Francis Beldi. Among other places visited, he came to Economy. On the way to the village he kept asking people about the Harmonists. Apparently all kinds of answers were flying about and the joking became so intense that "one traveler who spoke merrily at first, turned silent and sullen and finally said that he should be qualified best to know the answers as he was a member of the Society." In turn Farkas and company became silent, but eventually tried to calm the man. He then did answer questions willingly, but expressed regret that they were coming to visit "with such prejudices."[5]

William Faux displayed a shade of this attitude:

> The spell, or secret, by which these people are held in voluntary slavery, is not to be known or fathomed by inquiry. We asked if strangers were permitted to go to their church tomorrow. 'No, ' was the answer. This is unprecedented in the civilized world.[6]

This inhospitality obviously was not always the case, for Melish records being conducted by the innkeeper to a seat appropriated for strangers, and after the service being asked by the guide to remain a little, as they had on his account asked the band to play. He says:

> They assembled before the pulpit with their various instruments, namely three violins and a bass, a clarinet, a flute, and two French horns. On these they entertained us with a great variety of airs, the most of them of the solemn kind, and some of them accompanied by vocal music.[7]

Melish also gives a splendid account of the service and his reaction to it:

> The church was quite full, the number of persons being not less than 500. The women sat all in one end, the men in the other. They were singing a hymn in which they all joined with one accord; .... After prayer Mr. Rapp delivered a sermon with great animation, to which all the congregation paid the most devout attention; after which, with a short prayer and benediction, he dismissed the assembly. [8]

Elias Fordham has this to say about a service he observed in Harmony, Indiana:

> Men sit at one end of the church and the women at the other; and Mr. Rapp sits while he preaches in a chair placed on a stage, about one yard high, with a table before him. When I heard him one weekday evening, he wore a linsey-woolsey coat and a blue worsted night cap. Their singing is very good. [9]

Morris Birkbeck also recorded his impression of the effect the Sabbath had on the Harmonists. According to his notes he did not attend the service, but observed the people as they came from worship.

> ... This day, being Sunday, afforded us an opportunity of seeing grouped and in their best attire, a large part of the members of this wonderful community.... Soon the entire body of people, which is about seven hundred, poured out of the church, and exhibited so much health, and peace, and neatness in their persons that we could not but exclaim, surely the institutions which produce so much happiness must have more of good than evil in them; and here I rest, not lowered in my abhorrence of the hypocrisy, if it be such, which governs the ignorant by nursing them in superstitution; but inclined in charity to believe that the leaders are sincere. [10]

William Owen, in his diary, has several reports on services he attended:

> About 11 we were summoned by a psalm tune

played on a keyed bugle and a French horn to a
meeting.   Mr. Rapp spoke from the 169th psalm.
[? There are only 150 psalms!] He also said that
whoever does wrong disturbs the harmony of the
Universe and in order to restore it again we must
either do something, or if that is not possible, we
must suffer something. On the whole as a sermon
it was good and practical, with comparatively little
fanaticism about it.

I went to hear Mr. Rapp preach.   His sermon was
concerning the millenium.[11]

For that same Sunday, December 19, 1824, Donald
MacDonald had the following to say:

... Mr. Frederick Rapp sat at an elevated desk
and gave out the psalms and preached.   His
sermon was about friendship, working for one
another, having common property and the approaching Millenium, which would be brought about by
these and such like practices and method of life.
There was a mildness and amiable expression of
countenance in the whole congregation which was
extremely pleasing. Several of both the males
and females were good looking, strong and
healthy, and a very general contentment seemed
to prevail among them.   The service lasted about
an hour and a half. We were about 500 persons
present. We dined between eleven and twelve.
Between twelve and one the village band, consisting of eight or ten wind instruments, assembled
in front of Mr. Rapp's house, played one or two
slow movements and then preceded us into the
church. We were followed by about 300 of the inhabitants, mostly of the younger part of the
population. We remained there between one and
two hours which time was devoted to music and
singing psalms.[12]

Buckingham gives the most detail:

At the sound of the bell the dwellings began to
pour forth their inmates, all neatly dressed, the
females all with snowwhite caps, and each with
a book under the arm....   When all were seated,
Mr. Rapp entered, with his hat on, keeping it on

his head till he reached the platform, when he un-
covered. ...

The service commenced with the singing of a
German hymn; and as every individual had a book,
the page and number, and first line of the hymn,
was sufficient to be given out; as after that, all
could proceed, without having the lines repeated.
The singing was sufficiently good for the simple
melody of the hymn--tune, without the aid of instruments, or any attempt at harmony by singing
in parts; and it was very effective, as every individual of the whole assembly appeared to join
cordially in the exercise. Everyone sat during
the singing.

... The sermon followed immediately after this.
It was preceded by the reading of several verses
from St. Paul's Epistle to the Corinthians; and the
sermon was a running commentary on these, the
preacher sitting at the table on the platform during
its delivery; and though given in a loud and firm
voice; and with great vigour of tone and decision of
manner, it contained nothing, in act or gesture, of
which the most fastidious could complain; having
no reference to any peculiarities in their own mode
of life, but being just such a sermon on the general
doctrines of Christianity as any other Lutheran
minister might preach. To the sermon succeeded
another hymn, which was also well sung; and by
a quarter before 11 the assembly was dismissed;
so that the whole service lasted about the same
length of time as that of other churches.[13]

When the Rev. William A. Passavant of Pittsburgh
came for a visit the following year, he was not as compli-
mentary as Buckingham had been. He obviously had different views of religious life, and took particular issue with the
Harmonists' celibacy and distilling of whiskey. Aside from
this emotionalism, however, he gives a valuable account.
He says:

Through the influence of an acquaintance I was permitted to attend church on Wednesday evening, a
time at which no strangers are suffered to be
present. For some time before the bell rang for
worship there might be seen numbers of aged

women dressed in dark clothes, and walking at
a snail's pace and leaning on their staffs. After
these came the other females of the society and at
the first notes of the bell the men old and young
were seen collecting from all quarters. Presently
old Mr. Rapp, supported by two of the members,
entered the church and took his seat directly before
the Bible which was placed on a desk on the platform.
He was dressed in the common garb of the society
and wore a woolen night cap which he always removed before praying. His sermon was excellent
and he enforced the duty of following the Savior
and of living near the cross, with great earnestness. He remained seated during the whole discourse and when the subject seemed to demand
greater animation, his eyes flashed with intelligence
and his voice was raised to a high pitch that would
be deemed almost incredible for a man in his nine-
tieth year. [Wrong. Rapp at this time was 83
years old.] During the course of the discourse he
took occasion to introduce his favorite doctrines
and asked with seeming indignation, 'Was Christ
married?' His stupid congregation had not the
sense to see through his empty reasoning and
swallowed the remark entire. It would seem that
one who strenuously insists on following Christ in
his habits of love, would not enter so deeply into
the whiskey business--but precept and practice are
two different things in his creed. The appearance
of Rapp is well calculated to the situation he occupied. Though his age is now ninety, his step is
still firm and a snow-white beard reaching down to
his waist gives the appearance of a venerable
prophet.[14]

From a business-personal letter sent by Henrici to
Romelius Baker, the business head after Frederick Rapp's
death, one can see that the sermons presented to the people
were often discussed at table. Passavant reports that George
Rapp spent much time in reading the latest religious works
from Germany, so these table talks of the Luther and German
tradition must have been engrossing.[15] From the following
letter it is evident that unity and brotherhood for Christ was
their all-consuming passion:

... I am looking forward to soon having your company again at mealtime for the spiritual discussions.

Much has come forth since your departure.
Romelius, you often spoke and thought about the
restoration of all things in which God will be one
and all.   As father preached recently from 1st
Corinthian (on the 15th), all the destructible and in-
destructible, and all the perishable until finally
death comes is conquered in the battle; and from
now on through the corridors of time people will
willingly submit themselves to Christ and to the
community till finally everything is one; so that
no one, not even the smallest creature will display
any adversity or disturbance, but instead will be in
the purest, most blessed, most complete form of
harmonious unity where a master is not needed because everything is permeated and affected with the
finest being of the Father and in conformity with a
part for the whole it manages, produces and lives:
this we saw for the first time as the complete goal.
For the end, greetings and a few words which we
sang at last Wednesday's hour service:
> 'Blessed, blessed, blessed is he
> Who a follower of Solomon's be. '
> (signed) Jacob Henrici

P.S. by Father:
Creation is a whole (circle), and we are in the
middle. Don't the near and far both feel the bond
of unity when some of the members, because of
the necessary need of the whole, must go out to
the periphery to carry on the business? Therefore
we are happy to soon have you again in our midst
to eat together the bread of God at our common
table which I presume will taste very good although
you are in the whole blessed and happy. I know
beforehand that the nearer you can see the completion of your business, the more intense is your
attraction (to the Society) so that with the wings of
an eagle you would make your return voyage to the
place where the magnet of love unites us; so we
hope soon to see you well in our midst.
> Hearty greetings from the entire House
> of Peace.
> (signed) Georg Rapp[16]

From the Owen diary and a letter from Gertrude Rapp
to Rosina Rapp it is evident that in the absence of George
Rapp, Frederick took on the religious leadership. In a

short chatty letter to Rosina, Gertrude reports that Frederick
delivered a marvelous Christmas sermon with Isaiah 11 as
his text and that everyone was much taken by it.[17] In passing, it should be noted that Isaiah 11 speaks of the peaceable
kingdom and the victorious restoration of Israel, the latter
being a major tenet of the Harmonist "credo."

In George Rapp's "diary," which consisted of letters
to Frederick written in the spring of 1823 with a running account of happenings, Rapp refers to sermons and Sunday activities, as the following excerpts show:

... On the 13th [April] I spoke on Isaiah 25,
verse 4, and the afternoon finished all.... At
12:30 we started and went to the 'cutoff hill' for
reading--into the peach grove, because on account
of the height it was not so cold there, and all the
little bushes are in bloom there and it was very
pleasant for it was pleasant weather. In the
evening around six, music began to play in the upper story of Number 2 [dormitory] and all people
gathered there uncalled, and I was very cheerful
and happy for the oldest men and women sat in the
hall to the right and left and there was discussion
about the beginning of Harmonie. And the young
people sang several songs from the Harmony Song-
book. Then we prayed. After that all the inhabitants
of the house came and shook hands and promised
not to break the bond of peace. And at 9:30 o'clock
we parted.
. . . .
The 16th (Wednesday) ... In the evening there was
a meeting and the discussion was on the Jeremiah
chapters 31, 32, 33, and 34, and the great difference
was pointed out that the Lord complained that He
had to force them but in the new covenant He will
search out from all nations these capable of receiv-
ing light and place 'my law into their heart,' that it
will not be bound to one people alone.
. . . .
Sunday (20th) there was a meeting as usual and the
discussion was about Zephaniah, chapter 3, verses
8, 9 etc. How true it is that the eighth verse is being fulfilled, especially how the kings of the earth
are brought together, for really everything is mixed
up in there, both the religious and the political,
for the scholars and philosophers have a task to find

a way in which the nations, especially Christen-
dom, may combine the political with the religious,
where this would be of communal interest to all.
Without this combining force revolutions cannot be
sufficiently guarded against or stopped. Behold,
gradually they are being brought together, probably
they will go too far and Christ and His religious
will be degraded too much so that the anger of God
will awaken and, of course, will preach quite differently after the judgment, perhaps as is being
preached in the Harmonie already, that He will
perhaps be [unclear] to us.
. . . .
In the evening [probably Wednesday] there was a
meeting and the discussion was about Romans,
Chapter 8, verses 18 and 19. This is chiefly our
concern; to bring into balance the suffering of the
time and the future glory.
. . . .
Sunday the 27th at 8:30 the meeting began and the
discussion was about Isaiah, chapter 55, verses 8 ff.
The 11th verse explains the meaning of the text.
In the afternoon I read about Solomon's fall and
sacrifice, by Klopstock, in the Labyrinth. [18]

These accounts are evidence that the subject matter
of the sermons was biblical, and not filled with instructions
relative to their secular affairs, as had been charged.

Aaron Williams throws a further light on the sermons
by explaining the Harmonists' allegorical interpretation. He
writes:

In their exposition of the Scriptures, especially of
the Old Testament, they make much use of the
allegorical method. While not denying the literal
verity of the historical facts, they seek a deeper
typical or symbolical meaning beneath the surface;
and thus they spiritualize the letter, and find the Old
Testament full of the richest gospel truth. In de-
fense of this practice they appeal to the example of
our Savior himself and his apostles, who thus
spiritualize the 'manna, ' and the 'tabernacle, ' and
'Mt. Sinai. '

To give a few examples: They regard the process
of creation--the 'spirit of God moving upon the face

of the waters' [or chaos], the breaking in of 'light'
through the thick darkness, etc., as symbolizing
the new creation, when 'God who commanded the
light to shine out of darkness, shines in our hearts, '
and the purifying fires of the final conflagration,
which shall prepare the way for the 'new heavens
and the new earth, ' as resembling that 'baptism of
fire' by which Christ will burn up the 'wood, hay,
and stubble' of his people here, through various
fiery processes, and will make even the 'fires of
hell' [as they suppose] a means of ultimate purifi-
cation to lost souls!

Again, they take Moses as the representative of
the law, and Joshua of the gospel. The exclusion
of Moses from the promised land, was not merely
a punishment for his offense in smiting the rock
[which would have seemed too severe], but a great
symbolical lesson to Israel, that salvation or
entrance into the 'rest that remaineth for the people of God, : the heavenly Canaan, is not by the
law, but by the gospel of Jesus, who is the Joshua
of the New Testament.' Comp. Heb. 4:8, 'For if
Jesus [i.e. Joshua] had given them rest, then would
he not have spoken of another day. '

Thus also Noah, Joseph, and Boaz, are types of
Christ.... [19]

The spiritual mantle fell on Romelius Baker and Jacob
Henrici when George Rapp died in 1847. They continued
preaching in the same vein of the millenium, communal life
and celibacy. One source that points to it is the Pulszkys'
account of their visit in 1853, six years after Rapp's death.
Writes Theresa in her diary:

... When I spoke about the communistic principle,
they [Henrici and Baker] said: they believed that
Christ is coming soon and therefore it is better
to prepare for the future world than to care for
individual property, family, and the external world.
I remarked to them that if they do not marry and
the day of judgment is yet delayed, their society
might be centralized at last, and absorbed by one,
perhaps very worldly individual, inheriting the fruit
of all their toils. But Henrici met my objection,
saying that as their motives were good, Providence

would take care of the results.[20]

She was most uncomplimentary about their singing, calling it a "nasal twang," and wryly noted Henrici's colorful language when during a sermon he said: "Asses, do you mean to be wiser than our Saviour? He was unmarried."[21]

That Father Henrici must have been "a character" can be seen from another anecdote recounted by Christiana Knoedler. It seems that Henrici would at times chastise some of the brethren for wearing clothing that was too worldly.

> For instance, Lena, a new girl in town, had a
> pale-blue woolen hood with blue ribbons, which
> she wore to church for the first time. While
> Father Henrici was talking he noticed Lena's hood.
> 'Who is that?' he demanded. 'And what is she
> wearing?' The entire congregation looked at Lena.
> No one answered. Lena looked at the floor. 'Well, '
> continued Henrici, 'if she is just visiting here, it
> is all right; she may wear it; but if she lives here
> she can't wear it. ' He continued his sermon by
> excoriating Eve, who tempted Adam to sin.[22]

While some of the practices became traditions, others changed. Duss in his memoirs remembers that, in contrast to earlier times, the bells were not rung until after the lay members had assembled and taken their pews; the women to the west, the men to the east. Seven elders occupied the front bench on the speaker's right, and prominent "fore-ladies," the opposite front bench. Newcomers were seated in the rear. Duss describes the typical service as follows:

> While the bells are ringing--in sweeps Gertrude,
> closely followed by Baker and Henrici. The Senior
> Trustee files to the right and ascends to the pulpit
> as Gertrude and Henrici to the left, ascend to the
> organ loft. The service opens with the singing of
> some stanzas from one of the Society's hymns.
> After a short prayer comes the sermon, preached
> in sitting posture--a desk being used instead of a
> pulpit. On said desk, particularly in winter-time,
> is a bouquet of flowers. After the sermon the re-
> maining stanzas of the hymn are sung, whereupon
> comes the benediction--which means that we are
> dismissed. Are we--and how! The woman nearest

the exit rushes forth; wide open flings the double
doors, through which the throng of women simply
pours.   A casual visitor, aghast, exclaims 'is
there a fire'--'Oh, no, ' he is informed, 'the rush
is in deference to the Trustees, who follow immediately and whose egress must not be impeded. '23

Although others held sway, the actual words of George
Rapp did not die; they did not even fade, for the Frederick
Rapp Library of the Great House has numerous school "Exercise Books" (für Schönschreiben) in which "the seven most
important points of Father Rapp's last sermon" are recorded
over and over. At random I picked up one dated 1888 and
found:

George Rapp died August 7, 1847

The seven most important points of Father's last
sermon:

1.   Suffer all misfortunes and be patient in your
distress for as gold is tested by fire so will you by
the fire of distress and will become pleasing to
God.

2.   All your purposes, regardless how good they
appear, and even though they are called splendid
by everyone, should be subordinated to God because you don't know if they agree with God's plan.

3.   Would you want one of our brothers to remain
in the clutches of Satan?

4.   Never allow the fire of the altar to go out.

5.   You must combine the warmth of your heart
with God's word if you want to become true and
one.

6.   You must fight two worlds--the sensual one and
the dark one--to arrive at the light of the world.

7.   The Lord bless you and keep you in the spirit
of community--brotherhood now and for all time.
Amen

According to the last will of our dear brother

Romelius the following three points should be added
to the above:

8. John 17:19 & 21: I heal myself for you so that
you also will be healed in truth; and so that they are
one as you in me father, and I in you; and that they
be one in us and that the world believe that you send
me.

9. Verses 22 & 23: I gave them the majesty of God
which you gave me so that they be one as we are
one: I in them and you in me so that they are completely one and let the world know that you send me,
and love them as you love me.

10. 1 Peter 4:8: Above all have love among you for
love covers much. [24]

C. Prayer

Häusliche Andachten by Gottfried W. Fink, which is in
the Frederick Rapp Library, could have been an inspiration
for George Rapp to pass on to his people as he supervised
the weekly meetings. That there are prayers for preparation
for the coming of the Lord is understandable. But it is interesting that the rest of the prayer-book is divided into
prayers for winter, spring, summer and autumn. Present in
these prayers is the same superlative, intense, emotional
comparison of God to nature as is found in the hymns. For
example:

Ich hang an der Natur. Unendlich ist ihr Reich und
überschwänglich gross ist ihre Pracht and Macht,
und unausprechlich ihrer Schönheit Fülle. Und
doch ist sie mit allen ihren Wundern, allen ihren
Freuden nur ein Wiederschein, ein abbild deiner
Herrlichkeit. Wer kann dich fassen und ergründen,
dich, den grossen Schöpfer einer solchen Welt!
Verloren in den Reitzen deines geheimnissvollen
Wirkens fall ich nieder und bete dich an.

I cling to nature. Abundant are her riches and
boundless is her splendor and might, and inex-
pressible her endless beauty. And yet, with all
her wonders, all her joys, she is only a reflection, a copy of your magnificence. Who can

fathom, who can comprehend you, the great Creator of such a world! Lost in the labyrinth of your
secret creations I fall down and worship you. [25]

Additional prayers probably used by the Harmonists
were those found in Johann Arndt's Paradiesgärtlein, also
located in the Frederick Rapp Library.

Included are prayers of every description--on the ten
commandments, thanksgiving, comfort, praise, joy, divine
service.   There are morning and evening prayers for each
day of the week.   The church prayers were set up for the
Evangelical Lutheran Church year.

The most fascinating factor of this prayer-book is the
introduction.   This reviews fourteen miraculous survivals of
copies of this prayer-book--thirteen in fires and one in a
flood.   In all cases the book was entirely untouched, just
like the three men of Nebuchadnezzar's fiery furnace.

Because there seems to be no record of actual
prayers it could be surmised that the Harmonists followed
Matthew 6:6, 7:

> But when thou prayest, enter into thy closet, and
> when thou hast shut thy door, pray to thy Father
> which is in secret; and thy Father which seeth in
> secret shall reward thee openly.

> But when ye pray, use not vain repetitions, as the
> heathen do: for they think that they shall be heard
> for their much speaking.

Among the travelers, Melish, Fordham, and Buckingham made comments about prayer.   And as mentioned above,
visitor Passavant took note that Rapp always removed his
"night-cap" while praying.   Fordham noted, "In praying the
Harmonists do not rise up nor kneel down, but bend their
bodies forward, almost to their knees. "[26]

If Fordham was correct, the practice had changed by
the time they returned to Pennsylvania.   In 1839 Buckingham
reports:

> ... but when prayer followed, every one rose, and
> joining their hands clasped in each other, and
> closed upon their breasts, they continued in this

attitude, with every appearance of silent, sober,
and sincere devotion, to the end, without sighings,
sobbings, or moanings, and in the most perfect
order and decorum. The prayer was fluent, copi-
ous, and fervent, without being violent; and such
as would have become any place of Christian worship.[27]

And Melish had written:

... After singing, they all knelt down to prayer.
We followed their example, and never did I pray
more devoutly. I did not understand one word of
the prayer;--but I saw that this interesting Society
was under the influence of the spirit of God, and
that they worshipped him with reverence and with
godly fear. Tears of joy came into my eyes, as I
exclaimed mentally, 'This, indeed, is true Christianity, --this, unlike the solemn mockeries of interested priests, who have turned religion into a
trade, and the temple of the Lord into a den of
thieves--this is worshipping God in spirit and in
truth. It contributes to true felicity here, and
prepares the soul for consummate bliss hereafter. '[28]

Notes

1. Evangelische Lutherische Kirche, Kleines Lutherisches
   Schul-Gesangbüchlein (New York: Hardter, 1866).

2. Elijah Lemmix vs Romulus L. Baker, et al., Circuit
   Court of the United States, Western District of
   Pennsylvania, Pittsburgh, 1854, p. 42.

3. Aaron Williams, The Harmony Society (Pittsburgh:
   W. S. Haven, 1866), p. 113.

4. James Silk Buckingham, The Eastern and Western
   States of America, II (London: Fisher, Son & Co.,
   1842), p. 221.

5. Karl J. Arndt, "Three Hungarian Travelers Visit
   Economy, " The Pennsylvania Magazine of History
   and Biography, Vol. LXXIX, No. 2, April, 1955,
   p. 199.

68   The Harmonists

6. William Faux, Memorable Days in America Being a Journal of a Tour to the United States (London: W. Simpkin and R. Marshall, 1823), p. 264.

7. John Melish, Travels in the United States of America in the years 1806, 1807, 1809, 1810, 1811 and Travels Through Various parts of Great Britain, Ireland, and Upper Canada, II (Philadelphia: 1812), 6-7.

8. Ibid., p. 7.

9. Elias Fordham, Personal Narrative of Travels in Virginia, Maryland, Pennsylvania, Ohio, Indiana, Kentucky, and a Residence in the Illinois Territory: 1817-1888, ed. F. A. Ogg (Cleveland: Arthur H. Clark, 1906), p. 208.

10. Morris Birkbeck, Notes on Journey in America From the Coast of Virginia to the Territory of Illinois (London: Ridgeway and Sons, 1818), p. 129.

11. William Owen, Diary of William Owen from November 10, 1824, to April 20, 1825, ed. Joel W. Hiatt (Indianapolis: Indiana Historical Society Publications, 4. No. 1, 1906), p. 54.

12. Donald MacDonald, The Diaries of Donald MacDonald, 1824-1826 (Indianapolis: Indiana Historical Society Publications, 1942, Vol. 14, No. 2), p. 220.

13. Buckingham, America, p. 222.

14. William A. Passavant, "A Visit to Economy in the Spring of 1840," Western Pennsylvania Historical Magazine, IV, No. 3, July, 1921, pp. 144-149.

15. Ibid., p. 149.

16. Letter, Jacob Henrici to Romelius Baker, Dec. 8, 1837, Old Economy, Archives, Box 45.

17. Letter, Gertrude Rapp to Rosina Rapp, Dec. 26, 1824, Old Economy, Archives, Series 2.

18. Karl J. R. Arndt, George Rapp's Harmony Society 1785-1847 (Philadelphia: University of Pennsylvania

Press, 1965), pp. 242-249.

19. Williams, Society, pp. 111-112.

20. Karl J. Arndt, "Three Hungarian Travelers Visit Economy," The Pennsylvania Magazine of History and Biography, LXXIX, 2, April, 1955, p. 215.

21. Ibid., p. 214.

22. Christiana Knoedler, The Harmony Society (New York: Vantage Press, 1954), p. 89.

23. John Duss, The Harmonists (Harrisburg: The Telegraph Press, 1943), pp. 162-163.

24. School Dictation Book, Old Economy, Frederick Rapp Library.

25. Fink, G. W.: Häusliche Andachten (Leipzig: George Joachim Goeschen, 1814), p. 3.

26. Elias P. Fordham, 1817-1888, p. 208.

27. Buckingham, America, p. 222.

28. Melish, Canada, p. 6.

Chapter VI

RITES OF PASSAGE

A. Baptism

As stated above, baptism was one source of the
Harmonists' irritation with the Lutheran Church. Rapp and
his followers believed that the clergy were not worthy to
baptize children, and that the children did not know what it
was all about anyway. So, what was the value? Nevertheless, for awhile the members baptized their own children at
an older age. But with the onset of celibacy this soon became
a minor problem. However, Arndt reports that if the records
are reliable, 262 children were born from 1805 to 1813;
sixty-nine from 1814 to 1824; twenty-five from 1825 to 1830. [1]
As there is no record of early baptism activity, it was probably frowned upon, as it had been in Germany.

B. Marriage/Celibacy

Perhaps this section should be called "celibacy."
Two years following their organization, the Harmonists made
a further advance toward the pure and holy life by abjuring
the use of tobacco and matrimony and further conjugal intercourse. However, families continued to live together as before, but "they that had wives were as though they had
none." [2] The men slept upstairs and the women downstairs.
Jonathan Lenz, a late trustee, made the observation that
young people, and not Father Rapp, had first conceived the
idea of celibacy because pregnancies rather hampered the
development of the wilderness with which everyone was
occupied. [3] The fact that Lenz himself was born in 1807 in
Harmony makes it evident that he is speaking of hearsay.
(He may have been inspired by Zoar, settled in 1817 by
fellow Württembergers. They found clearing their Ohio land
a difficult task, and solved part of their problem by declaring
a celibate state for all. When their wilderness began to
blossom, they abjured celibacy and returned to their wedded
bliss.) [4]

70

Whether the Harmonist celibacy was "a fresh revival
of religion" or just the expedient thing to do, it proved to be
a major problem for the Society until around 1846. Not that
celibacy is anything unusual in a communitarian settlement.
The Essenes practiced it in the 2nd century B.C.; early
Christians continually withdrew from the flesh; and the medieval Christians filled monasteries and convents. Nor is it
to be supposed that this asceticism could be carried out without occasional lapses. During 1805-1807 a number of marriages took place with Father Rapp officiating! Among
others was Rapp's son John, the father of the celebrated
Gertrude. However, according to Aaron Williams, thereafter no marriages were solemnized. Those who wanted to
marry had to leave the society. It was not that Rapp con-
demned matrimony for those who did not have the "vocation,"
it was simply that he expected the Second Advent and wanted
their number to be among the "hundred and forty-four thousand" who should "stand with the Lamb on Mount Zion," and
"who were such as were not defiled with women, but were
virgins."[5]

Karl J. R. Arndt speaks of the Berleburger Bible annotated by George Rapp in connection with the 144,000.
Since this Bible cannot now be found at Old Economy, the
facts must come from the Arndt work. He says that Rapp
makes special note of the root of 144,000, especially since
it is also the number of the tribes of Israel. The Berleburger
Bible continues:

> But in the twelve there lies a six double, and it is
> the number of man, for he was created on the sixth
> day. But since fallen man wanted to propagate
> himself, there was born out of this the mass of
> evil men. But if the sixth figure is again brought
> under the 12th figure, and thus is brought into 1
> and 2, it is corrected. This is done under Christ,
> the Lamb. Those who cling to him and unite him
> and in this way also are united with each other
> and become of one mind, these have found the
> right path. [6]

From the writing above a preoccupation with six can be seen.

In pursuing the material culture of the Harmonists I
discovered that the Harmony buildings using the Flemish bond
employed a unique brick structure. Five rows of brick are
placed horizontally (stretchers); the sixth row is placed as

with headers. This is true in Harmony, Pennsylvania; New
Harmony, Indiana; and Old Economy, Pennsylvania. Only oc-
casionally, as in the front facing of the Great House, is
there a difference. Perhaps in this case it was to affect dis-
tinction; perhaps it was the work of a hireling to whom the
number six was not significant. At any rate, the number
five plus one was not the building practice of the day. Oc-
casionally a former Harmonist house has been radically
changed, but can be recognized by this unusual building
practice.

    Those who left the society were not always happy be-
cause often the conscience developed by Rapp burned deeper
than the flesh. After the first heat of passion, the Harmonists were met by the cold facts of the alien world for
which they were ill prepared. The following letter tells of
one couple's distress:

                              Georgetown, Ohio 9/13/1841
    Worthy Friends:
        Since I left you five years ago like a link from
    a chain, I must now come to you as the prodigal
    son and must say 'Father I sinned before heaven
    and you' for I must turn to you for the waves are
    over my head, and in my sorrow I can go to no one
    for I have had no rest day or night since I left the
    society and God. I beg you, father, and all the so-
    ciety that you would be so good as to forgive me and
    my grave error. Everyday my husband has told
    me that I should have stayed at Economy; he would
    not have gone, so I must bear the entire blame.
    And so I must think it regardless what will happen
    to me because I deserve it for I agreed to all that
    had been taught, and I was certain it was the right
    way, but the devil approached so that I saw things
    the wrong way and I finally fell. Now I have no
    one to talk with because we live among people who
    mock us as the Harmonist slaves. Dear Father,
    in my need, I must call on you.
        Five years ago we bought 115 acres for $1600.00.
    This included a two-story house, barns and an
    orchard near Georgetown. We now have paid half,
    and the remainder is due, but we have had such
    poor times and crops that we don't have the money.
        Would you be so kind as to loan us money for the
    interest. Naturally we will repay you. We will
    give you the land as collateral because if we don't

get the money, it will be sold and we will lose all.
We beg you once more in the name of God to
help us. We beg you. Please write as soon as
possible. I could write more, but I hope soon to
be able to speak with you personally. Greetings
to all.

Christina Daum

Anna Katharina Müller
Address: Friedrich Daum
       Franklin Twp.
       Georgetown, Ohio[7]

Sometimes the couples asked to return, but this was
denied except in the Hildegard Mutschler--Conrad Feucht
case. Actually the entire Hildegard Mutschter story is
shrouded in enigma. That she was an unusually attractive
and talented girl and assisted Father Rapp in the laboratory
had been noted by the Duke of Saxe-Weimar, and no doubt by
all the Society. So when George Rapp reversed himself when
Hildegard started flirtations, he exposed himself to calumny
and caused a temporary breach between himself and Frederick. The year before, he had sent Jacob Klein away because
of his possible interest in Hildegard; she, in spite of the
rules, was allowed to stay. That Klein was bitter is easy
to understand. He even went to Attorney Bonnhorst who had
taken care of many Harmonist legal matters. The following
letters are a Klein receipt of his dismissal from Economy,
and the result of Klein's legal advice:

(At) Economy on 1st of September 1826 I, the
undersigned, received from Georg Rapp and Society
the sum of $150 in which sum was the $40.00 I
gave Frederick Rapp last April.

Jacob Klein

1827, the 17 of Nov. Received from Georg
Rapp and Society $40.00 in full which I certify
with my own signature.

Jakob Klein
[Note "c" in the first Jacob and "k" in the second.]

Sept. 15, 1826
I, Jacob Klein hereby declare in accordance with
the advice of Mr. von Bonnhorst that I will renounce all claim on Hildegart Mutzler; and that
with the said Hildegart; and that I will cause the
Society no concern over my escapade; and I hope
that Mr. Rapp and the Society members will forgive

me my inclination toward said girl which apparently was not mutual. I solemnly promise to remove
her from my thoughts so that I will not be looked
upon as an enemy of the society for I left the society in peace. I find no hate in my soul toward
the society. After all, my parents and siblings live
among you. How could I hate that where they are.
I certify this with my signature to convince the
Messrs. Rapp that I am cured of my brashness
and have followed the good advice of Mr. Bonnhorst,
in proof of which I have written the above and
signed it.
                                        Jacob Klein
Pittsburgh, the 15th of Sept., 1826
Counter-signature
Charles von Bonnhorst

                                        Sept. 15, 1826
My dear Mr. Rapp,
    I am enclosing a, which must not be an un-
welcome, copy of Jakob Klein's renouncement. He
came to me for advice. I advised him to seek
peace and drop his charges whereupon he wrote
the enclosed document.
    More about this when I'll have the pleasure
of seeing you. Best wishes to the old gentleman
and the family.
                                Most respectfully,
                                Charles Bonnhorst[8]

        But the most bitter turn of events came in 1827 when
Hildegard eloped with Conrad Feucht, one of the most prominent members of the Society. Instead of being glad to be
rid of them, as he was with others of like caliber, George
Rapp asked the Society to pray for them. This disillusioned
Frederick since it was contrary to all of Rapp's teaching.
Actually it confirmed his suspicion that the elder Rapp could
be blinded by flattery. Frederick's grief was intensified by
the knowledge that many of the Harmonists knew it too. In a
letter to George dated midnight of September 2, 1829, he presented the entire case of Hildegard to him. Nevertheless,
by 1834 the Feuchts returned to Economy. They had three
children; and much later, these brought one of the main suits
against the society. [9] Frederick's prediction of trouble had
been correct, not only for their present but also for the
future. The rigid system of celibacy had been given a severe
blow, and the contraries of man were more in evidence than
ever.

In spite of the gloom that appeared at times with this asceticism, wry humor, both ordinary and sophisticated, occurred. It should also be noted that the writers of the following letters obviously did not understand celibacy, and Lord Byron, while certainly well aware of European monastic orders, simply did not understand the Harmonists. It is indicative, however, of how widely the Harmonists were known. Byron would naturally assume that his readers knew of these celibates across the Atlantic when he wrote about them in Don Juan. First, an English letter:

> October 8, 1818
> Mr. Lyn, Sir, as I know you are a friend and a well wisher to the Harmony Society--I wish you to propose to the next legislature a Bill to disolve Mr. Raps restrictions on his people on their not marrying--as there is many young girls of excellent conduct and beheavour in hermony and many young men of good parts--make good husbands and wives--no doubt to me but wish to fulfill the command that God gave to Adam. Each to multiply and replenish the earth. The Harmonians being a peacable industrous virtious people to bring up young ones in the same way might in time become good citizens. It cannot be right not to perpetuat their specieous but the legislature that can disolve the marriage contract but that they may have power to give the youth of Harmony liberty to marry.
> A friend to the Harmony Society
> P.S. it is surely not right that those who are man and wife should not enjoy [each] other as such to please the old gentleman. [10]

A letter from twenty-five year old George Hatch wants to know all about the Harmonists. He says he has traveled all around and is looking for a place to settle down. The Harmonists interest him, but before he makes any move, he wants to know about this marriage situation--is it permitted or not? Some people have told him yes; others no. [11]

Finally, cynical Byron composes:

> When Rapp the Harmonist embargo'd marriage
>   In his harmonious settlement--(which flourishes
> Strangely enough as yet without miscarriage,
>   Because it breeds no more mouths than it
>   nourishes,

Without those sad expenses which disparage
What Nature naturally most encourages)--
Why call'd he 'Harmony' a state sans wedlock?
Now here I have got the preacher at a dead lock.

Because he either meant to sneer at harmony
Or marriage, by divorcing them thus oddly.
But whether reverend Rapp learn'd this in Germany
Or no, 't is said his sect is rich and godly,
Pious and pure, beyond what I can term any
Of ours, although they propagate more broadly.
My objection's to his title, not his ritual,
Although I wonder how it grew habitual.

But Rapp is the reverse of zealous matrons,
Who favour, malgre Malthus, generation--
Professors of that genial art, and patrons
Of all the modest part of propagation;
Which after all at such a desperate rate runs,
That half its produce tends to emigration,
That sad result of passions and potatoes--   12
Two weeds which pose our economic Catos.

C. Burial

From all accounts, none feared death. They believed
that all those who were true to the Harmony way of life but
were not permitted to live until the Second Advent, would be
raised up to meet Him at His Coming. Until then, when
their work was done, they would sleep in the orchard, for
such was their burial place. Hirelings of the Society often
used the terms Friedhof (Court of Peace) or Gottsacker
(God's Acre). To continue the practice of equality, no monument of any kind was placed on any of the graves in the three
cemeteries except one for John Rapp at Harmony, Pennsylvania. That one, for an unknown reason, is leaning against
the left side of the cemetery wall. It features the Harmony
rose. There are six roses: two on top, two at the center,
and two toward the bottom. The German inscription has been
translated by John Duss:

Here lies and rests in the cool bosom
of the earth
Johannes Rapp
who
was born the 19th of September 1783

> died the 27th of July 1812
> Here lies a clay upon the potter's wheel
> Until decay unlock
> The precious salt to a new body
> Which in the joy of life will then arise.

Originally there were no fences around the orchards; however, as time went on strangers disturbed the resting place, so fences of various types were erected. The first one to be built was in New Harmony, Indiana. Using bricks from their famous maltese cross church, which was being misused, they had a brick wall built at the cost of $143.57. Locusts having replaced the apple trees, Romelius Baker advised his friend Samuel Arthur to let only one or two sprouts of the locusts grow and that the burial ground could be used for pasture, but that he should keep it locked so that "ill disposed" people would not disturb it.[13]

The stone wall around the Harmony, Pennsylvania cemetery was built in 1870. This tree-filled cemetery is especially well known for its stone gate which swings on an iron pivot. Over the entrance are the following inscriptions:

[Top line:]
Here rest one hundred members of the Harmony Society who died from 1805 to 1815.

[Center]:
I know that my Redeemer liveth, and He will hereafter wake me from the earth. Job 19:25 Blessed is he and holy who has part in the first resurrection; over such the other death has no power but they will be priests of God and of Christ and shall reign with Him a thousand years. Rev. 20:6. Remain faithful until death and I will give thee the crown of life. John 11:25.

[Right small circle:]
In a moment, in a twinkling of an eye, at the last trump: for the trumpet shall sound, and the dead shall be raised incorruptible, and we shall be changed. 1 Cor. 15:52.

The third and final Harmonist cemetery is in Old Economy. It is surrounded by a chain-link fence so that the neighborhood children cannot play ball on the hallowed ground.

There are a few trees growing, and an attempt has been
made to plant some small flowers on each grave, which sometimes was done in the past as an "affectionate tribute." A
register was kept in which the name of the deceased was recorded with the date of his death and a number which served
to distinguish the grave in its row.[14]

The ceremony was simple. The elders and intimate
friends of the deceased came to the house where the body was
lying. After a few remarks, they followed the hearse to the
orchard. The plain hexagonal coffin, made to measure, was
laid over the grave, a hymn was sung, some more remarks
were made, a small bouquet of flowers was dropped into the
grave by each bystander and the grave was filled.[15]

John Duss, in his memoirs, remembers that an attempt had been made to regulate the number of mourners
escorting the body to the grave. This was due to their stress
on equality even unto death. The first attempt to do this was
"to count off twenty-four men from the cortege--these alone to
perform the last sad rites." At first it was successful, but
some folks had "a mere half dozen men." Then they tried in-
vitation. When this did not work out, they let the number be
whatever it happened to be.[16]

Christiana Knoedler adds the information that the body
was wrapped in linen, but that about the time of Gertrude's
death in 1889, regular clothes were beginning to be used.
She also speaks of the body being at home for three days, but
does not indicate when the custom began, although it goes
back at least to 1847. George Rapp died August 7 and
Baker wrote that they buried him on the tenth. With Gertrude's death came the custom of being buried from the church,
although it took time before this became a general practice.
The processions to the cemetery remained the same except
that in the later days more people attended the funerals. At
a child's funeral children followed first, the girls and boys
walking in separate groups. At an adult's death, the older
people followed first. In all cases, everyone carried a small
bouquet of flowers or (in winter) a sprig from the geraniums
which grew on every window sill.

Miss Knoedler writes that at the grave the spiritual
head would deliver the sermon. If the deceased was a child,
the children sang, the trustee first reading a line and the
choir singing after him. If the deceased was an adult, the
mixed choir, carrying their own hymnals, sang. Thereupon

each person dropped his flower, and another Harmonist "had
gone home."[17]

When writing a sketch about the Harmonists, with whom
she was in constant contact, Agnes M. Hays Gormly said the
shrouds used in Economy were the white robes made for the
Second Coming. (There is no place where one can corrobor-
ate "the white robe story," but neither can it be denied because, generally speaking, the Harmonists did not keep records
of this type of thing. Information turns up in the most unexpected places.) She also adds that unless one was asked to a
funeral, one did not go. Should one have received a note from
a trustee saying that someone had been called home and that
one should come, one dressed in the simplest dress, not
black, and, flower in hand, hastened to the house.[18]

When Frederick Rapp died, Romelius L. Baker spoke
the final words over the unmarked grave:

> Although our chain of brotherhood has suffered a
> violent break, we will not become either weary or
> lax in the battle; but the more firmly and intimate-
> ly united, that the bond of brotherly love and
> friendship be still more closely drawn....[19]

And when George Rapp died, Henrici delivered the address. Baker says:

> ... [it] touched the feelings of all members deeply
> and inspired the hearts on the occasion of the great
> common loss to renew the holy bond of brotherhood
> in common.[20]

And so in death, as in life, brotherhood in common
was the inspiration.

Notes

1. Karl J. R. Arndt, George Rapp's Harmony Society 1785-
    1847 (Philadelphia: University of Pennsylvania Press,
    1965), p. 418.

2. Aaron Williams, The Harmony Society (Pittsburgh:
    W. S. Haven, 1866), p. 30.

3. William E. Wilson, The Angel and the Serpent (Bloom-

ington: University of Indiana Press, 1964), p. 21.

4. Charles Nordhoff, The Communistic Societies of the
    United States (New York: Schocken Books, 1965),
    p. 102.

5. Williams, Society, p. 57.

6. Arndt, 1847, p. 417.

7. Letter, Christina Daum to George Rapp, Sept. 13, 1841,
    Old Economy, Archives, Box 52.

8. Letters, re. Jacob Klein, Sept. 1, 15, 1826, Old
    Economy, Archives, Box 6.

9. Arndt, 1847, pp. 429-432.

10. Letter, from a friend to Mr. Daniel Lynn, Oct. 8,
    1818, Old Economy, Archives, Box 2.

11. Letter, George W. Hatch to George Rapp, April 27,
    1840, Old Economy, Archives, Box 49.

12. Byron, Don Juan 15. 35-37.

13. Letter, Romelius Baker to Samuel Arthur, July 6,
    1848, Old Economy, Archives, Box 601.

14. Williams, Society, p. 115.

15. Ibid., p. 115.

16. John S. Duss, The Harmonists (Harrisburg: The
    Telegraph Press, 1943), p. 157.

17. Christiana Knoedler, The Harmony Society (New York:
    Vantage Press, Inc., 1954), p. 125.

18. Agnes M. Hays Gormly, Old Economy (Sewickley:
    The Harmony Press, 1966), n. p.

19. Duss, Harmonists, p. 91.

20. Arndt, 1847, p. 578.

Chapter VII

CALENDRIC CUSTOMS

The Bible-oriented Harmonists generally were not
given to festivals--religious or personal or civic--since they
could not be scripturally substantiated. But, like all people,
they chose what they wanted, and so developed seven festivals,
three of which were distinctly Harmonist in either origin or
form. The latter were the Harmonifest, celebrating their
inception on February 15, 1805; Erntefest--Harvest Home--
in the very early fall; and the Agape--Lord's Supper--in late
October. Good Friday, Easter, Pentecost and Christmas
were the Christian holidays observed in the early period.
(It would appear from accounts that Christmas as a "tree-and-
gift day" was a late development.) The fourth of July, their
only civic observance, was held not only because of the national significance, but also because it coincided with the arrival of three hundred of their number on the "Aurora" on
July 4, 1804 in Baltimore. They seemed to have the happy
facet of combining significant dates. Christiana Knoedler
reports that August 7th became the fixed day for the Erntefest
(Harvest Home) to commemorate George Rapp's death (which
occurred August 7, 1847.)[1] There is no record of their
honoring anyone else in such a manner.

A. The Feast Hall

On their festive days they assembled in the upper
room of the Feast Hall (the downstairs being a museum and
classroom) for singing, speeches, and feasting. Buckingham
describes the place and events as follows:

> Above the Museum is the large Social Hall, run-
> ning the whole length and breadth of the interior
> of the building, about 120 feet by 70, with a lofty
> arched roof well lighted and ventilated, abundantly
> furnished with tables and forms; and well warmed
> with several central stoves. This Hall is devoted
> exclusively to the general meetings of the

81

community, of which they have four in each year;
one being to commemorate the anniversary of
their foundation, the 15th of February, 1805;
another being about the period of Easter, a third
at the gathering in and completion of their harvest;
and a fourth at Christmas; so that gratitude and
devotion are the leading sentiments that direct
these festivities. Then they all dine together in
the Social Hall, and devote the remainder of the
day to music and social enjoyment. [2]

B. The Feast

Ross F. Lockridge, in The Labyrinth, speaks of the
Harmonist festival dinner as being "a rare stew which consisted mainly of veal and rice deliciously seasoned. "[3]   Karl
J. R. Anrdt writes of Romelius Baker noting in his book
that they had had "a supper of veal, rice, and pears. "[4]
Christiana Knoedler lists the menu as having thick rice soup,
roast veal, and roast beef (cooked together), a dish of
Schnitz, sauerkraut, white bread made with milk, ginger
cakes, and wine.   Also, two pitchers of wine and two pitchers of water were set on each table.   Knoedler adds that
the children ate the same food but had quince juice instead
of wine. [5]   Meals were sent to members who were too in-
firm to attend the festivities.   Any stranger and sojourner
among them was also remembered on this day. [6]   These
feast meals, taking several days to prepare, were cooked
in the large elaborate kitchen adjacent to the Feast Hall.

C. Harmonist Holidays

1.   The Harmonifest. --In his diary William Owen
gives us an account of the 20th anniversary of The Harmonist's Day.   That Owen observed this on February 17th
instead of the 15th indicates that it was a moveable feast
if the 15th did not suit them.   There is also a letter from
George Rapp to Frederick Rapp saying they will postpone
the Harmonifest until he comes home from his business
trip (see Chapter XI).   On February 17, 1825 Owen noted:

A beautiful pleasant day.   This day the Harmonians celebrated the 20th anniversary of their union
into a society.   They began with music between
five and six o'clock and at 9 they went to church;
at 12 they dined and remained together with a

short interval until near five o'clock; and at 6
they supped and remained together till after 9
o'clock.

What they were engaged in we did not learn as
they kept it to themselves, but they seemed to
think they had passed the day agreeably, and from
many expressions which they made use of, I
should conclude that the meeting, from some
cause or other, had tended to strengthen the bond
of Union subsisting among them. Part of the day
was probably employed in getting a knowledge of
the state of their affairs. They have now been
united 20 years. They transacted no business at
the store but many persons arrived on business
and were disappointed as they had not given any
notice of the intended holiday before. This the
American thought they should have done. But
they seemed to wish to throw a veil of secrecy
over all their proceedings. Before breaking up
at 5 o'clock, they marched out of the church in
closed ranks preceded by their music, all singing.
They halted before Mr. Rapp's house and sang a
piece of music and then dispersed. [7]

Some of the apparent secrecy may have been engendered by
the hostility of the Anglo-Saxon neighbors who resented
these strange, successful foreigners.

The following Baker letter shows that, even when they
were on a business trip, the Harmonists kept in close touch
during one of their special days:

Steamboat, Pennsylvania
Memphis, February 15, 1840

Father!
We wrote from Louisville to let you know how
we fared up to this point. So far we had no trouble at all with the boat, but on the 13th we had a
storm which made us anchor awhile. It was somewhat perious and dangerous because the drift wood
piled high in front of the boat. It stormed for 24
hours and therefore we could not leave the day
before yesterday. Today is the Harmony-feast.
It is a happy but cool day without a breeze; with
you it is surely a much happier day in the

brotherhood of all as you are renewing companion-
ship in the brotherhood-love. We are one, and in
this manner the richest people in the world, and
this we surely believe. The gift of your essay
[schriftliches Geschenk], dear father, made us very
happy and comforted us. We will read it often so
that we will fully understand the greatness and
importance of the group. We renewed our brotherhood faith thereon while thinking of you and the
piercing spirit of the World let us not be without
blessing.
    Since we left Louisville we have had no ice,
but plenty of drift wood and water. Today we ac-
quired in Randolph an Orleans price list in which
cotton brings from 6 to 10 cents, and sugar from
4 to 5 cents. It looks as if we will do better in
Natchez or Vicksburg than in New Orleans.
    We are well and cordially greet you all.
                          (signed) R. L. Baker[8]

    One might assume that the Harmonifest was the tra-
ditional day to join the society, for John S. Duss wrote:
"Wagner was to have joined the Society at the next Harmonie
Fest; instead, he went to the railway ticket-office and purchased a fare for parts unknown."[9]

    It became the custom to write a special hymn on each
anniversary in honor of the event. The following ode was
not signed by Father Rapp, but is in his handwriting, and it
appears to be the Harmonists' only actual expression of
Isaiah's peaceable kingdom which was made so popular by
Quaker Hick's painting. Their constant concern was with
the immediate Second Coming and the New Jerusalem itself.
That all would be peaceful seemed to be taken for granted.

    January 7, 1831

    Shouts of joy will fill your breast, O Harmonie,
    when you see the coming Jesus Christ on the
    clouds of heaven for He will keep his word; the
    freed people of God will rejoice with you; His
    goodness endureth forever will be the song of
    praise. Daughter of the Lord, you will hear His
    call when He comes. "Blessed are you of the
    House of the Lord" will be the greeting of the
    sanctified for each other; now is the time for the
    eternal communion so let us decorate the feast
    with branches and the altar with flowers to

celebrate the eternal Harvest-Feast.   Halleluja

Response:

Soon honey will flow from the rocks and in the
brooks; when Tabor and Hermon cover themselves
with blossoms and Carmel is heavy with fruit and
the lion has the lamb in his bosom, cows will
come in herds among which the lionesses and their
young will play.

Aria:

The dumb give praise; the lame leap like the deer
in the forest; the deaf hear our songs; the blind
see creation; trouble and plague are sore bound.

Response:

Pestilence may not creep upon us, the hot midday
kills not nor does it bring disease; so fly through
the heavens and be a happy and blessed people;
impervious to hurt you shall be high over the
houses where you'll see majesty.   Now peace returns; all discord is gone as it was in Eden.   Ei
ja, [used in singing; does not mean anything.]
earth and heaven are one, as in the beginning, a
choir-like hymn.

Gloria!   Our Shiloh is at pasture and his staff is
soft; the drover binds his colts to the vineyard
vine and washes the seam of his clothing in the
blood of the grape.

Jesus Christ has the power to make a garden from
this desert world: O, with what a multitude of
tongues your praises will be sung; take our happiness for praise; our happiness for thanks.
                    Father Rapp[?][10]

    2.   Erntefest. --Sources indicate nothing different
from the Harmonifest.

    3.   The Agape. --The Lord's Supper was celebrated
in the manner of an agape, a brotherly-feast before the
distribution of the bread and wine.   In preparation for par-
taking of Holy Communion they were admonished to recon-

cile all difficulties that had arisen among themselves.   This
was in conjunction with Matthew 5:23, 24:

> Therefore if thou bring thy gift to the altar, and
> there rememberest that thy brother hath ought
> against thee; Leave there thy gift before the altar,
> and go thy way; first be reconciled to thy brother,
> and then come and offer thy gift.

Should anyone have a serious sin that was bothering
him, he was urged to make a private confession of it to
the religious leader, as well as to God; it was believed that
without this confession one could not receive full forgive-
ness.   This is in accordance with Matthew 18:18:

> Verily I say unto you, Whatsoever ye shall bind
> on earth shall be bound in heaven: and whatsoever
> ye shall loose on earth shall be loosed in heaven.

After Father Rapp's death, this practice of confession diminished because in the eyes of the Harmonists none
could take his place. [11] Of interest here is an anecdote
Melish tells about confession.   For one thing, it has nothing
to do with the Lord's Supper.   Secondly, it has all the ear-
marks of religious enthusiasm, of which the Harmonists were
free.   Their inclination was toward mysticism.   Melish
writes:

> In the course of our journey the doctor told us a
> remarkable anecdote.   One of the boys at school
> one day was observed to weep; and one being
> asked what was the matter, he said he was afraid
> he had been very wicked.   A number of others
> caught the infection, and began also to cry.   It
> ultimately pervaded the whole school; and nothing
> would satisfy the children, until they called on
> Mr. Rapp, the pastor, and made a confession of
> their transgressions.   From the young the spirit
> of contrition fell upon the more mature in years,
> who one by one waited on Mr. Rapp to make their
> confession.   Of the number was the doctor, who
> told us he found himself impelled by an impulse
> which was irresistible, to wait on Mr. Rapp also.
> To him he laid open his whole heart:--on which
> the old man pressed him to his bosom; told him
> that now he knew his whole soul, and those of the
> other members of the Society, he had perfect
> confidence in them, and was assured that they

would persevere in the good work they had begun,
which would be a life of heavenly joy and rejoicing
in this world, and it would terminate in a state of
everlasting felicity in the next. [12]

It should also be noted that while the official Lord's
Supper was held in October in conjunction with the Agape,
it was possible to have it at other times. Since the Harmonists were a group unto themselves it mattered little on
what day an activity fell. During the tense time that followed the departure of Hildegard Mutschler and Conrad
Feucht (June 25, 1829), Baker added some Harmonist news
in his booklet of thermometrical observations, and one dis-
covers that on the nineteenth of July

a regular meeting was held and in the afternoon at
six they went to a supper of veal, rice and pears
with one mug of beer to a table. There were
thirty-three tables of men and thirty-nine tables of
women. All those over age took part in the Lord's
Supper, and at a quarter past nine they went
home. [13]

The separation of the men and women that Baker
speaks of continued well into the late 19th century. Christiana Knoedler writes:

At the front end of the hall was a large platform
on which stood two pianos. In front of the platform was a dais in the center of which was the
table. The Board of Elders and the Trustees sat
around the table on chairs, instead of the usual
benches, so that they faced the entire assembly.
From the platform to the rear the hall was bisect-
ed by a wide aisle. On the right-hand side were
tables for the men, with a special table for the
boys near the wall. The women and girls sat at
tables on the left-hand side of the aisle.

Before the meal a blessing was asked by the
trustee. After the meal a concert would be held,
with both band and singers, children and adults,
who sat on the platform, participating. This concert lasted until about two o'clock. Some of the
ladies and a few men remained to wash the dishes
and prepare for the evening meal, while the others
went home to perform their usual chores. At

about six o'clock the evening meal was served.
This consisted of leftovers from the noon meal
except for soup.   After it was over there was
more music by the band and choirs, and the
entire audience would sing from the community
songbooks. [14]

As stated above, hymns were composed for each of
these festivities.   They would be printed as flyers and dis-
tributed among the brethern.   Most are lost, but the following hymn was found by the writer.

For the Agape in the Autumn of 1834

Everyone:

Holy! holy! holy! Honor, praise and glory forever and ever for the Lamb that has been
slain.   Halleluja!

Congregation
(Melody: Comedy of Love)

O, Lord, how great was your desire after your
Last Supper! Then one saw your soul in balance
midst the holy disciples; you allowed the stream
of life pour from your holy mouth; such love
dissolves a heart and this is how we know you.

Choir

Whoever eats my body and drinks my blood, will
remain in me, and I in him forever and ever.

Song

Great is the love, yes, unmeasurable, that works
in such a way.   For you give of yourself to eat,
in bread and wine, your body and blood.   Was it
not enough, Faithful Lamb, that you died on the
cross for our sins?

Recitative

Honor and praise to the Lord who gave to His
people the promise to remain among them until
Judgment day

Song

What can we lack since you so love us? We find
peace and rest within You. It matters not that
there is trial and tribulation, with you we have
heaven here on earth.

Choir

The seal of the promise is the Holy Communion;
His living presence therein

Song

O heavenly secrets, O brotherly love! Yourself and your blessedness you give us in
Bread and Wine. Surely here is heaven's gate,
and there the Lord who has the secret of
eternal life, and none knows more than He.

D. Christian Holidays

1. **Easter.** --No special programs were found for
Good Friday and Easter, but the hymns in Chapter VIII
indicate the Harmonists' strong feeling in the matter.
Romelius Baker's letter on Easter Sunday of 1830 also reveals the depth of wonder about "the great plan for salvation." As always, it is interesting to note how religious
thought appears in business letters--ora et labora!

                              New Harmony--Easter Sunday
                              Evening
                              April 11, 1830
Frederick!
     On the evening of the 9th I arrived well after
spending my Good Friday in a small wagon from
Princeton. Yesterday and today I spent in the
country and just now returned from our cemetery
where I at sunset spent an hour of Easter-celebration. The young grass on the green sod of
the graves of our friends swaying in the cool
breeze, the festive solitude, the thoughts about
death and decay over which my feet trod, the
bodily resurrection of Christ and my loneliness
affected me so strongly that in a quiet wonder
about the great plan for salvation I returned to
my room a poor, poor man, yet not without

comfort.

I found your letters of March 22 and 26 in Vincennes after my return from Terre Haute. I'll see about the people. The patents & deed for MacLure are with Samuel Hall, Esqr. and will stay there until he receives the title and advice from you that the last note has been paid.

Taylor is gone. The Company is dissolved. Fauntleroy is handling it alone. Wm. Owen went to Orleans. They say he is expecting his father's return from Scotland.

Tomorrow I'll go to Ill. to Web as soon as I am finished there and here I'll go to Shawncetown; however, I will not get away from here till next Thursday since I still have to see a number of people. Because I came a month early this year, a number are not ready.

If there is a delay in Shawneetown I'll write once more. I am sending this letter with Mr. Lamfies, a tavern-owner who is going to Mt. Vernon & from there by water to Cincinnati.

Greeting to you & all friends,
(signed) R. L. Baker

P. S. My last letter was from Vincennes. The 2nd letter from the trip. [15]

    2.   Pentecost. -- A program flyer for Pentecost was tucked in a Gesangbuch. The program does not explicate, but it does give one an idea of the variety of music the Harmonists enjoyed.

Musical for Pentecost
June 7, 1829

1.	V. M. Billowing Fields	Nr. 32
	March 1 von Bonh	Nr. 192
2.	N. M. The Virtue March	Nr. 54
	The Peach March	Nr. 28
	Evening	
1.	Hanover March	Nr. 292
2.	Dream with Variation	Nr. 291
3.	Cantata: Come Holy Ghost	
4.	Sonatina	Nr. 258
5.	Cantata: Who, who can expr.	
6.	Impetuous Buoyancy	
7.	Choral: Halleluia, Honor, Praise	
8.	Blessed Flames	Nr. 250
9.	Beethoven's Minuet	Nr. 114

3. Christmas. -- For Christmas 1827 the following
hymn was composed:

> Jesus, you my throne of grace, you
> most blessed Son! You are my rock and friend;
> My darling child, and valiant hero. You have
> come to us on earth and now I fear no more.
>
> O, God's Child, the Light of my life, O, little
> Brother forsake not me; strengthen my faith
> And you shall be my song of praise; make
> me strong and well my whole life long.
>
> O, you my little child and man. Without
> you I care not to live nor can. You beautiful
> Morning Star! Messiah! Emmanuel! You
> have power over body and soul, you
> Sweet Almond.
>
> O, Son of Man, Glory, Standard-bearer, my
> dearest Child, guide me to you, my
> Priest and Prophet. Come! Open heaven's
> door and take me to the living, without
> you all is a wasteland.
>
> O, Jesus, my rose in the valley, You
> most beautiful one of all of Sharon's
> blossoms; into my weak heart
> flows oil and wine and
> you deserve the praise.
>
> O, dearest Child of the beloved ones, my
> turtledove, my appletree, my dewdrop,
> forget me not, watch my every step,
> in you alone I trust.

This Christmas hymn, like the Christmas hymn in Chapter
VIII, shows the Harmonist adoration for the Christ child,
a typical south-German devotion. It should also be noted
that among the numerous epithets for the Jesulein appears
"my rose in the valley, You most beautiful one of all of
Sharon's blossoms."

Christiana Knoedler writes that on all the church
holidays the band would play from the church steeple at five
o'clock in the morning. She also adds that their Pentecost
was a Memorial Day. At this time the band led the procession to the cemetery where the sermon was held and the

children sang; and then moved on to the Indian mound where
the service would be repeated. [16] This custom of a band
leading a procession to the cemetery is also found among
the Moravians of eastern Pennsylvania. But they do it on
Easter. The service in Lititz, Pennsylvania draws non-
Moravians, and news coverage.

John Duss, who came to Economy at age two in 1862,
also speaks of a Memorial Day, but he does not equate it
with Pentecost. He speaks of "the annual procession to the
Friedhof in the springtime." He recalls their being dressed
in their best silk. Romelius Baker would have a short service, followed by a hymn (no mention of children). Then
they would proceed through the orchard to the Indian mound
for a repeat service. [17]

E. Civil Holiday

1. Fourth of July. --As was stated above, on this
day in 1804 three hundred dissenters of the Lutheran Church
who were to be known as the Harmonists arrived in Baltimore on the "Aurora." It was a day to celebrate; that it
also was a national holiday was a happy coincidence. And
they could show a friendly spirit to the neighbors. This
does not mean that they were not serious about their new
country. There is a letter from Frederick Rapp to James
Drake of Mt. Vernon concerning citizenship certificates:

> August 1, 1828
> Mr. James Drake, Mount Vernon
>   You will no doubt recollect that in the year
> 1824, a number of our people came to Springfield,
> and made declaration to become citizens of the
> United States.
>   Shortly before our removal you furnished me
> with certificates to that effect for each of them
> except for Leander Ebner and Anshelm Voelm.
> I therefore request you to have the goodness, and
> send me two certificates by return mail for these
> two persons with your bill.
> Frederick Rapp[18]

The Wabash celebrations must have been gala affairs.
In 1815, one hundred and fifty persons came to see, talk,
listen, and drink. [19] In 1822 a correspondent for the Cory-
don (Indiana) Gazette wrote: "... they honored the last

anniversary of American independence and furnished a free
dinner and plenty of beer to all who pleased to visit them,
treating them, also to fine music from their band. "[20]

In 1833, the Harmonists and their guests were treated to a reading of the Declaration of Independence followed
by a fiery patriotic speech laced with the foresight of the
importance of preserving the culture of ethnic groups. [21]

While the Harmonists did not have a calendar full of
"red-letter days," they had what Von Ogden Vogt calls
"unconscious celebration"--rest after toil and a well-being
and a quiet singing happiness. [22] Nor did they renounce
the song of life, "the festal celebration. "[23] As a matter
of fact, they had their singing and feasting well spaced in
their calendar year, starting with their Harmonifest in
February, and ending with Christmas. It is interesting
that both of these festivals--the beginning and the end--are
especially oriented toward brotherhood and love of fellow
man which achieves for man "the true spirit of Harmony."

Notes

1. Christiana Knoedler, The Harmony Society (New York:
   Vantage Press, Inc., 1954), p. 93.

2. James Silk Buckingham, The Eastern and Western
   States of America, II (London: Fisher, Son & Co.,
   1842), p. 226.

3. Ross F. Lockridge, The Labyrinth (The New Harmony
   Memorial Commission, 1941), p. 75.

4. Karl J. R. Arndt, George Rapp's Harmony Society
   1785-1847 (Philadelphia: University of Pennsylvania
   Press, 1965), p. 427.

5. Christiana Knoedler, Society, p. 127.

6. Aaron Williams, The Harmony Society (Pittsburgh:
   W. S. Haven, 1866), p. 113.

7. William Owen, Diary of William Owen from November
   10, 1824 to April 20, 1825, ed. Joel W. Hiatt
   (Indianapolis: Indiana Historical Society Publications, 4, No. 1, 1906), p. 105.

8. Letter, R. L. Baker to George Rapp, Feb. 15, 1840, Old Economy, Archives, Box 49.

9. John S. Duss, The Harmonists (Harrisburg: The Telegraph Press, 1943), p. 155.

10. Harmonie Ode, Jan. 7, 1831, Old Economy, Archives, Box 29.

11. Williams, Society, p. 114.

12. John Melish, Travels in the United States of America in the Years 1806-1811 and travels through various parts of Great Britain, Ireland, and Upper Canada, II (Philadelphia, 1812), p. 8.

13. Arndt, 1847, p. 427.

14. Knoedler, Society, p. 127.

15. Letter, R. L. Baker to Frederick Rapp, April 11, 1830, Old Economy, Archives, Box 27.

16. Knoedler, Society, p. 124.

17. Duss, Harmonists, p. 157.

18. Letter, Frederick Rapp to James Drake, Aug. 1, 1828, Old Economy, Archives, Letterbook 1828-1820.

19. William E. Wilson, The Angel and the Serpent (Bloomington: University of Indiana Press, 1964), p. 38.

20. Ibid., p. 61.

21. "A Patriotic German-American," Western Pennsylvania Historical Magazine, II, 2, April, 1919, pp. 107-114.

22. Von Ogden Vogt, Modern Worship (New Haven: Yale University Press, 1927), p. 6.

23. Ibid., p. 5.

Chapter VIII

MUSIC

A. Significance

In Germany music is a tradition. It is a vital part
of every German's life, and it may be his "escape" from
his methodical and organized way of life. At least, so it
would seem to have been with the Harmonists. William
Owen, in his diary, complained:

> We find it uncommonly dull and stupid having so
> little to interest the mind. The body may be
> exercised by walking, but the mind gets dissatis-
> fied under idle speculations or a dull routine of
> doing nothing. [1]

Expressing themselves in song, the Harmonists
achieved a dual purpose, a respite from the sameness in
their being and a call to worship. Song for them spelled
charisma, whether it was a psalm or a song of their own
composition. It not only drew them to it, but to each
other, creating the unity and brotherhood of which they
sang. They became one in spirit, synthesizing their beings
for a state of harmony where the love of God reigns supreme. This state of harmony was not limited to voice;
the pianoforte, flutes, horns, violins, and bassoons were
often used. Nor was singing reserved for formal worship;
it was a way of life, as was noted by many travellers.
Buckingham wrote:

> In the intervals of our agreeable conversations,
> we had vocal and instrumental music, all
> German, and admirably performed: Mozart,
> Meyerbeer, and Beethoven, were the chief com-
> posers from whose works and instrumental pieces
> were selected; but many of the hymns and anthems
> were of Mr. Rapp's composition as to the poetry,
> Mr. Henrici's arrangement as to the music, and
> the execution devolved on Miss Gertrude Rapp, as

leader on the pianoforte which she played admir-
ably, accompanied by male performers on the
flute, horn, and bassoon; and by three male and
six female voices, from the younger members of
the community, from 20 to 25, who had been invited to join our party for the purpose. [2]

Elias Pym Fordham wrote:

They are great musicians, and many of them
study music as a Science. Once a week they
have a concert at Mr. Rapp's, to which I am invited. [3]

William Faux laconically commented:

After dinner a band of musicians entered. [4]

William Owen recorded:

We were then shown the flour mill .... the
women stopped work to sing for us. Those who
work together learn to sing with each other thus
forming a number of small singing parties. [5]

Karl Bernhard, Duke of Saxe-Weimar, was more
critical of his former countrymen at a concert conducted
by Dr. J. C. Müller, and no doubt was thinking of the
Moravians when he wrote:

The music was really not so good as we had
heard in the preceding autumn at Bethlehem. [6]

But he also was moved to emotion as he writes:

Mr. Rapp finally conducted us into the factory
again, and said that the girls had especially requested this visit that I might hear them sing.
When their work is done, they collect in one of
the factory rooms, to the number of sixty or
seventy, to sing spiritual and other songs. They
have a peculiar hymn-book, containing hymns from
the old Würtemberg collection, and others written
by the elder Rapp. A chair was placed for the
old patriarch, who sat amid the girls, and they
commenced a hymn in a very delightful manner.
It was naturally symphonious, and exceedingly well

arranged. The girls sang four pieces, at first
sacred, but afterward, by Mr. Rapp's desire, of a
gay character. With real emotion did I witness this
interesting scene. [7]

The duke also wryly noted that Father Rapp was very
fond of psalmody and concluded his observation with:

In this hymn-book are some pieces, which, if the
perfect child-like innocence of these maidens be
not recollected, might appear rather scandalous.
For instance, there is a literal translation of the
song of Solomon, among others. [8]

The most amusing anecdote to emerge from the singing practices is related by John S. Duss in his memoirs.
It appears that Dr. Müller had some of the members hum
their traditional tunes. These he transcribed. Jacob Henrici, the next music master, corrected some of the Müller
errors. The fun started when Romelius Baker, the titular
head after Father Rapp's death, chose one of the revised
hymns for a morning worship. By this time, to stabilize
the congregational singing, two pianos with reed attachments
had been purchased. Henrici and Gertrude Rapp played the
hymn the new way while the Harmonists, having no written
music before them, sang it the old way. In the midst of
the confusion Baker turned to the organ loft, shouting in
Swabian dialect:

Hei, Jakob, was machts den du?

Jacob arose and in purest high German politely
explained, 'You see, Romeli, these hymns are
not properly arranged; this one, for instance, I
even had to put into correct time.' (He used the
German word 'Takt,' which also stands for 'step.')

'Ei was,' retorted Romeli, 'what do we know about
takt--play it the way we are accustomed.'

The title of the hymn was 'And entire nations still
are marching, in night and darkness round about.'
Henrici, who had a fine sense of humor, at once
took his pencil and added, 'aber nicht in Takt.'[9]

And that really did not matter, for as John Melish
recorded:

They were singing a hymn, in which they joined
with one accord; and so simply, yet so sweetly
did they sing, that it brought to my recollection
the passage in Burn's Cotter's Saturday Night:

They chant their artless notes in simple guise,
They tune their hearts, by far the noblest aim. [10]

The comparison need not stop here. Other lines of
this poem strongly reminiscent of the Harmonist philosophy
and language are:

10th stanza:
O happy love! where love like this is found;
O heart-felt raptures! bliss beyond compare!

15th stanza:
The priest-like father reads the sacred page,
How Abram was the friend of God on high;

16th stanza:
Saw in the sun a mighty angel stand,
And heard great Bab'lon's doom pronounced
by Heaven's command.

17th stanza:
There ever bask in uncreated rays
No more to sigh, or shed the bitter tear,
Together hymning their Creator's praise,
In such society, yet still more dear;
While circling Time moves round in an eternal
sphere.

20th stanza:
What is a lordling's pomp? a cumbrous load,
Disguising oft the wretch of human kind,
Studied in arts of hell, in wickedness refin'd. [11]

Remembering these homilies when reading the hymns
below, the reader can readily see that the Harmonists were
a guileless people who moved with folkways and yet, una-
wares, were lifted into metaphysical spheres when their
hymns took flight in extravagant images.

B. The Composers

Anonymity shrouds their hymnal. It is assumed that
George and Frederick Rapp composed most of the hymns.
However, since the Harmonist belief in common ownership
and self-denial was all embracing, it follows that no personal glory was expected from authorship. They were sac-
ramental acts of private devotion showing much spiritual
passion. Christoph Müller no doubt also composed, as probably
did Jacob Henrici and other unsung mystics. Mystics they
were.

The composers' hymns are uneven in quality and
phrasing. They share the metaphysics' language of extreme
images and extravagant figures of speech, especially those
related to Sophia, their personification of wisdom. They
express the anguish and tension of the search for that harmony which would prepare them for the immediate coming
of Christ.

George Rapp especially instilled harmony into his
flock. His religious enthusiasm brought the mysticism of
the 17th century to his followers. According to Karl Arndt
and John Duss, we know that George Rapp wrote the hymn
"Kinder seid nun alle munter" while he was in Washington
in January, 1806, presenting to President Jefferson a peti-
tion instigated by his people, which requested permission
to purchase 30,000 acres of land in the Western Country
for the chief purpose of cultivating the vine, since Butler
County was unsuitable. While the bill was debated (and de-
feated by a tie vote) Rapp wrote twenty-four impassioned
stanzas about the destiny and purpose of the Harmonists.
He included the theory of the biune nature of Adam, now
separated by Adam's desire but soon to be re-united, and
the entire philosophy he later expressed in his (again
anonymous) Thoughts on the Destiny of Man, published by
the Harmony Society in 1824 in Indiana. It is a philosophy
of hope, for it says man will be punished, but not forever.

C. Hymns

"Kinder seid nun alle munter" and twenty others
follow. They are taken from the Harmonisches Gesangbuch
published in 1827 by their own printing press at Economy.

They had had an earlier Gesangbuch published in
1820 by Heinrich Ebner at Allentown. The chief difference

between the hymnals is the large number of hymns in the
1827 book. For example, the 1820 version had ten hymns
about "faith"; the 1827, twenty-five. The 1820 had twelve
"searching for God"; the 1827, twenty. The 1820 had
twenty for "the love of Christ"; the 1827, thirty-seven. The
1820 had four for "the following of Jesus"; the 1827 thirty-
four. The 1820 had twenty-two about "wisdom"; the 1827,
forty-three. And the 1820 had ten songs about spring; the
1827, twenty-eight.

As was stated above, the linguistics of these hymns
bear a strong relationship to folk usage and metaphysical
poetry. Common words of the German folk-song texts
and the Harmonists, as well as of the metaphysical poets,
are: nature, garden, rose, rosy-selfe, rosie leaves,
wreaths, gold, golden, glorious, enflame, blushing leaves,
perfume, perfumes flow, sweet, buds, celestial, heaven,
dove, Holy Spirit, bright sun, flashing rays, love, nightingale, Adam's fall, "I am the Rose of Sharon," the Lily of
the Valley, bride, bridegroom, warm embrace, desire,
dawn, light, dew-pearled, renunciation, ad infinitum.

The hymns have numbers; their titles are taken from
the first line of the hymn. As none of the hymnals have
music, melodies, either their own or familiar ones, are
indicated. However, satisfactory translations cannot be
made because their own melodies are always noted with the
laconic Eigene Melodie, and the other titles are abbreviated,
making a complete translation impossible.

In the archives of Old Economy are a number of
handwritten hymnals, obviously pre-dating the printed ones.
Quite likely these had been school exercise books, serving
a double purpose. Also to be found in the archives are a
few hymnals with transcribed notes. One of these books
belonged to Gertrude Rapp, the gifted granddaughter of
George Rapp.

It is here also where some of their folk-art found
expression. In addition to the 1820 published Gesangbuch,
until 1827 each member of the Society had his own manuscript hymn book. The end papers of these were often
decorated with Fraktur. Their decorative writing and design
chiefly used roses and other flowers. Several dozen of these
examples have survived in the music archives. For a Ph.D.
in Music, Mr. Richard D. Wetzel is working with these
transcriptions and the work of William Cummings Peters,
who was at Economy for a short time in 1827.

D.   Feurige-Kohlen

Feurige-Kohlen (Glowing Coals) is another hymnal
printed by the Harmonists in 1826 at Economy.   There is
no attempt made at phrasing; it is more like a series of
prayers to be spoken rather than sung.   The subject matter
of these hymns is like that of the others.   It is filled with
passionate praises for Harmony and Sophia, although it also
has odes for Christmas, the Passion of our Lord, the Last
Judgment, spring, the nearness of God, psalm-hymns, and
eleven songs with music.   The latter, at least, is indicated
in the table of contents, but no music is present in the
book.   An example follows:

> See how wondrous is the bride of the Lamb; how
> magnificent her worth; how incomparable her
> beauty.   Even in calumny, splendor and glory full
> of harmony radiate from her.   Her bridegroom
> will ennoble her that all of earth's brilliance will
> be darkened; all slander and reproaches will not
> hinder her dignity.   Her walk in truthfulness and
> honesty is majestic; her cheeks glow like the roses
> of spring; her glance is pure desire; her garland is
> one of virginity.   With such jewels she pleases her
> friend, the soul; with such jewels she forgets the
> glories of the world. [12]

E.   Selections from the Hymns

A hymn of Hope (No. 250)
   Kinder seid nun alle munter
   Children, be now gay

This hymn propounds the theory that the sinfulness of
Adam will be redeemed and suffering will be at an end when
we find Jesus through self-denial and brotherhood.   It is significant to note that in stanza 17, "Now blooms the golden
rose" appears.   This became their trademark both physically
and spiritually in Harmony, Indiana.

> Children, be now gay and carefree
> For with love's inner spark
> Jesus again unites the parts;
> Sunlight flashes, rays agleaming
> Send forth spirit's sparks
> Unto the seed fields of paradise.

From the deepest world of love
Now emerge strong heroes from above
Whom God implored
His banner to carry high,
And to tell the folk
What his wisdom ordered

What role eternity has played,
What many sanctified have felt;
Yet darkness prevails.
This no longer can be hidden
Because the flowers do as bidden
And in the daylight they unfold.

Marvelous things you shall hear
While the spirit's breezes blow;
The air is clear enough above
The secrets to reveal
Through the means of love
That even the children will know.

What has long been hidden
In the secrets of the ages
Now is revealed to you.
Thus you see
How beautifully the lillies bloom
Greatness is upon you.

You shall clearly know,
Nothing is concealed;
It is God in the Holy Spirit
Who makes his mark on you,
And really touches you
His inner image to reveal.

That image you are yourself,
Yes, this pearl of the beholder
So are you in brethren spirit.
Within this fire you are consumed,
Yet you will find your life,
But only now your being knows it.

From the seed of God,
With the inner world
We will step with highest cause
Not only to look into Faith
And in promises to trust,
But also to embrace all with awe.

And all this in truth
To make your life gentle;
That it flows with brethren spirit
Essentially your body to build
In the image of Jesus;
This is the goal of his spirit.

This body is the brotherhood,
The beautiful, the only one
Which he formed himself
Through the spirit's works;
This body saturated with love
Is intoxicated with it.

How quickly can she forget
What she has known;
And even you ravish yourself;
Jesus's Spirit may try
As he leads the drunken ones
Toward the goal.

What a great wonder
That such a love spark cannot
Mellow the brothers;
Only when the hearts are in unison
And each man practices self-denial
Are hearts joined to hearts.

Then we will see Jesus
In the spiritual resurrection,
And personal manifestation of
His future plans,
What he wishes with his church
Will be established.

God, how long are the years
In the vast universe
Where the great plans are hidden.
But now it will happen
That Zion will see the bride,
That the Number will have its day.

O, what we have suffered,
What pain we have felt
In Babylon's days!
Let the sun send happy rays,
Let the future be her messenger,
Friend, come and bless us.

Soon better days are coming
For the inner light is shining
Closer to our planet.
Zion, you will be prepared
Where your Friend himself tended you,
Where one finds timely grapes.

Where is now your mourning-coat,
And the Adam turn-coat?
All's been burnt in judgement;
Now blooms the golden rose
On the earth's bossom
And your suffering is at an end.

In Sharon bloom the lilies of the field,
White, red blossoms
In their fragrance you delight,
Urge you to leap upon the mountain
And enter the heavenly kingdom
So that you may never more afright.

This has become your reward
Because you with the brethren
Have withstood all the test,
Here you shall have love
Which often seemed harsh,
Here you see it in white and red.

That you will find Jesus
In the common brotherhood
Will unite you into one;
For all the spirit's action
Brought it to the spring of love
And moulded it as one.

There you will forget the pain
And eat the heavenly fruit;
See you then who planted it
In the garden of the brethern;
Glorious purity abounds
And love surrounds it.

What desireth you more?
You should radiate as a bride
In the sweet heavenly peace;
In the arms of the beloved
You should have passionate embrace;
Rest and close your eyes.

Sleep in heavenly peace;
Here you cannot tire,
To follow here does not cause ire;
Quiet worlds are the homes
Where forever and ever eat
God's chosen ones.

So soon be pure,
And the bridegroom's only jewel;
Forget all, do nothing,
In love be dissolved:
This is the way
To spiritual union with God.

A hymn about Creation (No. 166)
Heilig sei dein Nam' in allen Welten
Holy be Thy name in all the world

This hymn speaks of the vastness of God's kingdom
and that there is glory in all His works.

Holy be thy name in all the world,
Clean and holy be every brethren heart;
You will give them glory in reward:
The removal of desire's pain.

Holy, holy sing through all the land,
From all good men you receive honor;
Many from nations and distant islands
Which did not know you before.

All the countries where the sun shines,
Where the moon the long night illuminates,
Where the northern light's beauty emblazons the air,
Where the ray of the sun vertically falls,

Where the morning-red the day announces
And the evening-red the night proclaims,
There is your kingdom where your grace commands
And what you command is fulfilled.

Everywhere your Holy Will is done;
You command: man thanks, obeys, and is silent;
The entire universe is hushed
When before you the brethren bow.

Peace, blessed peace wafts from the morning,
    noon, night, and the North;
Far from us are the sorrows;
No trouble makes life heavy.

All regents in heaven and on earth
Bow before your glorious radiance;
They are thine and will be Seraphimes
And glorified before thy throne.

Power and might is your scepter's strength;
Majesty envelopes the brother-hall;
Glory is in your works;
All acclaim you with exultation.

A hymn of Supplication (No. 3)
   Ach du Liebster
  O, Beloved

    This hymn asks for God's help, saying let no false-
hood mar this meditation, but lead us on.

O, you, Dearest One, how gently you waft
   unto your chosen lily-fields your scent from above!
Come to the hills to shepherd her
   who for you cries;
There she sits beneath the myrtle
   dreaming of your love.

Pour your peace, pure like the heavenly air,
   into our being
That with your presence our evening-song
   doth close;
Till lifts the dark veil that falls
   between the world and quiet meditation.

Let no falsehood mar this meditation,
Cover it with stars floating westward
   like the summer,
Cover it with peace that
   holds sorrow in its folds without a murmur.

Float down like a blossom,
The heart trembles happily to hear
   echoes of your heavenly goodness;
As in a dream we draw roseate
   sympathies from light chambers.

When under the cypress sadly we
     sit with sorrow
You will not forget us for thy will
     is good;
Lead us, Beloved, through
     darkness unto light with your shepherd's
     staff.

A hymn of Preparation (No. 303)
     O auserwählte Schaar
     Chosen People

     This hymn is a preparation for the Lord's coming.
Everyone should get ready--up, up and be quick about it.

                    No. 303. "O, Chosen Band"

O, you chosen people adorn
     yourselves with the finest;
Make haste, the watchmen from the
     high heavenly throne already are calling
     you to the wedding feast.

Up, up, and be quick about it
     that no one through over sleeping
     will be late;
Everyone refreshed with spiritual
     weapons be ready for your fate.

Open your heart and ear, and stretch
     out your hands;
See how the enemy's might
     and Babel's harlot-splendor
     come to the end in those lands.

Then, Jesus, your hero, who has
     chosen you as his worthy one is
     calling loud and clear,
That his chaste bride be attired
     as only deserving of such a one.

Well to him who has forethought,
     and keeps watch all hours and
     does not tarry;
He will not be missing when
     Jesus, our shepherd, his people
     gathers to marry.

His chaste bride who in him trusts with
    pure love,
Only to him will she be devoted
    without hypocrisy.

Pleased I am that I am chosen
    to be counted with the devout;
    the pure dove herself has chosen me,
    and no enemy can rob me
    of my rebirth.

Hymns about Harmony

No. 162
    Harmonie dein Gnaden Oel
    Harmony your state of grace

No. 163
    Harmonie du Bruderstadt
    Harmony you Brotherhood

No. 164
    Harmonie du gold'ne Rosenblüthe
    Harmony you golden rose

No. 458
    Wie schön sind Brüder--Harmonien
    How beautiful is Brother--Harmony

The following four hymns were written for annual
Harmony feasts, celebrated February 15. Numbers 162 and
458 are sheer tributes. Number 163 emphasizes the theory
that without Harmony existence loses all meaning. Christiana Knoedler says that this hymn was the most famous
song of the society. It was the one hymn that was sung on
all occasions.[13] Only six stanzas (2, 4, 5, 6, 8, 11) are
translated because John S. Duss closed his book The
Harmonists with a translation of six stanzas (1, 3, 7, 9,
10, 12). He also annotated the 1827 Gesangbuch to the effect that George Rapp composed stanzas 1, 4, 5, 7, 8
while Frederick composed stanzas 2, 3, 6, 9, 10. He
makes no mention of stanzas 11 and 12, nor does he tell
how he determined the authorship.

Number 164 is the most anguish-filled, indicating
that trouble still abounds. They ask God for a gentler pain,

realizing that those who stay will get the golden rose and Jesus.

No. 162

Harmony, your state of grace is here without fail,
Your rose-like beauty which by God Himself was made
    is reflected;
Through its fiery radiance God shines to earth.

Look at the flaming altar upon which God's just anger burns;
To his pleasure light an everglowing fire;
Even though love is here the banner,
God's anger also churns.

Look at the washtub and the ocean,
Both give us a lesson,
Like judgment and holiness an honor-dress should dress
    God's children;
What will mercy do at such a time when they receive the
    poor sinners?

Rays of God, you, yes, you--burn like those flames here--
Burn like diamonds when the sun shines upon them
Because you are chosen, that you now and forever go before
    the great majesty--
As a pair that God had united.

Harmony, your magnificent splendor shall be honored
    at all times,
And your white dress of chastity, shows its righteousness;
So will chastity triumph and belong to God's friend
    who is closest to him,
And at the next meeting will present you like a king.

Give praise to him for this time through the love of
    loveliness;
The singer's clear voice returned an echo to give honor
    to our king
Like the angel's choir in his heavenly domain,
All who belong to Him.

No. 163

Brethren, tarry not here to become citizens;
Everything is not yet executed that will be;

Only in Harmonie does the spirit find the meaning of
        existence;
All else is effort without growth.

You are clear and light without a spot;
You alone reveal that which wants to hide.
Without you all is pain; you are full of rapture.
Harmonie is blessedness in God's sun.

Harmonie, you house of God, full of light and blessing,
Through you flows the gentle rain of heaven;
Water that gushes from you is from primeval springs.
Harmonie, you reserve of joy, you greatest treasure
        of the soul!

Harmonie, who can describe you?
Harmonie, where eternal brotherhood will remain--
From you flee all enemies who love not the cross;
Those who join must love from the heart both friend and foe.

You are a ray of light, the light of lights;
Your face is light and clear;
You are a stern judge tempered with mercy,
But not so that you blindly follow.

O God, you Mightiest One, come to your people,
That we with the fire of your love may be healed,
That your will may come to us,
That we soon may see salvation.

No. 164

Harmonie, you golden rose,
Today we bless ourselves in filial feast;
Where true love glows in the fire stands God's house firmly;
Consanguinity throbs in its veins,
Its balsam resembles the heavenly grape that purifies the
        blazing sun.

Noble stay those with the group
Who do not shun the cross of adversity;
Love softly flows on their cheeks
Like a rosy-fingered dawn;
And how glad are your church members,
Charming like the heavenly rose fragrance;
From the unconscious we awaken
And refresh ourselves with pure air.

Holy Devotion, today teach us to pray,
Much has God wrought for us;
Devotion must redden our cheeks as we all look at heaven
Pouring light and strength from its purple rays onto the
    society;
All are full of a benevolent attitude
Working in your spirit.

Only the spirit of love shall bring us to a happiness
That finds a glad heart even though adversity yet often
    rages;
Grant us soon a gentler pain,
Let the spirit of devotion raise itself
Until all is given to the Lord, 'till completed is the
    great plan.

Your flaming eyes are the weapons which betray the
    enemy when he nears
So that your loving spirit can work within us
And guide us to the paths of duty.
God's peace may flow through us
For we are a group of the chaste;
So our hearts will melt when the sun sends her gold.

May bliss crown our conquest which we foresee,
Further strengthen us that we remain united in brotherly-
    love,
And when everything is gone
Send us a healing wind for all our pain.
Let the heavenly child greet us.

No. 458

How wonderful is brother Harmonie penetrated by the Cedars
    of Lebanon;
Its crown is refreshed
With dew from Zion's hills
Where God has his throne.

Here is where blessings are all around us,
Here sounds the sweet melody,
Here refreshed us life everlasting from the unity of harmony,
And lifts the whole choir into heaven.

Hymn of Brotherly Love (No. 1)
   Ach Brüder lasst am trauten Herd ein frohes Lied erschallen
   O, Brothers, let echo a joyous song from the hearth

      This hymn deals with brotherly love.   Brotherhood's
spirit should be on every hearth.

         O, Brothers, at the hearth sing a joyful song;
         He who teaches the birds to sing
         Is glad when heart and voice sing
         Praise and thanks in unison.

         Love warmly weaves us into a garland;
         Each radiant face reflects the flames;
         Instruction nods her head and points
         That we from heaven came.

         Brotherhood's spirit, true and mild,
         Warms every humble home,
         Beams like the sun into our midst.
         In her reflection justly reigns holy tradition.

         From the low hearth she stretches heavenwards;
         So strives the heart to rise from dust
         That clean and clear
         As an altar of God it may be.

         Unchanged and silent, in quiet sincere union
         Young courage and strength shall prosper
         In an earnest pilgrimage;
         The maiden pure and gentle; the youth, clever and
            wise.

         The hearth is our altar in holy union;
         Like grapes they embrace him in the trusted hour.
         Such a hearth is worth its weight in gold;
         Sing praise with heart and voice.

Hymns about Sophia

No. 343
   O Sophia! Wann die Liebes Hände
   O, Sophia, when thy loving hands

No. 362
   Sag' wo find ich deines gleichen, Sophia
   Tell me where do I find one like you

No. 394
   Sophia, aus deinen Blicken
   Sophia, from your glances

No. 395
   Sophia, du Auserkohrne
   Sophia, you chosen one

No. 396
   Sophia, du weisst mein Leiden
   Sophia, you know my suffering

No. 397
   Sophia, edle Braut
   Sophia, noble bride

No. 398
   Sophia, ich kann's nicht lassen
   Sophia, I cannot let go

These are hymns about wisdom, the personification of
which is Sophia. Here one finds the most extravagant projection of the figure of speech and emotion. Sophia becomes
the sun-clad figure of Revelation; the positive feminine symbol of the Harmonists' spiritual world. Chapter II discussed
this symbol more fully.

No. 343

O, Sophia, when thy loving hands
   carefully have guided my path
Through the thorny rose-bush,
Let my shadow soar;
You, the Harmonists' goddess, play
   now your golden strings;
Bind with loving golden chains
   those who follow you to the designated   goal.

O, you adornment of the house of God,
Let us soon take the pilgrim's staff,
Escort us with your shimmering goodness, given
   for us by God.
Strengthen the courage of the fighter
   coming to full circle.
That your people with good deeds
   will bless your approaching feast.

Where the day happily kissed the light,
And the first born of the song are
    exhilarated with love,
And purified and freed from all
    wild desire,
All, free like brooks from the
    rocks, plunge into the full stream;
Such is the bliss which runneth over.

Fairest one, you bring about in
    inner stillness
The laceration of a fiery prayer!
Sacerdotal is the fulness of your heart
    for sick mankind;
You have with compassion
    so much grace combined with our spiritual strength
That often with the swing of the rod
    your pity cries.

How wisely you watch our tents
    that no clever enemy will catch you therein;
When justice compells us to scold,
You deftly include grace;
I, the true, loving, pure, gentle godly groom;
Let joyful tears fall, for your
    faith has no limit.

Let us cheerfully greet you, you
    life's only peace;
You, O, Sophia, are the means of joy!
You protect the banner of truth,
You no enemy ever has frightened;
Nothing diverts your visionary plan;
Our hope lies in your goal.

Now in your arms we are at rest,
Now in your grace we are bound;
Your eyes are full of mercy as your
    presence tells us;
Often you dry the pale cheeks and
    wipe tenderly the tears;
Nothing now holds my spirit captive; it
    escapes from the decaying grave.

No. 362

Tell me, where do I find one like you,
    Sophia, whom all revere,
Whom shall I entreat to show
    me, you, you angel?
You must be a goddess of
    radiant beauty
Who receives all who see her.

First prize belongs to the beauty
    to whom none can compare;
No flower, not even the jasmine comes close;
Nor the moonlit night nor the morning-
    star's glow,
This all does not compare with
    her splendor.

You won my heart from hearsay
    before I saw
Entranced the queen of the sun.
Who can bear to stand where
    such pure breezes blow
And see a sight from which such beauty flows?

Which artist could paint a picture so angel-pure,
One that pierces my heart with love's rays?
All becomes gentle as if this were
    the heavenly-kingdom,
And I have reached my rest.

Such feelings bring heavenly pleasure,
Let me always look at you;
To part from you, Sophia, would be
    a deadly pain;
I follow you, beautiful goddess, and ever
    will be alert.

Take me along in your fields where
    the happy songs are sung,
And the morning-dew your tired
    pilgrims guides;
Most beautiful one, you will escort me
To the spring--happiness where we
    will never part.

Your friendly behavior tells me that
    you like me;

What does your eye betray?
When you love me, you are mine.
Such balsam breezes make the air
    holy, and close the dark gorges.

Gentle love and purest virtue, pour
White locks of beauty on youth's
    rosy-cheeks;
Fragrance from the jasmine
    wafts around the pretty ones;
Let us ever bloom in you.

No. 394.

Sophia, from your glances rapture flows into my
    heart
When a friendly love delights my soul;
O the pure instincts your charm arouses in me;
This flame feeds the blessed heavenly love.

You surmise in silence all wild passion,
And uncover what is hidden within us;
For my endeavors rob me of all rest;
Beloved, would you desert me if I am unwise?

Beloved, let me experience the gentleness and faith
    if we were united,
With your sweet caress many an anxious hour would
    flee,
My wounds would be healed,
Pure fire would be drawn to love.

Your demeanor reveals that your heart treasures me;
What joy, what rapture when you are close to me.
If kings would offer me crowns instead of your love,
I would cast them at their thrones
Since happiness is only when you are my own.

ιs spring gently wafts in the ether,
ʊo does my heart filled with your love;
As the rainbow melts into a noble hue,
So am I made complete by Sophia in the valley of
    the lillies.

Dip your brush into the rays of the sun to paint me
    your lovely picture;

Your lips and cheeks scarlet,
Should my mouth and heart be pressed thereon,
My soul and spirit would be refreshed.

O your walk is without care; your work is the joy of
    love;
Gentle and white as the lily is your sign on my breast
For the hand of harmony is the throne of love com-
    plete;
Beloved, if you live with us, you are our spiritual sun.

No. 395

Sophia, you chosen one,
Your brotherhood's first song;
Shine through the dawn to awaken life,
An early rising springs from the dream of the night
    before.

Delicate blossoms tumble from above
O'er which the spirit of the brothers softly whispers;
From a wild arbor rings triumphantly
The faith taking on life's traces.

Gracious love wanders softly from the
    shadows of the brush and nightingale;
Through the clearings see the joy of living
Jubilantly like enchanted dreams.

Warmth of the sun floods the fields;
The mighty songs of the forests stir;
The tips of the hills glow like sacrificial flames,
And flash into the dew-pearled valley.

Ebullient sacrificial flames are in the great temple;
The earth is a consecrated altar.
See the priestess is surrounded with radiance,
And sinks her gleaming crown
    into her hair.

Dressed in radiance, she steps from darkness
    toward her altar.
Incandescent clouds of the East
Strew themselves like scarlet blossoms on her path.

Sophia, Chosen One, come from the East,
Bring the brethren comfort of the soul!

Also beckon the friendless a joyful hope
With your wreath of roses.

No. 396

Sophia, you know my suffering
    for I have entrusted myself to you;
My praises of love shall resound from my lips
    for you;
What every prodigal avoids confessing,
I shall confess today.

I acknowledge that I love
Like I conceal the pain coursing through
    my quaking heart;
It sees and drives with mighty step, glance and hand
Toward one goal above.

Separate I myself from you,
    my limbs anxiously quiver;
My cheeks become pale and wan,
    and from my eyes death shivers;
I sway weak and dying
    resembling a moribund figure

Yet the bridegroom's fearless arm
    full of warmth and kindness,
With eager desire can embrace me
    with his goodness;
But when your arm touches me
    I am already charmed.

On you cling mouth and eyes;
    and the firmly pressed bossom
Quickly returns fire, joy, color,
    and life blossoms;
My cold blood warms
    with the ardour of your love.

May the storm of the north-east howl,
Send the Arctic bear, snow, ice
    and frost,
If only I can remain with you;
I'll renounce all joy, bird-song, and
    flower-fragrance.

Reward always with constant fire my
    pure tenderness;
No creature far and wide
    loves more sincere than I
You, beloved Jesus, my heart's life.

No. 397.

Sophia, you noble bride,
You have illuminated my heart with
    your loving ray,
And you have moistened my parched
    spirit with your oil;
My being is irrevocably bound in yours with
    love and duty.

My love for you enables me
    to bear all, whether bitter or difficult;
If only you come to me, I will
    be cheerful and daring;
The bitter will be sweet,
The heavy burden will be light.

I feel within me the striving of pure love,
    O noble spirit!
With ease I can reject this world
    and carnal love;
Yes, such banishment comes
    from my bossom

O, stay with me, Sophia, let
    me flee what is distasteful to you--
    no matter what it be;
My heart will withdraw, O, pure
    Bride;
O, make me free from all chains.

Let no Delilah sneak into
    my heart, and rob me of my strength!
Let me be constant and true,
Let nothing ever weaken me
    through its false brilliance.

Let without exception my ear
    and being bent to your will;
Let me with earnestness and diligence

seek to fulfill what in us speaks
Your word, your light.

Protect my heart from
the poisoned arrows of
Satan, the flesh and the world;
Should such a one, sometime
o'er take me
Do not push me from your loving care.

O, heal what was wounded,
cut what is unclean!
Give me, noble Virgin, a virgin-heart;
Give me a hero's spirit for my sufferings;
Let brightly burn in me the light
of truth.

I am aware that I can not
be spotless in my spirit, soul, and body;
It will be given to me by you, you
pure God's brilliance!
So, immaculate Spirit, mirror yourself
in me.

No. 398

Sophia, I cannot let go,
my heart burns with sweet fire;
My heart desires to hold you, and
wants to let go all the mire
Until my spirit rests with you;
Nothing but you I want to love,
My heart is refreshed with increasing fiery-zest;
Call me yours, then I am free.

Free from the shackles of falsehood
A new life sparkles for me;
No play, only purposeful goals and truth,
So flows life happily
and gently in the freedom-circle,
So the heart will be softened
When love through brotherhood arrives
at her goal.

Yes, more noble joys lift me to your
gracious breast;

All blessedness weaves into the simple life
   love and exquisite pleasure;
For the brothers' luck and blessing
Love the spiritual mind;
Then the sweetest reward leads to an
   even road,
And new achievement.

O, the pretty rose-time and
   the golden youth,
Love smiles and from a distance seems
   to envy my bliss;
Nature unravels the magic-chain
Which held me in bondage when
Looking into the alien world
   Almost ensnared my heart.

Sophia, the blessed, beckoned me;
Days quickly passed;
Often during the evening-red
   I would go to her in tribute;
So passed many a day that
   I do not now want;
Now in my cheerful face radiates
   my new life,
A higher, joyous, silver light.

For mankind, for the brothers
   the noble spirit now comes;
Friendly, active, great and proper
   is my wish,
Nevermore will diligence rest.
Never again shall a picture of the world
   delude me;
Never shall I the oath regret;
I will remain ever faithful
   and all time to her dedicate.

Hymns of Thanksgiving

No. 2
   Ach danket und rühmet den herrlichen Namen
   O, thank and praise the glorious name

No. 462
   Wir danken dir, mächtiger König!
   We thank you almighty King

These two hymns are hymns of thanksgiving, glorifying and praising God for his deeds and infinite power.

No. 2

O, thank and praise the glorious
    name,
You who are born of Abraham's
    seed,
And with me be designated to godly living,
Which Jesus Himself gave us
    from above.

We have seen many wonderful deeds
Which God rendered and bestowed;
Therefore we want daily to proclaim the
    wonder,
With thanks and praises loud.

Since we all have enjoyed his blessings
Which he has poured on us,
We desire to show the wonderful fruit
Grown in us in heavenly light.

We know that God Himself governs us
And has led us splendidly
Toward many holy ways
Through which we defied the enemy.

Therefore, let us glorify him
    with thanks and praise,
Thereby his name in us is
    exalted in love;
We will praise his wonderful name
With godly wisdom.

From within us burst forth
Many lovely songs to his pleasure;
And when we in united love are together,
Blessings through blessings enjoy.

Grow there in paradise's garden
Fruits of various kind
In honor of him who bestows us
    his blessing;
Let us in our heart's rejoice.

And daily high praise the wonders and deeds
Which for us so wonderfully succeed;
While we stay there edified by the Lord
All in the world's eyes looks on in
   amazement.

No. 462

We thank you, almighty King, and
   praise your infinite power;
Your governing knows no limits nor
   barrier through which our salvation and
   redemption is made;
The defiant heathen in us is raging,
   and struggling with you;
But your anger is more mighty
   and will extinguish the raging foe.

The time is at hand to judge the
   wicked in thoughts, words, and deeds;
The day is here now to destroy the demon,
   to help and strengthen the poor and depressed;
Yes, come, You Just One, to punish the despiser;
Ruin the ones which have caused the utmost
   pain and corrupted the soil of the heart.

We see the temple of the Lord rise
   which holds all the laws therein;
In the sanctuary revelations and voices are
   heard.
Our arch-priest, filled with blessing goes
   in the Holy One to serve and the purest
   offering to the Father to bring
And his mercy to implore.

Exalted Redeemer, You have selected
   us out of all races and generations;
You have christened us with fire
   and the Holy Ghost,
You have given us the taste of the
   heavenly meal;
How shall we repay You, we,
   your chosen ones?

Praise, honor, glory, grandeur
   and eternity be yours, God and your annointed
   ones.

Hymns about Christmas

No. 379
   Senke dich von Purpur--Wolken
   Descend from scarlet clouds

No. 380
   Sei uns gegrüsst du heil'ge Nacht
   Hail to you O Holy Night

      These hymns are lovely, gentle Christmas sentiments.
No. 380 clearly shows the southern German devotion to the
Christkind that comes on Christmas.

            No. 379

            Holy evening descend gently
            From scarlet clouds;
            Breath fresh air and
            Scatter dew and rose perfume
            From the fragrant ether above.

            No. 380

            Hail to you O Holy Night,
            Concealed lies earth's splendor,
            From the heaven high above
            Only the stars can see the little Child. Halleluja!

            We greet and bless you, Holy Child,
            Halleluja! We are pilgrims;
            You are the son of heaven;
            We, your kinsmen, welcome you in our pilgrim's land.
            Halleluja!

Hymn about Good Friday (No. 145)
   Golgotha, meiner Andacht wünsch't ich Flügel
   Golgotha, I wish my prayer had wings

      This Good Friday hymn has all the sensuousness of
the folk. It wants to feel, to kiss, to touch. The repetition
of blood completes the graphic picture.

            Golgotha, I wish my prayer had wings
            For I found your grave in the far distance;

Transported by my deep prayers, I will kiss the ground
Where the blood of my Savior is sprinkled.

Blood-altar, for so many pains you have suffered for
   all--
I think of thee.
I will give up my pleasure and carry my sorrows
As you want me to.

Martyrdom, sorrowfully I cry for your honor,
And my bitter tears flow for your agony;
Your pain increased as you carried the cross
And showed us how you loved us unto death.

Messiah, my prayers I multiply because much my
   fearful ear hears from Golgotha;
I will lean over your grave and will leave my tears on
   the dust of death
As many have done before.

Suffering, now I have seen the place
On which such salvation has transpired;
The holy place blessed by the righteous,
So grant rest to the lonely; you I honor for evermore.

Holy mountain, even though the floods are wild
The Savior's blood will forgive my many sins;
On the Mount of Olives, in the middle of Gethsemane,
I saw his sweat and blood.

Hymn for Easter (No. 407)
   Triumph, triumph

      This resurrection hymn speaks for itself with its open-
ing words.

         Triumph, triumph, the Blessed One has conquered;
         All you blessed by happy;
         Triumph, triumph, the dragon is defeated,
         Destroyed is the devil's realm.

         The strong seraphim rise in haste
         To judge by the Lord's command;
         One is calling to the other; holy, holy,
         Holy is the Lord of Sabaoth.

All the land as God has promised
Is full of God's glory;
No enemy can take Zion asunder;
God himself is its sun and shield.

Blessed you, blessed you in Jesus
You who know the Lord Christ's true light;
You are those whom Christ calls his brethren,
Through him you are free from judgement.

Now sing, sing: blessed the people! blessed, blessed
     the people
Who have this God for their God!
God makes Zion full of joy
For their living Bread is Jesus Christ.

Praise, honor, wisdom, gratitude, praise, courage,
     strength
Be with our God in eternity;
He showed his servants his works
That they live in him for ever.

Hymn for a Funeral (No. 75)
   Des Lebens letzte Stunde
   The last hour of life

     This funeral hymn, as the resurrection hymn above,
speaks about eternal life.   However, it also repeatedly asks
the poignant question, "Where shall we be next year?"

The last hour of life has struck;
The brethren send their blessing!
It will join the gray years of sorrow and woe
And will bring us nearer our goal.
Chorus - yea, joy and sorrow the hour brought,
     And took us nearer to our goal.

Fleeting time continually changeth;
It blooms, matures and disappears;
Writings scarcely accumulate on its decaying tombs;
And beauty, wealth, honor and power eventually
     sink into the night.
Chorus - And beauty, wealth, honor and power
     Eventually sink into the night.

Will we all be living a year from today?

Striving and happy--yes, many have departed and
rest now in peace
O, friends ask for peace in our friend's quiet
grave!
Chorus - O, friends ask for peace
in our friend's quiet grave!

Who knows which one of us within the year lies in
the grave?
Unannounced death carries men away.
In spite of springtime there are many faded leaves.
Whoever remains grants the friend in the grave
peace and tears.
Chorus - Whoever remains grants the friend in the
grave peace and tears.

The virtuous one closes his eyes;
God sweetens his grave with peaceful slumber
after this life of sorrow.
Then God awakens him to completeness in a better
world.
Chorus - Then God awakens him to completeness
in a better world.

Be of good cheer, Brethren, even when separation
threatens,
Whoever is good finds goodness in life and death.
There we will reconvene and sing songs of victory.
Now sing: to be always good is our wish the whole
year through.
Chorus - Now sing: to be always good is our wish
the whole year through.

Hymn about Prudence (No. 123)
Es blüht ein Blümlein irgend wo
There blooms a flower somewhere

Although this song is about modesty and prudence,
it is reminiscent of the "Blümelein" themes that abound in
German folksong. But Number 123 is pedagogical, while
the usual "Blumelein" songs are sentimental. If the Harmonists sang any of the latter, there appears to be no actual
record except for the Duke of Saxe-Weimar allusion that
Rapp liked gay songs which the psalms or the Gesang-
buch-lieder hardly were.[14]

There blooms a flower somewhere
    in a quiet valley;
It caresses eye and heart in
    this gay sun-valley;
More valuable than gold,
    pearl or diamond
It is called Modesty by
    everyone.

I could sing a long song of my
    flower's strength,
In body and soul what
    wondrous things it wrought;
No secret elixir can perform
What this unpretentious flower does.

Whoever carries Modesty in his bossom
    will an angel be,
This I've always noticed whether it be
    man or woman.
For all folks, be they old or young,
It is homage's talisman.

A haughty bearing, a proud head that
    lords it over all
It is not an asset for any man.
Should you through rank or gold to
    haughtiness aspire
Modesty will smite it and bow your head.

It makes your countenance rosy-colored
Shielding your eye from the harsh light.
It adds the flute's soft tone to voice
Changing stormy manner to that of a zephyr.

The harp is built like a heart
    for song and melody;
Yet joy and pain play not oft
    nor loud--
Pain, when gold flees from your desires,
And joy, when gold is drawn
    into the victor's garland.

O, Modesty reigns mild
    and lovingly   in the heart,
Interchangeably earnestness and
    caprice in its magic abound!

Anger is not spoken nor shown,
It achieves, but boasts not nor
    pushes ahead.

How friendly and peacefully one
    lives, and
How calmly one sleeps for
Modesty holds poisonous
    matter afar;
The bee, determined though it
    be, cannot find a place to sting.

Believe me, Brothers, I do not sing
    of fantasy
Though hard this is to grasp.
My song is a reflection of heaven's
    love,
Which blessedly strews modesty on great
    and small.

O, what wondrous strength
The flower has for body and soul;
It's more decorous than silk, pearl
    and gold;
Though I call it Modesty
    its proper name is Prudence.

Song of Spring (No. 496)
    Der schöne Maienmon't began
    The beautiful month of May began

    This spring song shows the Harmonist love of nature;
they can actually feel the great outdoors. It also has a
meditative mood, remaining true to their concepts.

The beautiful month of May began
    and everything was glad;
The sun came like a knight and
    winter fled;
Ice and fog withdrew; nature
    left her winter-bed
And instead of cold stars
    In a flower wreath was clad.

The bossom of the clover-covered hill
    is a verdant show;

The carefree deer nibbles the best that it
    can get;
Whispers rush through the groves,
    in a wink virtue is forgotten;
All see only play and the lovely
    morning glow.

Here, here in my shadowy glen
    I am unbound by
The rustling of the appletree and
    the murmuring of the brook,
And the glistening of the stream in
    the green wood
Where the nightingale her sweet melody
    resounds.

The beautiful golden morning sky
    pierces red through the trees,
And unites itself with the brilliance
    of a scarlet silver thread;
How smiles at us the budding twig,
    and the worm in the swaying grass!
And then for the flowering mass
    a well appears.

Rivulets gush o'er the flowers, leaving
    a blossom-fragrance;
The nightingale drinks in the mild
    evening air in its nest;
The rose which on the meadow green
    in hazelshadow rests,
Too soon will pale.

How tenderly flows the ether from its warm
    bossom,
It no longer rests on the wild plum, but
    all is fragrant with it;
The butterfly hovers o'er the grass and errs in
    the bushes;
How beautifully he lights on the grass, how
    delicately and gently!

The muffled voice of the dove is heard,
    while she gathers the twigs for the nest,
Very musical the woods resound
    while many a bird sings;
The wind in the grove and the leaves
    from the trees bring joy to all,

        Everyone feels the great outdoors
        and looks for the peace that matters.

     These hymns, like all the others in the Gesangbuch, reflect the real spirit of the Harmonists, for as a man is, so he writes. They reveal that at times all was not harmonious, but they show that their despair was healed with infinite hope in Jesus and His coming. It ultimately does not matter that there had been a disintegration in Adam, because the apocalypse will see the triumphant reintegration of the whole man. Such is the destiny of man.

     The serious tone of the message is negated by the type of melodies used. Ross F. Lockridge, the director of the New Harmony Memorial Commission, when writing his book The Labyrinth, had occasion to interview John S. Duss, a musician and a former trustee of the Harmonists. His comments speak of the adapting of street songs, a common practice among the folk:

     Although the Harmonists adapted many Old World
     melodies to their hymns, they practically excluded
     the magnificent chorals such as Luther's 'A
     Mighty Fortress is Our God. ' They had no patience
     with the slow, solemn tread of the sort of music
     which to them was representative of what they re-
     garded as head hanging or downcast Christianity, in
     other words, Hypocrisy. Hence they went to the
     other extreme--adopting folksongs and street songs
     and, as to the ordinary dignified hymns, they add-
     ed grace notes and turns and furbelows, and speed-
     ed up the tempo until both dignity and Hypocrisy
     were non est.

     True, there are a number of Minuets by Mozart,
     Beethoven, Pleyel; waltzes by Mozart, also others
     by Haydn, etc. But most of the music is of the
     ordinary type. The great number of pieces of
     dance music therefore can only be credited to the
     leaning away from the stately, the dignified the
     majestic, toward the lively and whatsoever was in
     lighter vein--the same tendency mentioned hereto-
     fore in connection with the music used in their
     religious service.

     I recall an incident in the 1870's when one of the
     supercilious hired hands [not a member of the

Society] took it upon himself to remonstrate with
Henrici about permitting the band to play this
music 'of the street and bawdy house.' Henrici,
with a twinkle in his eye replied, 'You evidently
know things that are not interesting to me.' As
for music itself, there is nothing low or impure
therein, and in any case we are not going to let
the Devil exercise preemptory rights when it
comes to a question of ownership in the realm of
music.' 'Amen,' said one and all to the Henrici
summing up.[15]

Notes

1. William Owen, Diary of William Owen from November
    10, 1824 to April 20, 1825, ed. Joel W. Hiatt
    (Indianapolis: Indiana Historical Society Publica-
    tions, 4, No. 1, 1906), p. 102.

2. James Silk Buckingham, The Eastern and Western
    States of America, II (London: Fisher, Son & Co.
    1842) p. 230.

3. Elias Pym Fordham, Personal Narrative of Travels in
    Virginia, Maryland, Pennsylvania, Ohio, Indiana,
    Kentucky; and a Residence in the Illinois Territory:
    1817-1888. ed. Frederic Auston Ogg (Cleveland:
    Arthur H. Clark, 1906), p. 207.

4. William Faux, Memorable Days in America: Being a
    Journal of a Tour to the United States (London:
    W. Simpkin and R. Marshall, 1823), p. 272.

5. Owen, Diary, p. 74.

6. Karl Bernhard, Duke of Saxe-Weimar Eisenach.
    Travels Through North America, during the years
    1825 and 1826. (Philadelphia: Carey, Lea and
    Carey, 1828), p. 164.

7. Ibid., p. 163.

8. Ibid., p. 165.
    Everyone had, in addition to the Gesangbuch, Der
    Psalter des Koenigs und Propheten Davids, ver-
    deutschet von Dr. Martin Luther, gedruckt bei Jacob
    Mayer Für Johnson & Warner, 1812.

9.   John S. Duss, The Harmonists (Harrisburg: The Tele-
      graph Press, 1943), p. 161.

10.   John Melish, Travels in the U. S. of America in the
      years 1806, 1807, 1809, 1810, 1811; and Travels
      Through Various Parts of Great Britain, Ireland
      and Upper Canada, II (Philadelphia, 1815), p. 6.

11.   Robert Burns, "The Cotter's Saturday Night," stanzas
      10, 14, 15, 16, 17, 20.

12.   Feurige-Kohlen (Economy: The Harmonists, 1826),
      p. 207.

13.   Christiana Knoedler, The Harmony Society (New York:
      Vantage Press, Inc., 1954), p. 79.

14.   Saxe-Weimar, 1825 and 1826, p. 163.

15.   Ross F. Lockridge, The Labyrinth (New Harmony:
      The New Harmony Memorial Commission, 1941),
      p. 82.

Chapter IX

HOME PATTERNS

A. Living Quarters

When the Harmonists first came to Butler County,
Pennsylvania, they apparently camped under the trees (see
Chapter I), and tradition had it that a few feet north of
dormitory No. 5 in Harmony, Indiana was a large oak tree
which was the camping ground of the members first to arrive in that area.[1] The spot continued to be a favorite with
the Harmonist band.[2] Later, in Economy, Christiana
Knoedler says that at French Point stood the famous "camping oak" under which the first contingent of Harmonists
camped when they arrived at their third settlement-to-be on
June 6, 1824.[3] In each area they were surrounded by a
wilderness but soon made it "blossom as the rose." In the
midst of this luxuriant growth they built villages that were
the surprise and envy of all.

First came log cabins, then houses. The six-room
houses, all alike in style, were of frame or of Harmonist-
made brick, two stories high, having but one door on the
side. There has been much speculation as to why there is
no front entrance in these private dwellings. (All public
buildings had front entrances. This included Rapp's house
because he entertained visitors.) There actually is no answer, but several can be proposed. First of all, it may
simply be remembered south-German-village design. The
pathway leads to a vestibule, a convenient house entrance.
Why put in a door that would never be used? And it would
take up wall space in the interior of the house. Secondly,
it reflects their utilitarian work attitude and practicality.
There is no need for more than one door. It assured more
privacy, cleanliness, and warmth. And there was the love
of flowers. This door led into the pleasure garden of the
"L-shaped" garden which each house had for beauty and the
kitchen. The former was filled with flowers and shrubs,
hiding the vegetables and herbs beyond. Since flowers
played such a large part in the life of a Harmonist, it

134

would please the householders as they passed them to enter
their dwelling. It was true to their spirit of combining simplicity, beauty and practicality.

The Bentel House in Harmony, Pennsylvania had one
feature that no other house had--the Virgin Sophia carved by
Frederick Rapp above the lintel of the doorway (see Appendix). As stated above, Sophia was in their very being, so
it is not surprising that she would appear on a building. The
only question is: Why did she not appear over a doorway in
each settlement, as she appeared in their song in each place.

Don Blair, of New Harmony, Indiana, has done extensive authentic Harmonist reconstruction in New Harmony.
(Charles M. Stotz of Pittsburgh is the expert for Economy.)
In Blair's excellent brochure, which is given to visitors in
this second settlement of the Harmonists (information taken
from his Harmonist Construction), he says the Harmonist
building plans are a composite of ideas from Europe, the
eastern United States, and experience. One thing certain
was the complete utilization of space and thought of comfort,
especially related to draft. The entrance and stairs are in
the vestibule. By removing the stair-well from the rest of
the house, an "air lock" is created. This makes the living
area more comfortable. The fireplace and doors are located
on the center wall, thus creating maximum wall-space and
also taking care of both cooking and heating. Mr. Blair
especially makes note of the fact that the chimney does not
support the center beam.   This additional weight of fireplace and chimney would cause differential settlement. Another clever device used by the Harmonists for insulation and
a fire deterrent was "the Dutch Biscuit," described by Blair
as follows:

> 'The Dutch Biscuit' was made by wrapping a wood-
> en board, one inch by four inches, and the neces-
> sary length, with straw and mud. The straw pro-
> vided the insulation, and the mud was the bond.
> Some insect repellent was incorporated in either the
> mud or the straw, as no evidence of attack by ter-
> mites or other insect pests has ever been found.
> 'The Dutch Biscuit' was installed in grooves cut in
> the sides of the ceiling joists. [4]

The trap door in the entry leading to the cellar is
further indication of their utilization of space and concern
about draft. Below would be a small root cellar with a

brick floor.   Evelyn Matter, a guide of Old Economy, who
has made an extensive study of the Baker House there,
throws more light on the cellar.   She says there are tunnels
from this area to openings on two outside walls, creating a
circulation of air which kept the cellar cool and the house
dry.   Mr. Blair also had made drawings of these.   Mrs.
Matter points to another trap door, this one leading to the
attic.   It is assumed that this area was used for sleeping,
or perhaps for storage. 5   However, most of their storage
space was the wooden family shed found behind every house,
although two houses may have shared one.   The shed,
divided in three parts, held firewood, tools, hogs, chickens,
and a cow (if there was no communal dairy).   The center
room was for the storage of food, and in the rear was the
"outside-plumbing. "   Below is another root cellar, and above
is the hay loft.

        The doors of the Harmonist houses were the common
"Christian Doors" used by many sects.   The six panels of
the door are divided into an upper half depicting "the Sign
of the Cross, " and the lower half depicting the open Bible.
Also note the number six discussed in Chapter VI.

        These popular 30 x 22-feet houses were prefabricated,
according to Don Blair, and were stored in a central re-
pository.   When a house was to be built a "hill of material"
was requested, and parts were delivered to the proposed site.
The framework was assembled while lying on the ground;
final adjustments were made before its erection. 6   This
would explain the speed with which the Harmonists were able
to build towns in three different settlements.   At Harmony,
Indiana, they also built four dormitories three stories high,
possibly inspired by monasteries, convents or the Ephrata
Cloisters in Lancaster County, Pennsylvania.   However,
this must not have pleased them.   When they returned to
Pennsylvania, they built only the popular six-room household
dwelling.

        The dormitories, three stories high, also had only a
side entrance.   MacDonald makes a special note of the
dormitories: "The larger dwelling houses are of brick.
Galleries run through the center of them.   The women's
apartments, opening one into the other, are on one side and
the men's on the other.   Stoves stand in the middle of the
rooms. "7

        Ross F. Lockridge, for some unknown reason, states

that the dormitories were for housing only men. In The Old Fauntleroy Home he refers to "four men's dormitories."[8] And in The Labyrinth he states: "The four large brick dormitories that the Rappites built for the housing of single men were material symbols of their practice of celibacy."[9]

The dormitories each had one large fireplace for cooking and a dining room on the first floor that served those who lived in the dormitory. Because the fireplace-ovens in the kitchen were relatively small, two community ovens fulfilled the needs of the harmonists.

Father Rapp's house in Harmony, Indiana was a two-storied brick house with verandahs on the south and east sides of the house and flights of stone steps leading to the two entrances--"a large pile of brick surrounded by shrubbery and pleasure grounds, but rather distinguished for capaciousness than taste," says Schoolcraft. Even the front room is uncarpeted.[10] In the cellar, wine and cider are stored. (Some detractors, who were more impressed with the house than Schoolcraft, like to say that worldly Owen, who bought Harmony from the Harmonists, did not live in a large house. What they do not say is that the Owen experiment failed within three years and Owen returned to Scotland.) The two most interesting facts about the Rapp house were not of the house but of its grounds, which were dominated by a fairly large greenhouse on rollers, and an unusual slab of limestone. Instead of the plants being moved about, the greenhouse was rolled to the plants and to exotic fig, lemon and orange trees to protect them from the inclement weather. In the winter this greenhouse was heated with tenplate stoves.[11]

While George Rapp was traveling, he found along the Mississippi at St. Louis a tabular mass of grayish-blue limestone, containing two apparent prints or impressions of the naked human foot. The impressions are "to all appearances those of a man standing in an erect posture with the left foot a little advanced and the heels drawn in. The distance between the heels, by accurate measurement is six and a quarter inches, and between the extremeties of the toes, thirteen and a half."[12] It must be noted these are not impressions of feet accustomed to the European shoe. Here the toes are spread, and the foot is flattened. Someone suggested it was done by a sculptor. This Schoolcraft thought ridiculous. But even more ridiculous was the gossip that sprung up, crediting Father Rapp with the story that the Angel Gabriel came to talk to him, and left his mark.

People loved this story, and even though Father Rapp himself
told of his having brought the slab from St. Louis, and although people like Schoolcraft pronounced the story foolish,
it persisted. People who knew nothing of Father Rapp's true
philosophy want to know about Gabriel's footprints even today. [13]

As soon as they began to substitute brick for log
houses in Economy, they built a "Great House" for Father
Rapp and his family. Actually it was not so much for the
Rapps as for the Society. The Harmonists needed a proper
place of reception for the many visitors coming to see
Economy. The house is a two-story center structure with
two wings, with a two-story house attached to the north wing.
This wing was the house of Frederick Rapp. Rooms of special interest are the Reception Room and Trustees' Room of
the center portion of the Great House. The Reception Room,
rear parlor, was used as a living room and "a place for
small business suppers" when they were about to close a
business deal. The front parlor or Trustees' Room was the
formal drawing room where all the visitors were entertained.
Here also the members of the Rapp household sang hymns. [14]
The Great House, like most of the buildings, had espaliers
for grapes. Again the Harmonists' practical mind could have
nothing just ornamental, as ivy would be. The grapes were
attractive, and because they were hugged by sun-warmed bricks
their sugar content was increased, thus producing a very high
quality grape. [15]

Everyone who saw the villages was amazed and delighted. Melish reports:

> The whole country from Pittsburgh to this place is
> rather rough and uncultivated; and land sells at
> from two to three dollars per acre. Beyond this as
> we continued our journey we found the country to
> improve; and approaching the precincts of the
> Harmonist Society, we passed some of their well-
> cultivated farms. Here the road passes over a
> considerable hill; and on reaching the top we saw
> at a little distance the town of Harmony, elegantly
> situated amid flourishing and well-cultivated
> fields. [16]

William Hebert found:

> Their little town, seen from the neighboring hills
> which are covered with their vineyards and

orchards, has an exceedingly pleasing appearance.
... The log cabins are giving place as fast as
possible to neat and commodious brick and framed
houses, which are extremely well built, the uniform
redness of the brick of which the majority of them
is composed giving to the place a brightness of
appearance which the towns of England are quite
destitute of.... The streets of the little town of
Harmony are planted on each side with Lombardy
poplars, but as these are found to die as soon as
their roots come in contact with the substratum of
sand, they are replaced with mulberry trees. A
town being thus planted with trees, has a very
picturesque effect from a distance, it appearing
to stand in a grove, beside the pleasant use of af-
fording shade and shelter when walking about it. [17]

Morris Birkbeck had an uplifting of spirits when he
saw the Harmonist clearings:

The view of that noble expanse was like the opening of bright day upon the gloom of night, to us
who had been so long buried in deep forests.... To
travel day after day among trees of a hundred feet
high, without a glimpse of the surrounding country
is oppressive to a degree which those cannot con-
ceive who have not experienced it. [18]

Charles Nordhoff noticed the marked difference between
the community on the edge of the Harmonist property and
Economy:

... and you wonder at the broken fences, unpainted
houses, and tangled and weed-covered grounds, and
that general air of dilapidation which curses a
country producing petroleum and bituminous coal.

Presently, however, you strike into what is evidently a large and well-kept estate....
....
The town begins on the edge of the bluff; and under
the shade-trees planted there benches are arranged,
where doubtless the Harmonists take their comfort
on summer evenings, in view of the river below
them and the village on the opposite shore. Streets
proceed at right angles with the river's course; and
each street is lined with neat frame or brick

houses, surrounding a square in such a manner
that within each household has a sufficient garden.
The broad streets have neat foot-pavements of brick;
the houses, substantially built but unpretentious,
are beautified by a singular arrangement of grape-
vines, which are trained to espaliers fixed to cover
the space between the top of the lower and the bottom of the upper windows. [19]

During Edward de Montule's travels from Pittsburgh
to Buffalo he stopped at Harmony, Butler County. In Letter
XX, while recounting his harrowing travel experiences, he
also has comments about the first Harmonist settlement:

... and arrived at dinner time in a pretty little
town whose aspect delighted and amply consoled me
for having chosen the longer route. This settlement, beyond a doubt the finest of its kind that I
have seen in the interior of America, is the only
one in which individual enterprise has been directed
toward the common good. The town is named
Harmony.

... the leader suddenly sold the holdings ... and
went off with his followers to clear another piece of
land on the Wabash.... These lands, in the hands
of diverse individuals, are deteriorating daily. [20]

Finally, George Flower, whose father had acted as an
agent for George Rapp when Harmony, Indiana was up for
sale, has a humorous anecdote to tell. And truly it is a
human comedy. He prefaces it with the observation that all
who came from the backwoods saw with surprise and wonder
what this group had been able to accomplish. They could not
help but compare these good houses surrounded by pleasant
gardens with their own log huts filled with dirt, desolation
and discomforts. It opened a new train of thought to one
young man who did not seem to come to a conclusion. He
just said to Flower: "I studies and I studies on it. "[21]

B. The Household

While communal groups generally dissolve all family
units, the Harmonists, with the exception of their Indiana
dormitories, kept the house. So the family became a
"household"; it being the smallest part of the Harmonist

Society. However small it was, it was an intrinsic part of
that larger organization. But names became unimportant.
The "brothers" and "sisters" were called by their first
names, even by children.[22] Each house was known by the
appointed head of it. When "the head" died or was moved
to another house for some practical reason or left the society, the house took on the name of the new senior member.
Generally speaking, the houshold consisted of five or six
members, but there could be as few as two and as many as
eight. Rearrangements were constantly made.[23] Many of
these were made because of the aged or helpless ones.
Williams reports that these were always carefully tended
and nursed. A few Harmonists had been bed-ridden for
twenty or thirty years, and were remarkable examples of
patient Christian endurance. It seems reasonable that
through the course of years the patient would have had
several nurses and thus several household rearrangements.[24]

        Victor Duclos, in his Diary and Recollections, and
William E. Wilson write about a hospital in Harmony,
Indiana. And Don Blair has the hospital on a copy of William Pickering's 1824-25 town map which is a Harmonist
brochure given by the Wilson Furniture Company of New
Harmony. Duclos described it as a one-story frame building about 30 by 60 feet.[25] Wilson says the hospital on
Brewery Street must have been in a pungent neighborhood
because in addition to the brewery there was a distillery and
a large piggery.[26] But nothing is said of the reason for the
hospital or of its major services. It is known that in Indiana
they had a large number of malaria cases every year. (This
was one reason for their leaving the area.) Their sense of
orderliness and efficiency probably prompted them to put all
the sick under one roof. This way they could have better
care. But there is no evidence that they had a similar
building in Economy.

        At Old Economy they have restored a typical dwell-
ing of the Harmony Society. Because it is the Baker House
it must be recognized that the furnishings may have been
somewhat better than in the others, since Baker was a trustee and a business man of the world. On the other hand,
Baker was deeply religious and completely dedicated to the
Society and its ways, so he may have refused anything better than the standard of the day.

            The living room (22' x 18') features: three
        ladderback chairs, one rocker, one arrowback

chair, one horseshoesplat chair, one Harmonist
made corner cupboard, one Harmonist made table,
one table where one sat up to the table, not with
knees under, one desk, one sideboard, one chest,
one bench, one Seth Thomas Thomaston clock, one
applebutter red wardrobe, one yarn winder.

The kitchen (11'3" x 11') features: one Harmonist
made table, two Windsor type chairs, one kitchen
type chair, one dark red sideboard, one hanging
cupboard, one open-shelf cupboard.

The bedroom (once 18' x 10'; now, with the parti-
tion removed, measures 24' x 10') features: one
bed with wooden pegs for role lacing rounded head
and foot board, one bed with four posts same
height as head and foot boards, one 1855 three
paneled wardrobe, one chair with woven seat, one
Harmonist made table, one decorated table, one
chest of drawers, one blanket chest, one small
chest with hinged lid with chain, one American
Empire mirror, one potty-chair.[27]

None of these items belonged to individual members;
they belonged to the Society. Whoever left the Society would
get a sum of money related to his service, worth or mood.
The archives are full of receipts from withdrawees, and
later, after they had thought better of it, their letters asking
for money, a bed or a chest. The answer from Economy
was usually a stoic silence.

Affection in the Harmonist household was a brother-
sister relationship, as discussed in Chapter VI. From
Elijah Lemmix's testimony under cross-examination in a suit
he brought against the Society, relationships were proper, for
he said men slept upstairs and women downstairs.[28] And
on March 4, 1825, William Owen, while watching some Harmonists get ready to leave for Pennsylvania on the "Phoenix,"
saw fond farewells, but "all the kissing that took place was
from man to man."[29] So, while this household was not the
conventional concept, it was nevertheless a unit in which one
had to develop an unselfish attitude and a genuine concern for
another's feelings. Only in this way would brotherly love
flourish.

C. Food

The Harmonists never were in want; in fact, they
lived well and enjoyed the south German cuisine. However,
travelers were not equally excited about it. Sometimes it
tasted much better than it looked, as was the case when
Melish arrived with a doctor at a patient's house just in
time for dinner. They were invited to dine, and tasted of
the dish called "noodles. " Melish has as good a translation
as can be found for what probably is the Swabian Spätzle:
"Noodles is made this way--A quantity of flour is kneaded
into a paste, and is cut into small slices; these are mixed
with small pieces of beef or mutton, and they are boiled
together, with or without seasoning, as the taste of the
cook may determine. "[30]

William Faux reports having had "bad beef, though
good bread. "[31] But Farkas de Bolon found "the table more
luxurious" than he would have thought possible in this simple
world. [32] It is perhaps to be expected that the Duke of Saxe-
Weimar found good German dinners and uncommonly good
wine. [33] The Harmonists themselves fared well on their
south-German cooking. If it was heavy on the dumpling side,
the great abundance of fruit they had counteracted any im-
balance in the diet. Nordhoff reported that all ate meat, and
only a few abstained from pork.

Their daily schedule was that of a German farmer.
They rose between five and six, depending on the season; ate
a light breakfast between six and seven; had a lunch at nine;
dinner at twelve; an afternoon lunch, called vesperbrot at
three (the lunches consist of a slice of bread and a mug of
wine, beer, or cider); supper between six and seven; and
went to bed by nine. [34]

Each household cooked for itself. Formerly there
were public ovens. Hebert observed that they were supplied
"... with public ovens, which are placed at regular and convenient distances from each other. "[35] But by 1875 there
was a general bakery, as well as a dairy instead of the house-
holder's cow(s). For cream and butter they skimmed the
cream from the milk allotted to them. When the butcher
was ready for meat distribution, a little boy was sent around
the village crying "Sollt Fleisch holen. " As the householders
came, each received sufficient for his number of people.
Other household supplies, except produce grown in their own
gardens, were dealt from the general store at given times;
but if necessary, they could be procured at any time. [36]

Needless to say, a record was maintained to keep people
from being wasteful or careless, not only at the beginning
of the society's days, but also at the end. [37]

The Society was apparently famous for its ginger
cookies, always part of the feasts. It is likely that each
household may have kept some of those on hand. At least
Gertrude Rapp did, for Agnes M. Hays Gormly remembers
visiting in the Great House: "... Miss Gertrude excused herself, and in a few minutes re-entered with a tray of wine
glasses through whose facets you see a ruby liquid. Then
she opens a long narrow closet door in the chimney corner
and piles ginger cakes on a pink 'Adams' plate.... "[38]
Gertrude Rapp's recipe for these round scalloped ginger
cookies is typical of early cookery: one gallon molasses,
one pound lard, six ounces of ginger, four ounces of soda,
eight ounces of water, enough flour to make stiff dough. [39]

While the Harmonist cuisine was not exotic, it was
wholesome, and on occasion they must have looked into cookbooks, for several are in the Old Economy library. [40]

No one ever went hungry unless he was being punished,
if Joshua Nachtrieb's testimony in his suit against the Society was accurate and not malicious in intent. He testified
that Father Rapp ordered a punishment of sustenance on
water and bread for backsliding members. [41] However, in
cross-examination he stated he was never present when Rapp
issued such orders. [42] A more common punishment, mentioned by Nachtrieb and also reported by Hebert, was refusal
of participation in the agape, the Holy Communion. [43] Hebert
says this refusal was accompanied with general social neglect
of the guilty person. This, with verbal reproof, was found
fully efficacious to reform. [44] Shunning (meidung) is also
successfully employed by the Old Order Amish.

D. Beverage

The Harmonists came from a country where alcoholic
beverages were part of life. They brewed beer, made
wine and distilled whiskey, all of which they sold. For
themselves they kept some beer and wine which they drank
moderately. They did not tolerate drunkenness. [45] They did
not drink whiskey because that drink was not customary in
southern Germany.

The travelers and abstainers who smiled, and in those
smiles said sermons when they saw the sign "Golden Rule
Distillery," should have remembered that in this, as in all
else, the Harmonists had biblical injunctions. Who does not
remember Christ's first miracle? And wine was their most
common brew.

The Harmonists used grinders to crush the grapes,
which they placed in large vats. After fermentation stopped
(a week or ten days), the wine was pressed in their laundry
because the steam engine used to operate the press was also
used for the agitator-tubs in which their clothes were washed.
(Before they had a steam engine, they used horse power.)
Then the wine was led by hoses into the tubs in the Wine
Cellar where it was aged. When it was ready for sale it was
put into casks and rolled up the rack on the stairs by means
of the windlass. At first the wine was sold by the barrel,
later in bottles bearing the "Economy" label. Much later they
sold the use of their name. For example, "Old Economy"
whiskey was made until prohibition was adopted in 1920,
fifteen years after the Harmonists were dissolved. [46]

E. Dress

The dress of the Harmonists was that of the 1804
Swabian country and village folk. Time and styles changed
in the world, but changes did not touch the Harmonists.
The general attitude of the group was indirectly stated in a
letter from Romelius Baker to Frederick Rapp. Baker was
in New York, and sending home a report. As always, he
included, in one way or another, his religious philosophy. On
this occasion he wrote: "In the churches here they still
preach a great deal about our Lord, our Savior, and His
merit; although they allow their followers more than we believe in. Their haughtiness, lavishness, and splendor in
dressing are exceedingly immoderate."[47]

When their European clothing wore out they made new
with materials woven on their premises. They had their own
wool (their merino sheep were the finest in the country),
bought the best cotton, and later were among the first to produce silk. So they had the finest materials, but not high
fashion. The Mennonites, with whom the Harmonists were
acquainted, also have always used the finest materials in their
regulation dress.

Travelers usually saw the Harmonists in their work
clothing. Henry Schoolcraft reports women clothed in gray
cotton cloth and very large straw hats (which they wove).[48]
William Faux, who did not think the West was a flower, had
the following impression carry over to the Harmonists and
working people in general:

> The people appear very saturnine, and neither
> very cleanly nor very dirty. They are dressed
> much alike, and look rather shabby, just as work-
> ing folk in general look. None are genteel. The
> women are intentionally disfigured and made as
> ugly as it is possible for art to make them, having
> their hair combed straight up behind and before,
> so that the temples are bared, and a little skull
> cap, or black crape bandage, across the crown,
> and tied under the chin. This forms their only
> headdress.[49]

In 1839 Buckingham found the situation as follows:

> The costume of the members is German, but
> without any very marked peculiarity. The men
> wear short jackets, or half-coats, and trousers,
> of gray cloth, with waistcoats of lilac or brown,
> and black hats and shoes of the ordinary kind.
> The women wear gowns with long sleeves, of a
> sort of light woolen cloth, like coarse merino, of
> dark colour, with a near handkerchief of silk or
> cotton over the shoulders, pinned down tight before,
> a plain white or checked apron, and a perpendicu-
> lar German cap of black when in their labouring
> dress, and white in the evenings and on Sundays.
> The men wear their beards under their chins, and
> round the lower edge of the face, of different
> lengths, but shave the cheeks and upper lip down
> thus far; and the older men have also their white
> locks hanging down over their shoulders. The
> women wear their hair parted in the middle, and
> combed back smoothly under their plain caps; in
> both sexes the characteristics are simplicity,
> neatness, comfort, and economy; but there is not
> the slightest particle of taste or elegance in their
> apparel; and though their forms are robust and
> healthy, it would be difficult to light upon 500
> persons anywhere else, I think, with so little of
> either masculine or feminine beauty. They appear,

however, to be very happy.... [50]

Richard Flower, George Rapp's real estate agent in Harmony, Indiana, had been intrigued with their Swabian work clothes, which reminded him of the Norman peasant. In fact, since they were all of the same style and color, he thought they could be called a uniform or costume. Waxing romantic as he remembered the Harmonists marching to the field to work, he wrote: "The men marched first, the women next, and the rear rank composed of young women, with each a neat ornament of striped cedar wood on their head, formed one of the prettiest processions I ever witnessed."[51] That was in 1819. In 1835 some lady visitors were intrigued with the bonnets. In fact, they could not get them out of their minds. So, on April 2, 1836, a Mr. J. C. Reynolds wrote the following letter to Romelius Baker:

> I wish to procure from your Society four Bonnets for some ladies who visited your little town last summer when they saw and admired them exceedingly. They wrote to me the other day to procure if possible for them the Bonnets. I have therefore to request you if it will be agreeable to send them.
>
> J. C. Reynolds
>
> The price will be no consideration if you can send them. [52]

It was a few years later that Buckingham wrote that they had no style or elegance (see above). Considering the above "worldly" order, one is apt to observe that imagination was lacking either in Buckingham or in the tilt of the lady's bonnet.

Notes

1.   No. 5 Dormitory is a misnomer. The Harmonists built only four dormitories.

2.   Victor Colin Duclos, From the Diary and Recollections of Victor Colin Duclos. Copies from the original manuscript by Mrs. Nora C. Fretageot (Indianapolis: Indiana Historical Collections, III, 1916), pp. 540-541.

3.   Christiana Knoedler, The Harmony Society (New York:

Vantage Press, Inc., 1954), p. 72.

4. Don Blair, "Building Brochure," New Harmony,
    Indiana, Gift Shop, n.d.

5. Evelyn Matter, "The Baker House," (Ambridge: Old
    Economy, 1968), p. 4. (Mimeographed.)

6. Don Blair, private interview, New Harmony, Indiana,
    July, 1967.

7. Donald MacDonald, The Diaries of Donald MacDonald,
    1824-1826 (Indianapolis: Indiana Historical Society
    Publications, 1942, Vol. 14, No. 2), p. 219.

8. Ross F. Lockridge, The Old Fauntleroy Home (New
    Harmony: New Harmony Memorial Commission,
    1939), p. 6.

9. Ross F. Lockridge, The Labyrinth (New Harmony:
    New Harmony Memorial Commission, 1941), p. 69.

10. Henry R. Schoolcraft, Travels in the Central Portion
    of the Mississippi Valley Comprising Observations on
    its Mineral, Geography, Internal Resources and
    Aboriginal Population, Performed Under Sanction of
    Government in the Year 1821 (New York, 1825), p.
    171.

11. Ibid., p. 170.

12. Ibid., pp. 173-174.

13. Frances Lewis, private interview, New Harmony,
    Indiana, July, 1967. Dale Owen (American Journal
    of Science and Arts, Vol. 43, July 1842) wrote ex-
    tensively on Gabriel's footprints and definitely estab-
    lished them as Indian petroglyphs.

14. Daniel B. Reibel, A Guide to Old Economy (Ambridge:
    Pennsylvania, 1968), p. 17. (Mimeographed.)

15. Ibid., p. 10.

16. John Melish, Travels in the United States of America
    in the Years 1806-1811 and Travels Through Various
    Parts of Great Britain, Ireland and Upper Canada,
    II (Philadelphia, 1812), p. 2.

17. William Hebert, A Visit to the Colony of Harmony, in Indiana in the United States of America (London: George Mann, 1825), p. 329.

18. Morris Birkbeck, Notes on a Journey in America (London: Ridgway and Sons, 1818), p. 110-111.

19. Charles Nordhoff, The Communistic Societies of the United States (New York: Schocken Books, 1965), pp. 63-64.

20. Edward de Montule, Travels in America, 1816-1817, translated from the original French edition of 1821 by Edward D. Seeber (Bloomington: Indiana University Press, 1951), pp. 146-47.

21. George Flower, History of the English Settlement in Edwards Co., Illinois (Chicago: Fergus Printing Co., 1882), p. 281.

22. John S. Duss, The Harmonists (Harrisburg: The Telegraph Press, 1943), p. 29.

23. Ibid., pp. 121-22.

24. Aaron Williams, The Harmony Society (Pittsburgh: W. S. Haven, 1866), p. 116.

25. Harlow Lindley, ed., Indiana as Seen by Early Travelers (Indianapolis: Indiana Historical Commission, 1916), p. 539.

26. William E. Wilson, The Angel and the Serpent (Bloomington: Indiana University Press, 1964), p. 43.

27. Evelyn Matter, House, pp. 10-13.

28. Elijah Lemmix vs. Romulus L. Baker, et al., Circuit Court of the United States, Western District of Pennsylvania, Pittsburgh, 1854, p. 78.

29. William Owen, Diary of William Owen from November 10, 1824 to April 20, 1825, ed. Joel W. Hiatt (Indianapolis: Indiana Historical Society Publications 4, No. 1, 1906), p. 122.

30.   John Melish, Canada, p. 8.

31.   William Faux, Memorable Days in America Being a
      Journal of a Tour to the United States (London:
      W. Simpkin and R. Marshall, 1823), p. 264.

32.   Karl J. Arndt, "Three Hungarian Travelers Visit
      Economy," The Pennsylvania Magazine of History
      and Biography, LXXIX, No. 2, April, 1955, p. 202.

33.   Bernhard, Duke of Saxe-Weimar, Eisenach, Travels
      through North America during the Years 1825-1826
      (Philadelphia: Carey, Lea and Carey, 1828), p. 161.

34.   Charles Nordhoff, States, p. 87.

35.   Hebert, America, p. 329.

36.   Mrs. E. A. May, private interview, Patterson Heights,
      Pennsylvania, August, 1967.

37.   Hebert, America, p. 330.

38.   Agnes M. Hays Gormly, Old Economy (Sewickley: The
      Harmony Press, 1966), n. p.

39.   Mrs. E. A. May, private interview, Patterson Heights,
      Pennsylvania, August, 1967.

40.   Two such cookbooks are: a) Neues wohl eingerichtets
      Koch-Buch aus mehr als fünfzehen hundert Speisen
      Bestehend, oder Nachrichten von allem ersinnlichen
      Koch und Backwerk in Zwei Theilen (Tübingen, 1769).
      b) Caroline Elenore Grebnitz, Die Besorgte Hausfrau
      in der Küche, Vorrathskammer und dem Küchengarten
      (Reutlingen: J. J. Macken'schen, 1831). On the
      flyleaf of this cookbook is written the recipe for an
      interesting layer-torte: "1 cup of sugar, a good
      tablespoon of butter and an egg are thoroughly
      mixed. Add a cup of sweet milk. To this add
      1-1/2 cups of flour and two teaspoons of baking
      powder. Bake in three flat pans. When cool,
      spread two of them with either apple, quince or
      currant jelly. Place on top of each other. On the
      third sprinkle sugar. "

41.   Joshua Nachtrieb vs Romelius L. Baker, et al.,

Circuit Court of the United States, Western District
of Pennsylvania, Pittsburgh, 1849, p. 58.

42. Ibid., p. 53.

43. Ibid.

44. William Hebert, America, p. 330.

45. Elias Pym Fordham, Territory, p. 208.

46. Daniel B. Reibel, "A Guide to Old Economy" (Ambridge:
Pennsylvania, 1968), p. 9. (Mimeographed.)

47. Letter, Romelius L. Baker to Frederick Rapp, Sept.
26, 1821, Old Economy, Archives, Box 3.

48. Henry R. Schoolcraft, Travels in the Central Portion
of the Mississippi Valley Comprising Observations on
its Mineral, Geography, Internal Resources and
Aboriginal Population, Performed Under Sanction of
Government, in the Year 1821 (New York, 1825), p.
171.

49. William Faux, States, p. 266.

50. James Silk Buckingham, The Eastern and Western
States of America, II (London, 1842), p. 218.

51. Richard Flower, Ruben Gold Thwaite's, Early Western
Travels, 1748-1846, X, (New York: Ams Press,
Inc., 1966), p. 99.

52. Letter, J. C. Reynolds to Romelius Baker, April 2,
1836, Old Economy, Archives, Box 42.

Chapter X

ACTIVITIES

A. Work

The Harmonists were founded on a religious life, but
it did not call for a life of meditation. It is thought that
Father Rapp himself expressed the need for work in the unsigned Thoughts on the Destiny of Man:

> The heavenly Kingdom admits of no idle time.
> Let it not be thought that men were simply cre-
> ated for mere contemplating, admiring, rejoicing,
> and enjoying. How could that be without objects?
> Man is man and will continue to live as such even
> after death, only in a more refined and perfect
> state, of which he is susceptible.
>
> His melioration consists of progressive activity in
> a direct course towards the perfecting of all the
> faculties of his nature, to become a united member
> of the whole, and a great, coherent, symphonious,
> intimately connected part of a universum: conse-
> quently a being of everlasting persevering and in-
> creasing activity in the human sphere, pressing
> forward upon an always enlarging scale, towards
> substantiality and efficaciousness, wherein he
> lives and moves without restriction.
>
> This is the eternal life destined for mankind, the
> truely [sic] good and beautiful, for which the founda-
> tion is laied [sic] here by good men.[1]

And so the Harmonists worked and hoped. They worked
not as slaves, as some of the recorders would have us believe, but as the methodical, persevering Germans they were.[2]
William Faux said, "they worked very gently, but constantly."[3] As a matter of fact, considering the day and age, they
had excellent hours. Buckingham reports that the men worked
about ten hours a day; the women in the cotton factory, only

eight; and those in the dwellings even fewer hours. Everyone
had several leisure hours a day, and they retired at nine.[4]
While working in the fields they would have rest periods for
their Vesperbrot, and would even sing after eating as they
had sung going out to the fields and would sing coming back.
Much has been made of a megaphone Father Rapp supposedly
used at both Harmonies to admonish the men at work.[5]
Actually, considering their work-hours, Vesperbröte, and
affinity to singing, Father Rapp, if he used the megaphone
to admonish, probably had to, to get any work done. That
Father Rapp was concerned for his workers is rather clear
in the following letter written to Gertrude in 1824 when the
third move was in progress:

> I can hear you chattering, singing and laughing ...
> our girls have too much to do, for 20 women are
> too few for 70 men. They can do nothing aside
> from their housework. By the time they are
> finished with the washing, mending and cooking the
> week has passed especially since the people tear
> so much of their clothing. But they get plenty of
> practice. The younger ones can cook for 14-15
> people just as readily as the older ones. It is as
> nothing for them. The same can be said of other
> household activities. And I have not heard a word
> of discontent--everyone is peaceful, willing and
> obedient. I bought three dozen chickens for them,
> and the young girls have to gather the eggs every
> day far and near because the chickens are not as
> yet fenced in and the chicken houses are just built
> on to the gable of the house.
>
> We have been living in the village the past five
> days. Rosina and Regina are well and they have a
> beautiful house, yard and quite a large garden
> which they have fenced in. The garden is plowed
> but not a blade of grass is to be seen. Yesterday
> the girls and I laid out the garden and planted
> lettuce around the fence. Now, my dear child, the
> foundation of your training on which you now stand
> is about to develop that the light and truth will
> show you your own conviction. [For the next 12
> lines 2 to 3 words are missing at the end--it has
> been ripped off and therefore difficult to establish
> the thought of the long involved sentence. But the
> gist of it is: "You have many talents which will
> let you make many discoveries; choose a system of

perseverance that truth, goodness and beauty are
united and do not give up the belief of the love and
hope in the Lord Jesus--strength in harmonious
behavior; perfection in symmetry, and . ?. which is
so becoming to woman and makes you beloved by
God and man and a God's peace will be your reward here and beyond"] ... and so with these wishes
I greet you heartily, also all those of our house;
say hello to Frederick for me. Farewell
                                       (signed) Ge: Rapp

The girls say hello to you, and would like to hear
from you.

[It should be added that Gertrude at this time was
17 years old.]6

Years later, in the 1880's, when John S. Duss was
working for himself out in Nebraska he was joined by his
mother and Gottfried Lauppe who were unhappy about the
modernism that was creeping into Economy. But Lauppe was
not happy in Nebraska either. Missing his Vesperbrot, he
complained that three meals a day were not enough. "And
look how they rush about," he would say. "This is no way
to work."7

So even though everyone at Economy had to work, it
was not unduly demanding. It certainly proves what organization and constancy can produce.

This organization carried over to the dogs. Melish
reports observing a dog turning a wheel for blowing the
bellows. 8 In Indiana, Schoolcraft saw several dogs working.
To supply the cattle with water and to save the labor of driv-
ing them to the river, which was near, deep wells had been
dug, stoned, covered, and furnished with pumps and pipes,
which conveyed the water to all parts of the yards. The
water which supplied the distillery was pumped by a large
dog running in a wheel, and one of the bellows in the blacksmith shop was run the same way. 9

Children did not escape either. MacDonald, who had
come with Owen when Harmony, Indiana was for sale, kept
a diary in which he has an excellent accounting of the planting of corn. He noted that planting corn in this way was a
pleasure.

> Four boys or lads carried poles with small flags
> which they placed four and 1/2 feet apart, then
> followed four ploughs forming furrows in the direc-
> tion of these marks. These furrows crossed other
> furrows which had been made the day before. Thus
> squares of 4-1/2 feet were formed by the crossing
> of the furrows. A female with a small basket on
> her arm, full of corn grains, walked along each
> furrow dropping 4 or 5 grains in a square at each
> crossing furrow. Behind her came another with a
> hoe to cover them over. Two girls went before
> with pumpkin seeds of which they dropped 2 or 3
> grains at every third crossing. Fred Rapp took off
> his coat and walked along with them, sometimes
> conversing--sometimes dropping corn. I took off
> my coat, got a basket and went in my own furrow.
> We sometimes worked fast and when a few fur-
> rows in advance assisted our neighbours. At four
> o'clock we sat down under a shady tree, had some
> bread, butter, cheese, apples and beer, and a
> song in chorus, and continued work till near sun
> set. This method makes the business of corn
> planting really a part of pleasure, and is a very
> expeditious process.[10]

Besides having "fun" with corn, small boys also had
"fun" with peach kernels. The Harmonists had been manufacturing oil from pumpkin seeds. Somehow or other they
discovered that they could get oil from "well dryed peach
kernels." An anonymous article found in the Old Economy
archives says that "upon the first trial they have pressed
out of seven pecks of such kernels five gallons [of] excellent
oil which is very little inferior to sweet oil."[11] It goes on
to say that small schoolboys do this to pass their time between school hours.

1. Individual tasks. --Writers are continually using
the misnomer, "peasant," when describing the Harmonists.
From the above it is evident that they were clever farmers.
The Harmonists were also gardeners, tanners, shoemakers,
butchers, bakers, distillers, brewers, smiths, coopers,
stocking weavers, tailors, seamstresses, carpenters, brick-
layers, stonecutters, wheelwrights, cloth weavers, cabinet
makers, "teachers," clerks and herdsmen. The herdsman
rode to the pastures in "Noah's Ark," a small house placed
on wheels and drawn by cattle. The Harmonists, also, always had a doctor.

Business became a very important part of their work,
so Frederick Rapp appointed a foreman in each department of
business who was responsible for its proper management and
for the distribution of goods to the members.[12] The Old
Economy Archives contains thousands of business letters concerning merino wool, woolen cloth, cotton cloth, satinette,
apple trees, hogs, whiskey, beer, wine, and silk.

There is no outline of the work followed by the "teachers," who, except for Johann Christoph Müller, Jacob Henrici,
and John Duss, probably had little or no training. However,
they were probably as well prepared as the average country
teacher of the period. Obviously, the students would have the
basic three "r's." Music was the one culture class. These
classes were taught in German, although English and even
French were taught to those who appeared more gifted.[13]
According to Elijah Lemmix's testimony, he (Elijah) was not
allowed to study English. Having asked Father Rapp for permission to start an evening English class, Rapp was to have
told Lemmix that he (Rapp) did not want his young people to
learn English, that "It [English] was enough for a business
man." In one way this was a means of group-control. On
the other hand, Rapp was following the only system of education he knew, the German. And he followed this rather
closely. At age fourteen the non-academic German student
was "apprenticed" to learn one of the crafts. The apprentice
continued his formal education in the Sonntags-schule, as
Lemmix testified he himself had done.[14]

There should be no question about the thorough training in the non-academic field. If the Harmonists did not have
the know-how for a craft, a master craftsman was hired to
teach them. They were proud of their craftsmanship, and
Economy work was highly prized. The following letter shows
what non-Harmonists thought of their training, work, and
products:

Honored friend Ludwig Pfeil,
I want to report that last Wednesday, Sept. 14th
a young man came here saying that he was from
Economy and that he had a machine to decorate
leather and was an artist in this field. He further
stated that he could work 150 to 200 pieces of
leather a day. We weren't too enthusiastic; then
he showed us a testimony signed by Baker. He said
he was 3 weeks with you and that he had received
$50.00 and several pieces of clothing. At first he

was all right, but we didn't like his work.   I think
we can do better with the patent knife.   Dear friend
let us know about this and him.
                                        John Breymaier[15]

   2.   Folk Medicine. --The Harmonists always had a
trained doctor; first Dr. Johann Christoph Müller, then
Dr. Conrad Feucht.   At Economy can be seen the doctor's
office and apothecary shop.   There are medical charts,
medicine cabinets and an examination table.   While these
men were as scientific as possible, it is likely that a large
number of folk medicines crept in.   From an 1814 manuscript
medicine notebook it is known that the Harmonists made broths
and teas of oats, barley, rye, bran, and digitalis.   They
made a syrup from rhubarb and a bitters from boneset.   The
latter they also sold, but it is not clear whether it was sold as
a tonic or purgative. [16]

   There was a tremendous interest in purgatives, as the
remedies below show.   Not only was the Harmonist doctor interested in the medications, but Frederick Rapp was, too.
A book covering the usages of bitters bears his name in his
handwriting. [17]   That interest in folk medicines continued after
Frederick's death can be seen in the library's editions of
homeopathic healing and folk-healing. [18]

   The following folk-healing methods are certain to have
been used in all three settlements.   They are found in a three
and three-fourth-inch by six-inch hand-sewn booklet. [19]

Colic

One takes a quarter of a pint of stomach tincture or
bitters, and a warm drink such as rye tea.   If it is
not better within a half hour, take two to four tablespoonful of oilmixture which is a reliable remedy
for it.   Following the oilmixture, one can also take
several teasponsful of cramp-drops.   Drink increasingly warmer tea.   Glycerine also aids the
curing of this.   As improvement occurs, give the
mixture slowly, and toward the last only 1 tablespoonful every three--four hours.   Take care not to
travel for several days.

Cough, Chestpains

If the coughing is accompanied with headache and
sleeplessness take a vomit-powder.

Six hours after the vomitting one can either drink
half of the chest drink (a fourth of the chest
powder with six cups of water cooked till reduced
to four cups) or one takes one teaspoonful of the
chest powder in a cup of barley broth every two--
three hours.   If constipation is present, take a
laxative.

Coughing is relieved through: (1) Dover's Powder,
which is especially good at night; (2) cramp-drops
--one to two teasponsful--in any kind of drink;
(3) digitalis powder--a quarter of the powder in tea
every two hours. 20   This powder helps not only the
coughing, but also the heart.

Light chest pains are relieved through sour drops--
China Powder.

Cramps, Spasms
Menstrual Cramps, Gout

People whose nerves are on edge and thereby are
delicate are inclined to have the following ailments:
plethora (of blood), worms, colds, constipations
and a variety of cramps.   The attacks of the
cramps are never as serious as they look and feel.
A slight muscle spasm is relieved with Dover's
Powder dissolved in tea.   Cramp-drops, Courtier-
drops, a warm drink of bitters, or of strong-
smelling herbs will also relieve a slight attack.
If, however, it is a severe knot, apply heat pads.
Wash and rub the part of the limb so affected.
Liniment may also be rubbed on.   It also is a good
idea to give an additional Dover's Powder.   If the
patient is constipated use glycerine and oilmixture--
two or more tablespoonsful--every half hour.   This
is not only for the cramp and constipation, but it
also cools, reduces the fever, and is a poison for
worms, and besides it is not in the least harmful.
One can take it any time.

If the cramp is too severe and won't relax, give
the patient half of a Datura Powder; a half hour
later the other half.   But one cannot give more
Dature Powder for another twenty-four or forty-
eight hour period.   It could otherwise have unpleasant results.

If the patient for some reason cannot take medicine, rub cramp salve on the chest, stomach, abdomen and backbone. Only use this, if it is absolutely necessary as it is expensive.

Diarrhoea, Stomach Ache

Diarrhoea usually results from an upset stomach. Taking a half teaspoonful of rhubarb syrup several times will stop it.

If it is more than an upset stomach rhubarb syrup will not be sufficient. Take a vomit-powder prepared with Ipecac. Hours after regurgitation one teaspoonful of laxative is taken. Later drink a cup of barley broth or soup so that the laxative will work gently. Sour drops also help the healing.

Earrache

I have often observed that the most effective way of relieving the terrible pains of earrache is to cause regurgitation either with vomit-powder or tartar powder. Place a poultice on the back of the neck, and insert cotton dipped in cotton oil into the ear. Blowing tobacco smoke into the ear will also relieve the pain.

Eye Infection

If the eyelids are red and the eyes full of matter, rub eye salve the size of a pea once or twice daily into the eyes. But if the white of the eye is red, place cloth dampened with eye-water on the eye. Wash the eye often--five to eight times a day--with cold water.

If a headache, fever, and sleeplessness accompanies the infection, cooling powder or tartar must be taken.

Erysipelas

Erysipelas is a painful redness which starts on the foot or anywhere around that area and spreads. Very little of the healthy flesh is touched. It eventually turns light or brownish-red. The heat

in this inflammation and pain are exceptionally
great. If you place fatty salves or poultices on
the infected spots, it becomes worse, turns to
festering, and may take months before it is healed.
However, when one takes dry sacks filled with roast-
ed bran or warm ashes and places it on the parts
as warm as the patient can stand it, it will disappear in three to five days.

Should fever, and a headache, and a loss of appe-
tite accompany the redness, as well as redness in
face and body, then the patient must regurgitate
several times and take fever-reducing powder and
a laxative.

Erysipelas usually stems from a gall infection,
therefore powders for regurgitation are useful.

Fever

Check first if a purgative is necessary. If so,
give it to the patient as directed. Then every
two--three hours give the patient one teaspoonful
cooling powder in a barley or oat drink. And six
to twelve fever drops.

If constipation is present, administer every two
hours one teaspoonful Glauber's salt [sulphate of
soda] or a laxative powder either with or without
the cooling powder. If fever is too high and the
pulse too fast give a cooling powder with digitalis.

The fever of children is broken only through
purgatives. Also cooling powders have much more
effect on children than adults.

Menstrual Flow

Every two hours take half of sugar of lead powder
[contains four grams of sugar of lead]. Stop taking
it as soon as the flow stops. There should be no
other medication at this time. If headaches and
heat flashes are persistent Lochian Powder may be
taken.

Pleuritis

Drink as much tea as you want made from digitalis
powder (half of the powder cooked with six cups of
water until four remain). If there is no relief,
place a poultice on the painful spot. If necessary,
give a purgative. Sour drops may also be taken.

If women complain about pains in their sides during
the menstrual period, none of this has to be taken.
They should drink tea made from herbs and take
Lochian Powder.

Regurgitation Remedies
When and Not to take them

The symptoms telling us when to take purgatives
are revolting--a feeling of fullness in the stomach,
a coated tongue, feverish eyes, and at awakening
a bitter taste in a phlem-filled mouth. When these
symptoms exist, a tartar is prescribed for regurgitation. One doesn't give the complete dosage
at once, and furthermore, all these individual
powders are for adults containing six to eight grams
of tartar. For a two-year-old child two grams
are sufficient.

Dissolve a powder in a cup of warm water. The
adult should drink half of it; the rest he should drink
in three sips with a half hour between each one.
Only drink it all if it is necessary. After each
vomitting drink a sip of warm water. This is the
best.*[sic] The patient should vomit four to six
times. Should cramps and diarrhoea be present
Ipecac is called for.

*Children get one to three teaspoons every quarter
of an hour until they have had relief.

Laxatives

These are used when constipation is present.
Should it be a constipation without heat-flashes,
fever, cramps and the like laxans may be used.
Take a teaspoonful in tea or any kind of broth
every two hours. When it takes hold, stop taking
the medicine. In case of diarrhoea one takes

several times a teaspoonful of rhubarb syrup.
Should fever and heat-flashes be present take cool-
ing-laxative drinks according to directions.

When one uses a purgative one must eat only light
snacks.   This may be done while taking the
medicine.

Glycerine helpful with colic is made the following
manner. Cook half of one of the Species with
three cups of water till reduced to two and a half
cups. Stir in some soap shavings; put through a
sieve, and when it is lukewarm apply the same.

Toothache

Place a piece of horseradish between the cheek
and the aching tooth; wash the temple veins with
cold water; rub yellow drops on the temple and on
crown of the head; drop several drops into the
ears. [21]   One takes Dover's Powder and one
smokes tobacco.

One takes toothache drops in the mouth and one
swallows it later, but one may not swallow more
than a tablespoonful.   Place tooth powder on the
painful tooth.

Urine Retention

Take every two hours sixty to eighty drops of
sweetened spirit of nitric acid in any kind of tea.

All sick cases were not taken care of at Economy.
Dr. Edward Acker of Monaca sent George Rapp a receipt
for $80.00 for treating the boarding Regina Smith in the
"Water Cure."[22]   And when there were critical illnesses
unsolicited cures were forthcoming. Such was the case
during George Rapp's last illness.   W. P. Baum sent the
following remedy for Father Rapp:

> Make a poltis of bread and milk; add to it one
> tablespoonful of ground allspice and one of clove;
> well mixed to be applied warm to the stomach.
> Great relief has been obtained by this applica-
> tion when other remedies have failed. [23]

And this remedy failed too, because Father Rapp left for
his heavenly peace the following week.

B. Play

As has been indicated throughout, the society was not
oriented toward play, but it has also been seen that they received an enormous amount of pleasure from music, flowers,
gardens, and their calendric feasts.   Also, for communal
interest Dr. Müller and Frederick Rapp had developed a museum.   Frederick procured from New York and Philadelphia
rare minerals, paintings, collections of birds, insects, and
shells. He also brought in Indian antiquities. A copy of
West's "Christ Healing the Sick" was a particular favorite
among visitors. [24] Another pleasure was the Deer Park and
the gold fish pond. [25]   Simple pleasures they were, but in the
days before mass media this was the nature of entertainment,
and even today people visit far and wide to see lovely gardens.
Noyes wrote that the Harmonist "museums and gardens were
the wonder and delight of the region around them. "[26]

Singing was most probably their greatest pleasure,
as Nordhoff discovered in his trip to Economy. A Mr.
Kappler, recounting the pleasures of the past, said, ". . . we
sang songs every day, and had music every evening. "[27]
The situation changed as the Society grew old, but it was in
the 1880's that, in order to keep the young people together,
"sing fests" were held. [28] Fun was not always found just in
singing. Miss Knoedler recounts that on one occasion one
of the girls threw her knotted handkerchief at the lad pump-
ing the organ. Instead of its mark, it hit the spittoon just
as Henrici turned around. "Ei, ei was war das?" asked
Father Henrici. And the quickwitted youngster replied,
"Some whitewash fell off the ceiling. " To which he replied,
"I will see that the ceiling is fixed. "[29]

Another anecdote involves an English teacher of the
1880's who was not of the Harmonist persuasion. She was
dressed in the height of fashion of the late 1880's. This
featured the bustle; hers, being an exaggerated one, served
as an excellent note-carrier as she walked up and down the
aisle. [30]

That this type of fun and games was not just a pastime
of the hireling children of the 1880's is attested to by a letter to

R. L. Baker in 1836. It appears that a letter to Frederick
Rapp was addressed to Zelienople. Obviously the writer did
not know that Frederick had died, nor where he had lived.
The postmaster could have forwarded the letter, but he wanted a reason to write to Baker, from whom he had been
estranged ever since his family left the Society. Among
other ways, he appealed to Baker with: "I cannot refrain
from reminding you that we were once [some thirty odd years
ago] schoolfellows, companions in mischief [my underlining]
and intimate, sincere friends."[31]

        According to Duss, who came to Economy in 1862,
children also played "Hide and Seek," and "Blackman" or
"What will you do?", abbreviated to "Warlyloo." He further
states that nutting in the fall, as all harvesting, was a gala
time. In winter there was sledding.[32]

        A rather surprising pastime described by Duss was
the fox-hunt of the winter. All male residents took part.
A line of men and boys extending a mile or more eastwardly
from the Ohio River along Sewickley Creek on the north,
would drive toward the center of the property where the
sharpshooters were stationed. However, individual hunting
was taboo.[33]

        When the children outgrew their childish pranks and
games they too turned to music and the gardens. And those
who wished to read found ample opportunity. While in
Harmony, Indiana, the Harmonists had a library of three
hundred and sixty books, subscribed to eleven newspapers
and sold in their store Plutarch's Lives, Pilgrim's Progress
and The Vicar of Wakefield.[34] For children they had a
number of copies of the Kinderspiegel, a collection of children's stories, songs, sayings, and the like. A number of
novels appealing to young ladies had "Elsie Dinsmore" over-
tones. Of course, almost everything, if not on the very
scholarly plane, was full of morality. At any rate, the
Harmonists took their library to Economy, where it grew.

        Gertrude Rapp (and likely, others) spent much time
with music, painting, embroidery, wax flowers, and the
making of silk purses. Gertrude exchanged many gifts with
the business people associated with the Harmonists. On one
occasion Mary Graff thanks her for silk stockings and men-
tions a purse Gertrude made.[35] Elizabeth Solms writes:
"I think your wax work very handsome and your fruit very
good. Our family are all in good health, and join in sending
their best to you all."[36]

Whether the Harmonist had prayed, worked or played, the day ended at nine with the night watchman calling out:

Again a day is passed and a step nearer our end, our time runs out and the joys of Heaven are our reward.

At twelve o'clock the watchman cried:

Harken unto me all ye people, twelve o'clock sounds from the steeple! Twelve gates has the city of God, Blessed is he who enters the fold, twelve strokes, all is well!

At three a.m. the cry was:

Again a day has come, our time runs away and the joys of Heaven are our reward. [37]

By the time Aaron Williams was in Economy, the watchman, as today in Old Economy, made his rounds in silence. [38] The old order was beginning to pass.

Notes

1. [George Rapp] Thoughts on the Destiny of Man (Harmony, Harmony Press, 1824), p. 17.

2. Henry Heald, A Western Tour (Wilmington: J. Wilson, Printer), pp. 12-15. [1819?].

3. William Faux, Memorable Days in America Being a Journal of a Tour to the United States (London: W. Simpkin and R. Marshall, 1823), p. 267.

4. James Silk Buckingham, The Eastern and Western States of America, II (London: Fisher, Son & Co., 1842), 218.

5. William E. Wilson, The Angel and the Serpent (Bloomington: University of Indiana Press, 1964), p. 56.

6. Letter, George Rapp to Gertrude Rapp, Jan. 22, 1824, Old Economy, Archives, Box 4.

7. John S. Duss, The Harmonists (Harrisburg: The Telegraph Press, 1943), p. 210.

8. John Melish, Travels in the United States of America
    in the Years 1806-1811; and Travels Through Vari-
    ous Parts of Great Britain, Ireland, and Upper
    Canada (Philadelphia: 1812), p. 5.

9. Henry R. Schoolcraft, Travels in the Central Portions
    of the Mississippi Valley. Comprising Observations
    on its Mineral, Geography, Internal Resources and
    Aboriginal Population, Performed under Sanction of
    Government, in the Year 1821 (New York: 1825), p.
    168.

10. Donald MacDonald, The Diaries of Donald MacDonald,
    1824-26 (Indianapolis: Indiana Historical Society
    Publication, 1942, Vol. 14, No. 2), pp. 228-231.

11. Anonymous Article, December 18 (Archives, Series 2:
    Old Economy, Ambridge, Pennsylvania).

12. Aaron Williams, The Harmony Society (Pittsburgh:
    W. S. Haven, 1866), p. 29.

13. Elijah Lemmix vs Romelius L. Baker, et al., Circuit
    Court of the United States, Western District of
    Pennsylvania, Pittsburgh, 1854, p. 79.

14. Ibid., p. 42.

15. Letter, John Breymaier to Lewis Pfeil, Sept. 17, 1842,
    Old Economy, Archives, Box 53.

16. A chemical analysis of the Boneset Bitters found in Old
    Economy has indicated 5% alcohol, 85% water. Mr.
    Philip Schreiner of Grove City College, Grove City,
    Pennsylvania, who is doing the analysis, has stated
    that it is exceedingly difficult to find the other ingredi-
    ents. At the moment he is testing a possible honey
    content and the amount of boneset. Duss said the
    bitters were a mixture of crab-apple cider, whiskey,
    sugar and boneset. [Duss, The Harmonist, p. 179.]

17. Johann Evangelish Wetzler, Ueber den Nutzen und
    Gebrauch des Pullnaer Bitterwassers (Augsburg, Jos.
    Wolff'sche Buchhandlung, 1828).

18. Johann Ludwig Haas, Repertorium für homoopathische
    Heilungen und Erfahrungen (Leipzig: Ludwig Schumann,
    1834).

Herrmann Boerhaave, Volks-Heillehre (Stuttgart:
I. Scheible's Buchhandlung, 1840).

19. Folk Medicine Recipe Book MS, 1814 (Old Economy,
Archives, Library).

20. Dover's Powder is a commercial product that was
much used by the Harmonists. It consists of 10%
Ipecac, 10% opium, and 80% lactose: found in
Merck's Manual (Rahway: Merck & Co. Inc., 1940),
p. 1365.

21. Ibid., p. 1374. "Yellow drops" was tantalizing. There
was no hint anywhere, but it may be Lanum anhydrous:
refined wool fat. Freed of water. --Yellowish,
tenacious, semi-solid fat; peculiar odor; consists of
cholesterin, and isocholesterin-esters of the higher
fatty acids. --Sol.: Benzene; chloroform; ether; car-
bon disulfide; acetone; benzin; sparingly cold, more
sol. in boil., alcohol. Uses--as of the preceding.

22. Receipt, E. Acker to G. Rapp, Oct. 27, 1845, Old
Economy, Archives, Box 57.

23. Letter, W. P. Baum to R. L. Baker, July 29, 1847,
Old Economy, Archives, Box 59.

24. Aaron Williams, Society, p. 67.

25. Ibid., p. 67.

26. John Humphrey Noyes, History of American Socialisms
(New York: Dover Publications, Inc., 1966), p. 32.

27. Charles Nordhoff, The Communistic Societies of the
United States (New York: Schocken Books, 1965), p.
77.

28. Christiana Knoedler, The Harmony Society (New York:
Vantage Press, Inc., 1954), p. 93.

29. Ibid., p. 93.

30. Ibid., p. 98.

31. Letter, H. Muntz to R. L. Baker, July 23, 1836, Old
Economy, Archives, Box 42.

32. John S. Duss, The Harmonists (Harrisburg: The Tele-
     graph Press, 1943), pp. 131-133.

33. Ibid., p. 127-128.

34. John A. Bole, The Harmony Society (Philadelphia:
     American Germanica Press, 1904), pp. 88-89.

35. Letter, Mary Graff to Gertrude Rapp, Sept. 11, 1830,
     Old Economy, Archives, Box 28.

36. Note, Elizabeth Solms to Gertrude Rapp, Oct. 15,
     1835, Old Economy, Archives, Box 41.

37. William Owen, Diary of William Owen from November
     10, 1824, to April 20, 1825, ed. Joel W. Hiatt
     (Indianapolis: Indiana Historical Society Publications,
     4, No. 1, 1906).

38. Williams, Society, p. 115.

Chapter XI

COMMUNITY RELATIONSHIPS

The Harmonists were in the world but not of it. Yet,
like everyone else, they soon learned that the world is a
necessary "evil." At least their leaders knew this to be true.
The following two rambling letters give a good idea of the
variety of schemes in which they were involved, including
getting articles for the museum discussed in Chapter X. A
postscript also bears out an earlier comment about their
feasts being moveable even though they had fixed dates.

A. Business

[note: no salutation; date at the end of the letter;
obviously written to F. R.]

The above writing no one but you can answer
therefore, we are sending you a copy for you to
decide if it must be taken care of right away.
Otherwise everything is much the same. Mr.
Ott wants to know if he should come now or wait
till you return from Philadelphia. I told him to
come right away because five machines are already set up and sometimes seem strange to our
people who would like to know if they are operating
them properly. Gann, Baker, & Adam Geier
handle them quite well, if they only didn't have to
stop so often, but they are hopeful for the coming
of Ott. Coal has not arrived.
How does it look in the world? Did you per-
chance meet wise and learned men who made lovely
plans for mankind's brotherhood? You will have
opportunity enough to observe and judge if they have
the happy thought of unity and peace among them
and how it is carried out--about which I am uncertain. Both of you also will find out that the spirit
of these times will become more stormy politically
as well as morally even though the world believes

that it soon will merrily be in a blooming valley
full of beautiful fruit. I hope that you have your
compass with you that you will always recognize
the cause and reason & secret through which the
visible and invisible are woven inextricably together, the cause of which is Jesus. Take courage
that the world will soon realize that the Christian
religion is a means for godly living and that the
nations will be bound by its strength.

If you could get the seed for the peach--apricot,
called apricot peach, get some. This fruit is
larger than the usual apricot; its meat is reddish.
Also ask about the common barberry bush; they
have pretty red berries with sour juice said to be
very useful.

According to Mr. Ritter's correspondence of
Saturday, February 4 you'll be getting a book list
from which you will want to order some. There
also will be some for the piano. I noticed lately
in the paper that Ritter still has some of our books.
If they are so unpopular, I think we should take
them back, if you agree. We are well; I know no
other news & Romelius's little family is well again
& are busily working & greet you. Greetings to
you. We hope you are well.

the 12 February 1826   Ge Rapp[1]
P.S. The Harmonifest will not be celebrated till
you return.

[Note: the above writing mentioned in the letter
refers to a Mt. Vernon business letter which was
written in English.]

                              Economy, Feb. 16, 1826
To Frederick:
Your letter from Baltimore arrived yesterday
to the satisfaction of all the family relative your
health and trip; I am only sorry that you had to go
by land to Phila. I want you to know that our cotton is soon depleted; we have only twelve bales
left. Yesterday as I watched all the machinery
going at top speed, I suddenly thought about the
cotton supply. After checking I found we had
13-1/2 bales. Every three days two or more are
used so I told Feucht to write to Nahwill to send
fifteen to twenty-four bales; also that he should
write to Hay to inquire if he has any on hand.

Otherwise we soon would have to stop and that
wouldn't suit me at all. Perhaps you also could
send a letter from Philadelphia since mail is so
irregular at times.
      You reported interesting things in your letter
about the Czar of the Russians. It seems everything has a plan & our anticipation and wishes will
be fulfilled one after another for the occurence
will produce many events in all walks of life o'er
the world; I just wonder and pray. No serious
illness here, but some still have a virus; yesterday George Dechler died from appendicitus,
probably because he was not taken care of in time.
      F. E. Sturm wrote a letter from Steubenville,
dictated on Feb. 13, about his Natural History Museum. He is offering it for $3,000. He says he
has 12 glass cases of ?   and butterflies & 8
glass cases of seashells from all over the world
& that if you will get them from Pittsburgh he
will give you the lot plus minerals for $3,000.
I can't do anything about it because I don't know
nor understand the value of the cases; perhaps the
value is much. I would have bought it had he
not added anything, but as is, I will write to him
that I can't do anything about it because you are in
Philadelphia & will not be home for 4 weeks, and
that you had made plans to see him, but events
prevented you from seeing him, and that if he cannot stay in the area, he should let you know when
you can meet. You can write him too; perhaps he'll
stay that long in Steubenville.
      You have a letter here from Louisville; I think
you can handle it best. Feucht will probably write
to you.
      The weather has been cold; today it is snowing
hard. Scheible is in a hurry with his coke; today
he had brought 8 wagonloads before I knew it.
Tomorrow I want to try it in the hearth to compare it to the Pittsburgh brand. This evening I
threw some into the stove and it burned well.
      The glass over the wax flowers is broken, so
it is necessary for you to bring another.
      We have tried a new muslin [the figures that
follow I do not understand.]
      We are well and greet everyone.
                                           Ge. Rapp[2]

Members had fewer contacts with the outside world, but it was impossible to be entirely aloof. With strangers they appeared to follow the old rule of speech being silver, but silence, golden. In their case it was a protection, a withdrawal into an inner circle. But work always brought them out again. Work they could not abolish, for Thoughts on the Destiny of Man had told them, "No sluggard can live in this amicable confederation, for permission is never given to anyone, to eat his bread in sinful indolence."[3] But even if their labors had not produced the surplus that brought business people, they themselves would have drawn curiosity seekers. Wrote Father Rapp as they were building Economy: "As soon as the streets are opened many people will come; some in distress, others for curiosity."[4] It probably was with this in mind that a hotel was always one of the first buildings to be built.[5]

The hotel service of the Harmonists was highly favored in the two Harmonies, and the future of the one in Economy promised to be no different, since it was a source of work and income. But William Hebert did not like to pay. He objected to having to pay since the Shakers, a communal group he compared to the Harmonists, entertained strangers gratis. He further found the Harmonists' "trading spirit" excessive and in conflict with their professed way of life. The Shakers on the other hand, he said, "were not merchants nor money changers."[6] The Shakers themselves must not have found the Harmonists' business ability unpleasant because they were interested in having a merger of the two groups. But the Harmonists were not interested. Shaker Elder Henry Clay Blinn tells why the Harmonists refused his proffered hand:

> Their reason for not uniting with the Shakers was that all the little places on the earth where, purity is the object, are like so many flowers, though of different hues, yet all are beautiful in the sight of the Heavenly Father. And that they were one of these flowers in the great boquet [sic]. If they moved from the place where they reside, they would lose their identity and be as lost from the boquet, and if this was made of all white, all yellow, all blue or any other color, it would not be so pretty as though it was varigated.[7]

The sharp business practices alluded to by William Hebert also touched Morris Birkbeck. Frederick Rapp cashed two drafts for him on foreign exchange for $2,150;

when the drafts were returned, he charged Birkbeck over
four hundred dollars, basing it on a bill which entitled him
to "20 per cent damages on the principal of the protested
bills beside the interest from the date the bills were made
until paid."[8] Some scholars find this sharp-dealing of
Frederick's very un-Christian, but for vindication Frederick
only has to turn to Luke 16:1-9 where the false steward was
being praised by the master for being clever. On the other
hand, Frederick was well aware of good business sense and
relationships. At one point he informed John D. Hay that
he had instructed R. L. Baker to lower the price of import-
ed goods:

> ... which will enable you to reward the hostilities
> practised by your antagonists, as respects the
> prices of our own manufacture. I am confident
> they are as low as can be obtained anywhere else
> and I am determined to continue in that course.
> I am perfectly willing that you should alter the
> sign over the store door and leave it entirely to
> your own and Mr. Caldwell's discretion, either
> to put my own name, or Economy, or only cash
> store in place of it, whichever you think most
> suitable or advisable. I am perfectly satisfied
> that the adjoining country stores, should be regu-
> larly supplied with our manufacture and am much
> obliged to you for the interest you entertain for
> our society in gaining these customers....[9]

And by May, 1830 Frederick Rapp noticed, when going over the accounts, that Hay had many chronic debtors.
He proposed enforcing payment, or getting as much as possible; and if the debts were lost, striking them off the
lists.[10] It would seem that by October, 1830 the situation
had not improved, as someone had wanted to buy the Society
property in Vincennes, as the following letter shows:

> October 8, 1830
> Mr. William Burtch--Vincennes
> Your letter dated the 26th has been duly re-
> ceived. In reply to the same I have to remark
> that as soon as I returned home I made enquiry
> of our Society respecting the sale of our property
> in Vincennes and find the majority of them opposed
> to a sale, since our old friend J D H would by that
> step be thrown out of a home and be deprived from
> making a living which we can't do with propriety
> at this time.   Frederick Rapp[11]

So everyone did not experience the sharp dealing Birkbeck had encountered.   But Birkbeck also saw the value of
the Harmonists.   He says:

> This colony is useful to the neighborhood--it fur-
> nishes from its store many articles of great value,
> not so well supplied elsewhere; and it is a market
> for all spare produce.   There are also valuable
> culinary plants and fruit trees for which the neigh-
> borhood is indebted to the Harmonites; and they set
> a good example of neatness and industry, but they
> are despised as ignorant; and men are not apt to
> imitate what they scorn.   Ignorant as the mass of
> Harmonites may be, when we contrast their neat-
> ness and order, with the slovenly habits of their
> neighbours, we see the good arising from mere as-
> sociation which advances these poor people a cen-
> tury, probably much more, on the social scale,
> beyond the solitary beings who build their huts in
> the wilderness. [12]

Ignorance is a relative thing.   Looking at the Harmonist villages and all that went with them, one has to
acknowledge that these people were not ignorant.   Even if
they were, they would have been a part of the crowd, for
the average frontiersman was neither a scholar nor a gentleman.

W. E. Wilson is convinced that George Rapp's every
move was governed by his determined hold on the Society.
He suggests that had slavery come into the Indiana section,
the Harmonists would have asked themselves, "Are we any
better than slaves?"[13]   Anyone who thinks this does not
recognize that some people have a desire for a secluded,
monastic-type religious life.   The Harmonists' communitarian living was the means to that end.   In the 19th century
there were many people searching for answers, and some
found them in religious communities.   These communities
had no trouble enforcing their own disciplines because America was a vast open land where they could settle unmolested.

It was hard for many to believe that such unity could
exist altruistically in a group.   Schoolcraft reported that
there were many "who believe that the cloak of religion has
been assumed only to conceal from their followers the sure
but cautious steps which they are making towards self-
aggrandizement. "[14]   Schoolcraft felt unable to give an opinion

on the matter, but he was impressed with the Society.[15]

William Cobbett, on a tour to see what the American farmer was doing, came upon the Harmonists and their success. He thought it a wonderful example of skill, industry and force. He even thought them ingenious, bold, crafty. However, he thought their effect on others would be nil. He says:

> But their example, I believe, will generally only tend to confirm this free people in their suspicion that labour is concomitant to slavery or ignorance. Instead of their improvements, and their success and prosperity altogether, producing admiration, if not envy, they have a social discipline, the thought of which reduces these feelings to ridicule and contempt: that is to say, with regard to the mass; with respect to their leaders one's feelings are apt to be stronger.[16]

Harriet Martineau, like many others who seemingly could not accept that there are people who prefer a monastic type of life, pondered the question of the "hold" Father Rapp had over his "subjects." Not understanding charisma, she finally decided vanity was the answer:

> At first I felt with regard to both them and the Shakers, a strong respect for the self-conquest which could enable them to endure the singularity --the one community of its non-intercourse with strangers; the other, of its dancing exhibitions; but I soon found that my respect was misplaced. One and all they glory in the singularity. They feel no awkwardness in it, from first to last. This vanity is the handle by which they are worked.[17]

Frederick Rapp naturally looked at the matter differently. Writing about the group's third move, he said: "... Harmony will keep on to be prosperous. Nothing can disturb our harmony. It will be a demonstration to other people, who do not believe it possible that one group of men can unite like ours, and be successful in their undertaking."[18]

This same brethren spirit is seen in the following Romelius Baker letter:

> Schreiber & I are well & we have arrived at our

new location on the Ohio between Pittsburgh and
Beaver. We have taken charge of various com-
missions from Frederick which will keep us busy
until the arrival of the first transport of our
brethren.

We have had to manage business transactions
of which I had no idea, when I departed from
you, but in reality it makes no difference, when
or how we serve our brethren except that outside
of our group one always has more responsibility
and one must exchange ones association from true
friends to either rough-necks or dandies. Such
extremes cause unpleasantness, but if properly
evaluated they are the motive powers making a
Christian disappointed with this world and con-
centrating his being to a power above him from
where help comes. This is also our fate.

If it should happen that we remain here--send
our beds & clothes;

The shepherd from Gronau is in Philadelphia,
but he will not come to us because after being
investigated he was found unfit.

Doerrer is willing to join us next fall & bring
his entire family and one of Christoph's daughters.

Baker[19]

B. Charity

Then as now there were many people who were disappointed with the world. They sought refuge in the Harmonist settlements where there would be no anxiety, where
there would be food, shelter and clothing. Buckingham saw
it this way:

The great charm about these labours of the Rap-
pists is, that no one appears to be over-worked
or under-fed; none are without abundance of
clean and comfortable apparel; there are in their
factories no children, whose strength is taxed
beyond its power to bear: there is no anxiety on
the mind of a single being, as to a stoppage of
the works, a loss of employment, a reduction of
wages, or any of those vicissitudes, which place
before many an English operative the choice between a prison, a poor-house, or emigration.
There is no drinking to intoxicate old or young,
and to produce the disease and misery which that

> engenders, no confined air and heated atmosphere
> to oppress respiration and vitiate the blood: no
> want of medical aid, rest, and recreation, if sick-
> ness should require absence from labour: and no
> fear of want resulting from loss of time. No
> political questions or party contests ever agitate
> their passions or inflame their ill-will. The
> day glides on tranquilly; and after light labour and
> sufficient food, mingled with the enjoyment of a
> cheerful walk in the open air or music practiced
> in concert, they retire early to rest. [20]

The archives are filled with requests for admissions.
There were requests from orphans, widows, deserted wives,
and entire immigrant families. Now and then human comedy
crept in. Such was the case with Johannes Killinger who,
describing the glories of Economy, wrote: "wo beinahe alle
weltliche Sorgen weg sind." Then, having thought better of
it, he crossed out the "beinahe." Apparently writing paper
was too scarce to merit another sheet, even though he had
made such a tactical error. [21]

At times Economy sounded as if it were a school for
correction. A Mary Ann May writes from Pittsburgh, "John
had improved so much that he must remain there"; and, "As
Anderson is rather headstrong, particularly about catching
snakes, I hope you will endeavor to frighten or persuade him
from such occupation of his time as being dangerous." [22]
This knowing how to handle children also appears in the following letter:

> July 30, 1830
> To George Rapp
> This morning Frederick Henderer was here and
> complained about his son, saying since the death
> of his wife he has had nothing but trouble with the
> boy. But I think he just doesn't know how to
> handle children; he is too permissive. Now he
> says he would like to apprentice the lad so that he
> could learn a trade. So I told him he should send
> the boy to Harmonie where he actually belonged
> and where he also could learn a trade and perhaps
> he [Henderer] would get $75 or $50 for having
> raised the boy. He said if he knew that he would
> get $50 he'd let the boy go right away, but if he
> wouldn't he'd apprentice him to a shop.
> I thought I'd write this to you because I know
> you are inclined to raise orphans and take a soul

from the world as well as helping an old widower
who with difficulty has to earn his daily bread.
        If you want to do something, let me know right
away as Henderer is leaving and will apprentice
the boy before he leaves or send the money to
Wm. Grand and he'll let the boy go right away.
At any rate let me know what you will do.
                        (signed) Yohannes Maier
                                (Confectioner)
                        Related to C. Feucht[23]

        And there was integration among the Harmonists.   In
the archives is a letter from a Kentucky gentleman asking
for the admission of a free Negro woman and four children. [24]

        The requests often show frustration, as the two fol-
lowing letters indicate.   That Frantz Weinberg wrote to
Bäumle (whose name was Bäumeler and who was at Zoar)
and sent the letter to Economy is a clue to his confused
mind. Block House and other immigrant experiences probably made him that way.   Berton E. Beck, in "Tales of the
Block House, " says that Block House as a place name never
appeared on any Pennsylvania map.   However, "in the early
part of the 19th century the present borough of Liberty,
Tioga County, and the surrounding countryside of Liberty
Valley within a radius of five miles, part of which is in
Lycoming County, was known as the Block House. "   It ac-
quired the name because the first house was made of round
logs, and to the German workmen any house made of logs
was known as a "Blockhaus. " It caught on, but in English
it was known as Block House.   To this area a considerable
number of German immigrants came.   Having been lured to
Pennsylvania by "newlanders" like Philip Anthonyson who
earned a commission for every passenger on board ship, they
searched for this promised better life.   But in Block House,
as elsewhere, money was scarce and the settled English
were not too happy with the German newcomers.   To avoid
English discrimination, the Germans often turned to established German communities whether they understood the German sect or not.   It was a matter of survival. [25]

                                        Blockhause
                                        August 5, 1827
Most honored Mr. Bäumle,
    My wife with four of our children is with a
group of immigrants awaiting to go to your settlement.   As soon as I sell my land here, I will
follow with my 2 boys, aged 16 & 20.

My wife and family will make themselves useful in your society. I know the weaver trade,
and my boys can work with the farmers.

You may wonder why we decided to come to
your settlement. Your reputation led to our decision.

Please receive my family with love and welcome since I agreed to let (my wife and four
children) go to you.

Sincerely,
Frantz Weinberg[26]

October 1, 1827

Honored Mr. Rapp!

My wife and I separated without forgiving each
other. I wanted to forgive her if she just
wouldn't be so rude and crude as she has been
since we are in America. And she shouldn't
always claim to be right. I have no peace of
mind at all because of this.

All the families from the Blockhaus who
moved to Harmonie must bear witness that she
often was rude to me as she herself has to admit
if she tells the truth. It is for her peace of
soul if she admits her wrong and forgives me.
It is a great fault of my wife to turn the children
away from me and tell unpleasant things about
me. Lies! She, who when I was ill and asked
if she would make noodles instead of the water
dumplings which I couldn't eat even when I was
well wouldn't be considerate. But I am not going
to bother you with the sordid details.

I beg you, Mr. Rapp, to touch her conscience;
to confront her with her guilt. When she ac-
knowledges her fault let her write me just a few
lines to that effect and I will forgive her everything. At the same time I ask that my children
realize their misdeeds.

Should my wife still be stubborn, I will cut
off all contact. This I will do unwillingly.

I am much distressed because of the children;
Mr. Rapp, please give them my blessing.

I am,
Frantz Weinberg[27]

From the very beginning there were those who found
after they joined the group that life based on Acts was not

for them.   And from the very beginning this caused much
grief in the Society.   The first letter below shows what
hardship withdrawal from the group meant in 1806.   The
second letter is a type of receipt letter signed by leaving
members.   The two that follow the receipt indicate that
each member did not receive the same amount on leaving.
Following are letters asking for re-admission and the Society's reply.

          (Parts of the original letter are missing be-
     cause they had been cut out.)
                    10 April 1806

     Greetings my dear, good friend,
          I can report to you that your friends arrived
     safely and all are in good health.   Harlebans
     brought me your well wishes and your admiration
     for our work, and I was amazed to get a loan
     from you to be used by the society without inter-
     est.   It came at a time when it was sorely need-
     ed since we had three antagonistic families leav-
     ing.   They had come a year ago--we did not want
     them, had mistrusted them.   However, at first
     they were all right, but then they wanted a com-
     fortable living and they were accustomed to meat
     which we could not give them because our begin-
     nings were difficult since we divide everything and
     it takes much money until the land is paid and all
     the foundations of husbandry are laid.   They had
     contributed $2000, but we could not pay them.
     We asked the Lord for help (an angel of the Lord
     must have stopped by your house telling you to
     help us).   Within five days a friend of whom we
     did not know arrived with his family and $700.
     So we were able to give them a third of their
     payment, with a promise of another third next
     year, and the final third the following year.   How
     things will be then we don't know yet, but God
     does.
          Did you have a feeling when we called upon the
     Lord when we found ourselves in need?   You may
     follow your conviction.
          Otherwise things go well for us.   Our mockers
     are driven from us for as the Apostle says: See
     to it that you are not maligned with evil talk.   We
     are one and possess a deep peace in our Harmonie
     which is unlike others of the religious bodies; we

have a special feeling which is not of this time,
but belongs to another period for which we are
designated. We must be true to our convictions
regardless of the raging of the devil and his parties. We will not give an inch. Away with the
skin and the chaff; let only the best remain.
Christ's church will be renewed and from the root
it will be reborn. You must not look upon us as
we are now, but how we will become. You know
what faith can do when one is in the state of
Grace. As it was with Solomon's Temple, according to Jesus, no stone shall remain even less
from Cabel's Temple. Everything, everything
must go from inside out that is personal wealth.
Christ had nothing. Just as he served his brothers,
and as poor as he was, so must Christ's Church
be. Only in the beginning of love burns a fire of
love which serves its brothers unselfishly. See,
so will be the coming of Christ. Most of the people with their tradition-bound Christianity cannot
see this; even anger themselves, but I tell you
sincerely and surely that everything will be new.
You will say, yes, that I believe, but not yet; it
is a long way off. Yes, when you will experience
this rebirth you will belong to all time and you
may share with Cabel [missing paragraph]
Make Christianity visible through brotherhood
so that none will have any personal desires for
they must build the Temple of Christ. Of this
Isaiah says your builders must hasten, and he
who would rush must make certain nothing binds
him, and yet he must be bound, and should someone make the running difficult consider how the
child of destruction rushes to welcome his purpose.
[Words missing in the next 8 lines--torn from
edge of paper.] Call upon God and you will come
out of your darkness through the Revelation of
St. John ... the kingdom of Jesus Christ will develop to the 7th number. Darkness will be overcome and freedom won according to the letters to
the Romans, Chapter 8, verses 19, 20, 21, 22. At
this time the obsolete Church will be united with
us and through the will of God a holiness will be
created. Now God bless all and cordial greetings
to you and our other friends.

(signed) Georg Rapp[28]

Visit us when you can.

August 10, 1840

George Rapp,
   I have a request of you.   I wish you would be
so good as to give me my bed.   Why?   Because
I badly need it, and you yourself said that you
would give it to me if I would get married.   I
just haven't asked for it before.   (You should
give it to me) after all I served my term with you
and you always gave something to those who left.
I only received the $2.00.   Therefore I would be
thankful if you would give me my bed or some
money.   Why?   I didn't have any parents who
could give me something.   I hope you'll answer
me.
   Send the letter to: Schilz Postoffice, Margareth
Ingrem.   You called me Gerone Lemox.   I wish
you would write my name in English.
                     Margareth Ingrem[29]

August 12, 1832

George & Frederick Rapp
   We received your letter of July 27 from which
we can see that it is as we had suspected--none
of you wants to know anything.   You say we also
were present when the records were destroyed.
Your falsification makes it appear that we willingly agreed to it.   You write that you will not agree
with our ideas.   And we won't with yours; we will
not sign that receipt for $100.   Ask your con-
science if you don't owe us more.   Scriptures say
a man is worth his work.   You are not acting according to the teachings of Christ--love your neighbor as yourself.   You are acting according to your
own rules which are not God's commandments, but
those of man which will not hold before God.   If
we aren't worth more than $100 for all the time
we were with you then we must take the next step.
Our share is still with you; the receipt which your
agent Mr. Solms sent us clearly proves it.   Now
think about it--consider being just with us.   Send
an answer through the carrier of this letter.   Farewell.
                     (signed) Conrad Thorwarth[30]

   Today the 7th of January 1842 we the undersigned have withdrawn willingly from the Harmony

Society and have ceased to be members from the
same. Further, according to the society contract
we received $150.00 as a gift from Georg Rapp.
This takes care of any obligations he or any member of the society has for the undersigned.

Anton Kast
Theana Bohringer

[The following note is on the bottom of the letter.
March 23, 1843--they returned with $125. They
are staying where they had been.[31]]

November 16, 1844

Worthy father and friends:
I gather you did not receive my first letter. I
hope that this letter finds you and the entire society well. Since I left you I had a serious mis-
fortune for August became ill with a billious
fever, then another fever from which he suffered
nine days and died thereof on the 5th of October
at 10 o'clock at night. Now I am alone & know
no one except the family of Ekert, a master baker
for whom August had worked 12 years ago.
August on his death-bed asked this man to take
care of me until I again received permission to
return to the society. They all agreed to this.
Therefore, I long to return to you, as also August
wished it. On his death-bed with tears stream-
ing down his face August said, 'Oh, what have we
done! We were wrong. We trampled our good
fortune.'
So, I plead with you. Be good and allow me
to return. I have enough money to make the trip.

Greetings to all,
especially my father,
Maria Lemox[32]

I await a favorable reply.

10/14/1844

Mrs. Maria Weber (née Lemox)
Cincinnati, Ohio
Your letter to the leader of the society, (as
well as the enclosed letter from Mr. Ekert) and
to your and your husband's brother were received
and read before the entire society. The undersigned were requested by the entire society to

answer you in the following manner:
Your and your husband's brother do not want
the burial site of the dead man moved. They are
sorry that your wedded bliss was of so short a
duration, but it is duty to live with fate. The
community is in one voice in advising you against
re-entry into the society and under no circumstances will they grant it for we know you better
than you know yourself and know for certain that
you are less fit for our society than you are for
the place where you now are. Further, since you
withdrew the unbreakable rule that no one leaving
may return has been established. Therefore be
sensible and do not undertake a difficult and expensive journey to make something impossible possible. Instead, pull yourself together, take courage and make your present place your home. You
are clever and know how to make yourself attractive to all. Therefore behave properly and ap-
preciatively toward the people who in friendship took
you in. In time with their help you will find se-
curity, a home and family.
Your brother & your deceased husband's relatives
are well. They greet you and hope you will follow
our advice.

The whole society
Georg Rapp
Jacob Henrici
Conrad Feucht
John Schreiber
Christoph Weiber

We don't understand why you didn't get our reply
to your first letter. Here is a copy which also
answers your second letter. [33]

Withdrawals hit the peak during the Leon affair discussed in Chapter XII. People still asked to be admitted,
but the Society no longer was in the mood to take people in
need only to find that they were basically malcontents. In
1835, when George Rapp refused admission to A. F. Macklot
of Cincinnati, he told him that the Society had taken no new
members since 1832. [34] They kept to this rule. In 1844,
when Lorenz Schelling from Canton St. Gallen, Switzerland
wanted to become a member, he received the following polite
reply from the Society:

December 3, 1844

In answer to your worthy writing of last month I must tell you that we cannot grant your friendly request because some years ago a firm rule was set not to accept new members. [35]

All who wanted to come did not want membership. For instance, Thomas Foster asked to work for the society for a year and offered to teach them "... every art science and mystery of which I am in possession, relative to the different branches of manufacturing wool into cloth."[36] And John Schnee wanted to bring "a hatter, a tailor, and a blacksmith with their families."[37] As mentioned above, it was a haven for widows and deserted wives. A Catherine Rapp (no relative) asked for employment to teach school and do needle work to support herself and her two children.[38]

When Henrici sent Charles Nordhoff to the Economy Hotel, he did not tell him that he would have to eat punctually; but Nordhoff had to, and did, not knowing why. Later, when in his own room, he became curious as to the frequency of the ringing of the bell. Going downstairs, he found this surprising picture:

> I discovered there an extraordinary collection of persons ranged around the fire, and toasting their more or less dilapidated boots. These were men in all degrees of raggedness; men with one eye, or lame, or crippled-tramps, in fact, beggars for supper and a night's lodging. They sat there to the number of twenty, half naked many of them, and not a bit ashamed; with carpetbags or without; but all hungry, as I presently saw, when a table was drawn out, about which they gathered, giving their names to be taken down on a register, while to them came a Harmonist brother with a huge tray full of tins filled with coffee, and another with a still bigger tray of bread.

> Thereupon these wanderers fell to, and having eaten as much bread and coffee as they could hold they were consigned to a house a few doors away.[39]

Nordhoff found that the Society fed daily from fifteen to twenty-five tramps. The house set aside for them had accommodations for twenty men. In the morning they were to wash at the stable before a breakfast of meat, bread, and

coffee. The very needy also received some clothing. No
questions were asked, but they would not accept a regular
beggar. When Nordhoff asked if they were not imposed upon,
the answer was, "Yes, probably; but it is better to give to a
dozen worthless ones than to refuse one deserving man the
cup and loaf which we give."[40]

Those who asked for money were many and varied and
unexpected. For example, the Pittsburgh African Methodist
Episcopal Church asked for help in paying off indebtedness
incurred because of a church addition. [41] And Müllers from
Ohio wanted to buy land, but having no money, sent their
daughter to Economy to collect the expected amount. [42] From
a Norwegian settlement in New York came a cry for money
to help them get started. [43] And "Ora Labora," a sister-set-
tlement in Michigan, needed aid after a disastrous fire. [44]

But all correspondents were not in need. Harlow
Heard, planning to establish himself in the practice of medicine, asked if they raised Colchicum Autumnale (meadow
saffron). He says, "I understand you cultivate some or many
of the vegetable medicines, indigenous to this country, and I
should like to make an arrangement to purchase of you, if
you have them for sale."[45] Apparently, their folk medicines
discussed in Chapter X were well known.

Another of their products that was well known was
beer, which was sold far and wide. In connection with this
is an interesting letter from the West Liberty Temperance
Society. It certainly indicates that temperance means just
that, and not abstinence:

> We would like to purchase a few barrels of beer
> because some members of the society want to avoid
> giving whiskey to their hands. The beer made at
> Wheeling won't keep over the summer and ale and
> ports are too expensive. The Wheeling price is
> $3.50. What's yours plus transportation? ... Peo-
> ple are getting out of the habit of drinking whiskey
> and it would be a blessing if it were done away with
> altogether. [46]

Their silk also was well known and highly praised. It
increased the fame of Gertrude Rapp (whose hobby it was)
and that of the Society. In fact, a committee on exhibitions
for the Franklin Institute of Philadelphia wanted samples of
their silk. [47] And Governor Joseph Ritner was very much

impressed with the manufactured silk and the coat made for him, saying: "I may compare it with the German character which never gives more promise than can be fulfilled and which always is durable. "[48]

C. Politics

The manufacture of silk also brushed them with political maneuverings. They were interested in the legislature encouraging the culture of silk. In a letter written by Romelius Baker for George Rapp (who never learned English) they stated their reason for a high tariff.

> A German prince used to say: 'I live by my people, therefore, I must protect their industry against foreign competition.' We lament to see in many of our fellow citizens a very acute sense of artificial honour. Why are we not equally honorable to aid in placing our whole compact upon a true basis of honor, liberty, independence and self protection against a foreign competition who draws the life blood out of us by our own folly--self protection then is the grand principle of the American people individually and rationally. On that ground then, we unhesitatingly recommend a tariff. [49]

Actually, they were not political activists nor did they serve in the army. However, at that time one had a choice of paying a fine or serving in the armed services. And the Harmonists did pay the fines. [50] During the Civil War they contributed liberally:

> ... for the equipment of volunteers, for special bounties, for the support of the families of absent soldiers, and for the Christian, Sanitary and Subsistence Commissions, for the fortification of Pittsburgh, for the relief of the freedmen, for the support of soldier's widows, and the education of their orphan children. [51]

While in Indiana, Frederick Rapp was a delegate to the state convention in 1816 when Indiana was made a state. Four years later, Frederick was one of eight commissioners appointed by the legislature to choose a site for the capital. William Wilson, who has studied the Indiana political situation of that time, concludes that Rapp was not much moved by principle in public affairs, but had a strong sense of

expediency and much common sense.[52]   This no doubt helped
when Frederick Rapp was appointed superintendent of School
Section for Lynn Township in March, 1817.[53]   After Frederick
Rapp's death, any political activity fell on Romelius Baker.
So, during the Jackson campaign, Baker received a circular
with a long list of grievances against President Andrew Jackson.   In closing it read:

> The undersigned composing the Committee of Cor-
> respondence of the Whig Party of Beaver County
> for the present year, have taken the liberty of
> naming you as one of the Committee of Vigilance for
> your township, believing you to be a Whig in your
> principles.   They hope you will be vigilant and active
> until, and, at the election, doing all that lies in
> your power to preserve, protect and defend the lib-
> erties and best interests of the country.[54]

What Baker really thought of the ever-chaotic political
situation is neatly summed up in a business letter to Henrici:
"Das verwirrte Babel eilt stark an ihr Ende."[55]   Later there
were political-hysteria threats of burning Economy because
the Harmonists were Whigs.   But James Cameron of Pittsburgh suggested there was no real danger even if they were
Whigs, and that they should exercise their elective franchise
because they were under protection the same as anyone
else.[56]

D. Neighbors

In the midst of all this there came occasional letters
from religious enthusiasts who wanted to change Economy.
One such letter came from Andreas Bernardus Smolnikar who,
from 1838 to 1868, walked over Pennsylvania and adjoining
states preaching world federalism and ecumenicity.   Alfred
L. Shoemaker, who made a study of him, said that Smolnikar knew "every single crackpot of prominence," but no
one paid any attention to him.   It moved Smolnikar to write,
"I met everywhere with apathy and obduracy and all kinds of
abuse."[57]

5/9/1842
Worthy Father!
    I feel free to send you the 15 numbers of the
Message of Peace to all Nations. Father, you
should have read the three books I left when I was
at Economy in 1840 so that you would have learned

how Christ will appear. Actually at that time it
was too soon to say much for many things had to be
discovered and had to develop, and the hand of
Satan had to be seen. All of this is now evident for
the unbelievers, the believers, and those believers
who only hurt the cause of God. When I wrote to
you from Pittsburgh and explained the way of the
Lord to you, I received an answer from your group
which was evidence of the most terrible darkness.
I then mentioned your Economy so much in my
book One Thing is Necessary [Eines ist Noth] that I
thought as soon as you read it you would work with
me. Of course, I had no desire to send you the
book; you yourself should have concerned yourself
for the Lord. However, I have not been made aware
of the fact that you have done this. Dear Father,
at least take these 15 numbers of the Message of
Peace as a special sign of the appearance of our
Lord. You will find therein unexpected wonders
and signs of the resurrection of the dead and the
seeing of the blind through the magnificence of the
Lord who now reveals Himself in peace to all nations. You will also see how the people will not
listen to Christ's signs shown through me his
prophet. Neither have you because you haven't
taken the time to search for truth, but because of
this the Lord has given me time to make things
even clearer, and if you, dear Father, would
thoroughly study my three books you would see
that the Lord according to Scriptures, like a thief
in the night, appeared in 1836 and that 1842 is
also going to be a miracle year after which the
appearance of our Lord is to be spread over all nations. I hope that you as a protagonist for the millenium will soon send me a large sum of money to
carry on the work of the Lord. Let me know how
many books you need so that the great movement
can be carried on through you. I also hope that the
Emperor of Austria & the King of Württemberg &
other great ones will help spread the movement in
Europe. I hope, dear Father, to see you soon in
the peaceful millenium and be able to call all your
children of Economy my true brothers.
　　　Yours in Christ, Andreas Bernard Smolnikar[58]

　　　"The madding crowd" came closer, for here was a
folk whose "Divine Economy" did not always produce Harmony
for the outside world, because the outside world of western

Pennsylvania and Indiana was an alien world to the Harmonists'
communal religious concepts, culture, and nationality. But
as they moved from a settlement their worth was recognized.
MacDonald records in his diary Robert Owen's emotional reaction as the Harmonists were about to sail from Harmony.
He writes that Owen said he had never met with a people so
honest and affectionate. He also recounted their virtues of
justice and kindness. [59] Probably a more sincere statement
came from John D. Hay, with whom the Harmonists did much
business:

> ... they have my sincere esteem and best wishes.
> I feel under great obligation to them and would
> have been glad to have seen them before their de-
> parture. I am happy to hear that Rapp will soon
> return and that he intends to continue this establish-
> ment which I think will be increasing in importance.
> The people here (with a few exceptions) regret the
> removal of your society and begin to estimate your
> value in the state and community. [60]

But by the following year a great number of the people
in Posey County showed their envy. Frederick Rapp, in a
letter to Mr. Hay, indicates that this unpleasantness in their
neighbors was one of the reasons they left Indiana:

> ... I have never had a better opinion of the people
> of Posey County, and it was in a great measure
> the case that we left the country, although they have
> not the least cause according to our own conscience
> as we have never injured the community at large
> nor any individual person, but have rather benefited
> them, which every honest and good man must af-
> firm--they have never been very favourable to us,
> while we lived there, much less must they be since
> we left there.... [61]

As far as the Harmonists were concerned, those who
did not regret their leaving, or those who would be their
tormentors, were simply a manifestation of the beast of
Revelation, a trial they had to endure. In spite of the
"beast" they left their mark wherever they went, and even
where they did not go. For example, in 1914 Mrs. Rosa-
mond Dale Owen Templeton wrote from Mt. Carmel in the
Holy Land: There is a link between my native town of New
Harmony and my present abode. The upper story of the
hospital here is built with money sent from New Harmony by

George Rapp and his name is inscribed on the wall."[62] And at the Scalamandre Museum of Textiles in New York City are samples of their fine silk, for which Gertrude Rapp in 1838 received a gold medal from the Franklin Institute of Philadelphia; and two others in 1844 from the Boston Fair and American Institute in New York, respectively. (See Appendix for their silk designs.)

Buildings they built are still being used as dwellings in all three settlements. What is more, as Father Rapp predicted, many people are still coming to see the Harmonist way of life, but no longer "in distress"; curiosity perhaps. But not curiosity tinged with malice. It really is a human interest in unusual sects that left their mark on the American scene, and now serve as inspiration to the modern "dragon" fighters.

Notes

1. Letter, George Rapp to Frederick Rapp, Feb. 12, 1826, Old Economy, Archives, Box 6.

2. Letter, George Rapp to Frederick Rapp, Feb. 16, 1826, Old Economy, Archives, Box 6.

3. [George Rapp] Thoughts on the Destiny of Man (Harmony: Harmonist Press, 1824), p. 34.

4. Letter, George Rapp to Frederick Rapp, Oct. 12, 1824, Old Economy, Archives, Box 4.

5. Ibid., Box 4.

6. William Hebert, A Visit to the Colony of Harmony in Indiana, in the United States of America (London: George Mann, 1825), p. 337.

7. Shaker Elder Henry Clay Blinn Mss Journal, Shaker Museum, Old Chatham, N. Y., "Journey to Mt. Lebanon (Ky.) in a Carriage in 1853."

8. William E. Wilson, The Angel and the Serpent (Bloomington: University of Indiana Press, 1964), p. 67.

9. Letter, Frederick Rapp to John D. Hay, Nov. 7, 1826, Old Economy, Archives, Letterbook 1825-1828.

10. Letter, Frederick Rapp to John Hay, May 21, 1830, Old
     Economy, Archives, Letterbook 1828-1830.

11. Letter, Frederick Rapp to William Burtch, Oct. 8,
     1830, Old Economy, Archives, Letterbook 1828-
     1830.

12. Morris Birkbeck, Notes on a Journey in America,
     from the Coast of Virginia to the Territory of
     Illinois (London: Ridgway and sons, 1818), pp. 130-
     131.

13. Wilson, Serpent, p. 66.

14. Henry R. Schoolcraft, Travels in the Central Portions
     of the Mississippi Valley. Comprising Observations
     on its Mineral, Geography, Internal Resources and
     Aboriginal Population, Performed under Sanction of
     Government in the Year 1821 (New York: Collins and
     Hannay, 1825), p. 166.

15. Ibid., p. 166.

16. William Cobbett, A Year's Residence in the United
     States of America (London: Sherwood, 1818), p.
     291.

17. Harriet Martineau, Society in America, II (London:
     Saunders and Otley, 1837), p. 64.

18. Letter, Frederick Rapp to J. Solms, May 11, 1824,
     Old Economy, Archives, Box 4.

19. Letter, R. L. Baker to John Baker, May 12, 1824,
     Old Economy, Archives, Box 4.

20. James Silk Buckingham, The Eastern and Western
     States of America, II (London: Fisher, Son & Co.,
     1842), pp. 233-234.

21. Letter, Johannes Killinger to George Rapp, May 14,
     1827, Old Economy, Archives, Box 18.

22. Letter, Mary Ann May to R. L. Baker, July 1, 1833,
     Old Economy, Archives, Box 36.

23. Letter, Johann Maier to George Rapp, July 30, 1830,
     Old Economy, Archives, Box 28.

24. Letter, Wm. Chambers to George Rapp, Jan. 15, 1816, Old Economy, Archives, Box 2.

25. Berton E. Beck, "Tales of the Block House," Pennsylvania Folklife, XV: 2, Winter 1965-1966, pp. 20-21.

26. Letter, Frantz Weinberg to Joseph Bäumle, Aug. 5, 1827, Old Economy, Archives, Box 7.

27. Letter, Frantz Weinberg to George Rapp, Oct. 1, 1827, Old Economy, Archives, Box 7.

28. Letter, Georg Rapp to Jacob Neff, April 10, 1806, Old Economy, Archives, Series 2.

29. Letter, Margareth Ingrem to George Rapp, Aug. 10, 1840, Old Economy, Archives, Box 50.

30. Letter, Conrad Thorwarth to George Rapp, Aug. 12, 1832, Old Economy, Archives, Box 33.

31. Receipt, Anton Kast to the Harmony Society, Jan. 7, 1842, Old Economy, Archives, Box 52.

32. Letter, Maria Lemox to George Rapp, Nov. 16, 1844, Old Economy, Archives, Box 55.

33. Letter, George Rapp et al to Maria Weber, Oct. 14, 1844, Old Economy, Archives, Box 56.

34. Karl J. R. Arndt, George Rapp's Harmony Society (Philadelphia: University of Pennsylvania Press, 1965), p. 546.

35. Letter, Harmonists to Lorenz Schelling, Nov. 21, 1844, Old Economy, Archives, Box 56.

36. Letter, Thomas Foster to Frederick Rapp, Aug. 28, 1829, Old Economy, Archives, Box 25.

37. Letter, John Schnee to Frederick Rapp, Oct. 27, 1819, Old Economy, Archives, Series 2.

38. Letter, Catherine Rapp to George Rapp, April 24, 1824, Old Economy, Archives, Box 4.

39. Charles Nordhoff, The Communistic Societies of the
    United States (New York: Schocken Books, 1965), p.
    66.

40. Ibid., p. 67.

41. Letter, Z. W. Vashon to George Rapp, June 28, 1839,
    Old Economy, Archives, Box 46.

42. Letter, Michael Müller to George Rapp, June 18,
    1843, Old Economy, Archives, Box 54.

43. Letter, Frederick Rapp to Clang, Peerson & Co.
    July 10, 1826, Old Economy Archives, Letterbook
    1828-1830.

44. Ora Labora Article, n.d., Old Economy, Curator's
    File.

45. Letter, Harlow Heard to Frederick Rapp, Nov. 23,
    1833, Old Economy, Archives, Box 36.

46. Letter, Temperance Society to Frederick Rapp,
    June 16, 1829, Old Economy, Archives, Box 25.

47. Letter, C. A. Walburn to R. L. Baker, Sept. 15,
    1843, Old Economy, Archives, Box 55.

48. Letter, Gov. Joseph Ritner to George Rapp, April
    16, 1838, Old Economy, Archives, Box 45.

49. Letter, George Rapp to Thomas Henry, Jan. 24,
    1842, Old Economy, Archives, Box 52.

50. Receipt, Inspector Adams to the Harmonists, n.d.,
    Old Economy, Archives, Box 54.

51. William A. Hinds, American Communities (New York:
    Corinth Books, 1961), p. 21.

52. Wilson, Serpent, p. 65.

53. History of Posey County, Indiana, Illustrated (Chicago:
    The Goodspeed Publishing Co., 1886), p. 304.

54. Circular, Whig Committee to R. L. Baker, Oct. 1,
    1834, Old Economy, Archives, Box 38.

55. Letter, R. L. Baker to Jacob Henrici, Jan. 1, 1842, Old Economy, Archives, Box 52.

56. Letter, James Cameron to R. L. Baker, Oct. 24, 1844, Old Economy, Archives, Box 56.

57. Alfred L. Shoemaker, "Andreas Bernardus Smolnikar God's Ambassador Extraordinary," The Pennsylvania Dutchman, March 15, 1952, p. 1.

58. Letter, Andreas Smolnikar to George Rapp, May 9, 1842, Old Economy, Archives, Box 53.

59. Donald MacDonald, The Diaries of Donald MacDonald, 1824-1826 (Indianapolis: Indiana Historical Society Publications, 14, No. 2, 1942), p. 293.

60. Letter, J. D. Hay to J. L. Baker, June 1, 1824, Old Economy, Archives, Box 4.

61. Letter, Frederick Rapp to John Hay, Nov. 10, 1825, Old Economy, Archives, Letterbook 1825-1828.

62. Letter, R. D. O. Templeton to the Editors, June 9, 1914, Evansville (Indiana), The Evansville Courier.

Chapter XII

THE END OF THE SOCIETY

The Harmonists were one unit; the beginning and the
end in themselves. There never was a question of a future
other than the one in the New Jerusalem and heaven. When
the question "How did they expect to perpetuate themselves?"
arises, the answer is simply, "They didn't." Their entire
credo was based on a communistic Christian way of life that
expected to be rewarded by the Second Coming in their lifetime or shortly thereafter. However simple this was, there
were forces which did not allow this credo to run smoothly to
its end. The demonic in man reared its ugly head. As
George Rapp wrote: "It is decreed, that the whole Human
Race shall become united, by the sacred bond of mutual interest, and brotherly affection; but few indeed, have yet attained their destiny."[1]

The struggle for this destiny was, as in all religions,
not a matter of clarity and reason, but of faith, a faith in an
inner growth which cannot be forced unto man. So, from the
beginning there were those who had been carried along with
the Württemberg-religious ferment, but once they found themselves in the wilds of America their enthusiasm cooled.
Realizing that they preferred another way of life, they withdrew. And there were the children who had no conviction of
their own at the time of emigration, and who, as they grew
older, wanted lives of their own choosing. Added to these
were the latecomers who really did not have the harmony-
spirit and understanding of the founders even though they
were Württembergers seeking religious thought. Finally,
there were the hirelings, apprentices and indentured servants.
The population was in constant flux. Everyone who wrote
about the number of Harmonists would say "about," "some,"
"almost," but never the exact number, and only William
Hebert thought this uncertainty about the number strange. He
wrote, "Our guide informed us that their number was a little
above seven hundred, but that he did not recollect the exact
number, which last part of his communication I thought
somewhat strange in an elderly and influential associate."[2]

196

Among such an admixture there were bound to be
"cracks in the cloister." This in itself would have been
tolerable, but bitterness and greed crept in. The less noble
souls made charges against the Society and some brought
suit. The first to do this was Eugene Müller in 1821. There
was also the Jacob Schreiber case of 1835. The most celebrated cases were the Nachtrieb and Lemmix cases, 1849
and 1854 respectively. The court, after long battles, upheld
the Harmonists in all cases.

Apparently, after the Müller suit of 1821, Father
Rapp grew more wary and dogmatic. In 1827 he drew up
new Articles of Agreement which emphasized the founding
principles. 3 It was this emphasis which disturbed many.
From all accounts, members were reluctant to sign, but
615 did. Arndt reports that forty-two members withdrew. 4
But John S. Duss reports the withdrawal number as 52.
Duss also points out that in 1826, the year Rapp was showing
his new strength, twenty-six members withdrew. 5

With such unrest, the setting was right for Count de
Leon, alias Divine Messenger, alias Anointed of the Lord,
alias Broli, alias Bernard Müller. This Enthusiast impos-
ter had had his adventures in Europe, and now decided to
try America. His long-range planning started in 1829 and
culminated in 1832 when 250 left the Society with him.

Leon's first contact with the Society came through a
letter written by his secretary John George Göntgen, Ph.D.,
in which was stated a great reverence for George Rapp and
his Society. Leon, "the Appointed of God," was to see that
"the golden rose" should in truth come upon them. 6 Two
years later, with much fanfare, Leon and company arrived,
but not before more unrest grew. Besides, Frederick Rapp
and Romelius Baker, being wise in the ways of the world,
feared a fraud. The following letter shows the secrecy that
was afoot:

Oct. 2, 1831
Frederick!
My last writing was Sept. 28 and since then re-
ceived your letter of the 23rd. The wool and a box
of No. 1 blue cloth is shipped. I wrote to Walter
Forward [sp?] that he should write to J. & M.
Brown and M. D. Lewis about the wool.
We have heard nothing more about Count de Leon
and Göntgen except that we read in the paper that

he has traveled to Pittsburgh and was looking for
some land in the neighborhood. Father has not
told anyone that he received a letter, nor that those
people are around. However, he is hurriedly
completing the empty houses & has asked me not
to tell anyone. Many of our dismissed members
are in Pittsburgh--Henning, Philena Stark &
Christina Wolfert left together 2 days ago. He is
working at McClurg & Pratt. Zeno Schnabel came
for Dorothy Mutschler last Sunday and the next
evening they were married. Elias Steifel and
Andreas Boger also went down the river with their
brother. Other than that none left since my previous report. Father nor anyone else knows that
I wrote you these facts.

Greetings,
(signed) R. L. Baker[7]

It was soon thereafter that Leon arrived. He was
saluted with fine music from the church tower. When he
entered the church, where the Harmonists were eagerly
awaiting him, he made a few pompous statements instead
of the momentous pronouncements they had been prepared to
expect through Father Rapp's enthusiastic preaching.[8] But
within a short time, Leon, with promises of a more ma-
terialistic life and marriage, had won a considerable number of the Harmonists. It was only because of the oncoming
winter that Father Rapp allowed Leon and his entourage to
stay. By January 17, 1832, Frederick Rapp had publicly
written:

> ... until the Count completely and satisfactorily in
> deed and truth proves that he is the messenger and
> the appointed of the Lord and that he is of the
> House of Juda I will strongly protest all his pre-
> tentions--civil and religious--and treat him as an
> ordinary person.[9]

To add to the confusion Leon said he had the answer
to the Philosopher's Stone and could extract gold from stone
and base metals, a project Father Rapp had been working on,
and in which Frederick also had great interest[10] (see Chapter I). Finally, a paper was drawn up naming Leon as the
head, and all outstanding bills were to be sent to him. A
counter paper extolling the virtues of the old order was drawn
up. The Society was divided--250 for Leon; 500 for Rapp.
A compromise was ratified on March 6, 1832, giving the
leaving members $105,000, to be paid in three installments,

and their personal clothing and household furniture.[11]

The 250 who left settled Phillipsburg (now Monaca)
but their new-found happiness was short lived when they
found "the Appointed One" had clay feet and was spending all
their money. Furthermore, they came to the realization that
he could not make gold either, after he tried to fool them
by showing them gold in the crucible which he could not explain. In desperation, the deserters decided to demand
more money from the Harmonists, but the latter were pro-
tected by their non-Harmonist neighbors, who drove the in-
vaders out of town "before drum and fife, to the tune of the
Rogue's March."[12] George Rapp's version of the Prolli (or
Broli) affair follows:

October 12, 1834
    I received your letter dear friends, and I
would like to honor your request to hear from me
since you heard reports [about me] which puzzled
and dismayed you. And rightly so. As far as I
am concerned, I am well, and although I am approaching 78 I can carry on my spiritual and
worldly affairs as well as I did 30 years ago.
Don't you believe the evil reports that the Harmony
Society and I are at odds. What came to pass had
to be for the Old and New Testament are to be fulfilled that in the last days we would be tested to
become worthy of God; so all the trials and tribula-
tions of life are nothing more than the testing
ground and development toward our higher spiritual
life. Of course, it is always only a small number
which willingly leaves the broad highway of life for
the narrow footpath of Christ's followers. And so
it would be that the spirit of Jesus wants to prepare us for the higher step into the spiritual house
of the beginning of life.
    You accuse me, and at the same time you want
an explanation for your judgement! Your aim was
not good, and your hit even worse. I am inclined
to defend myself, but let me tell you that from
the first glance I recognized Prolli for what he was
and that to the praise of many of the society the
manly thing was done and during the first ten days
many reported him. But the bad fellows, for whom
the road of conversion was too straight and narrow,
united themselves with him and the 40 cohorts he
brought with him because he promised them to
make much gold and said that all the secrets he

possessed were given to him by God to establish
the millenium.   He said he already had 5 million
and a thousand other great treasures which I consider trash for his fraudulence is too apparent. He
said he was sent here by God to be a new leader
of the Harmony Society and to build a temple for
the City of God, the new Jerusalem for which
great work Rapp was not the builder so he [Rapp]
would have to be removed either dead or alive.
But the greater number of good people were on my
side and my enemies were shamed and mocked and
the judgement of God will go hard with them. Because they were not able to find any evidence against
me, I advised them to invent all sorts of malice,
error and wickedness about me and to swear by it,
and that they should make every attempt to present
me as a villain. This was done and it was published in the newspapers and the public was informed.   And this is the diatribe you read.
Enough of that.   Nothing further happened here
but that our society was cleansed of rubbish and
thereby strengthened its growth.   New is our
ground which we founded 30 years ago according
to the Scripture that no one have any personal be-
longings, but that there be spiritual and bodily
brotherhood so that we can see and know the power-
ful and important 100,000 of the Lord for although
the brotherhood of the church of Christ was founded
in the time of the Apostles, it has become something
entirely new and different which is built on selfish-
ness and political freedom and explanations which
are surely beckoning apostasy in which the Church
of Christ will disappear. And because of this, it
behooves us to be on guard and to take heed of
John 14:16 and find a heavenly kingdom here on
earth where the tree of life can be transplanted
and where it soon will bear fruit and our brotherhood; actually our community already has such a
place in miniature because we have peace and unity
of action among us. A cross and attack unites the
same opinions.

I greet you and those to whom I still am of
some worth.   And I am happy that your old friend
still lives in your memory.

Your good friend,

(signed) Georg R. (app)[13]

The year this letter was written was also the year of
Frederick Rapp's death, and the beginning of the end of the
old order. The business end still had momentum while
Romelius Baker was around, but he was not the tower of
strength that Frederick had been, and George Rapp and
Jacob Henrici were not of this business world. In a letter
to Father Rapp, Baker added, "P.S.--If there are any notes
due don't forget to send them to the bank in time."[14] And in
a letter about spinning machine business he added the dry
comment, "If one has to deal with the world one must keep
ones mind on business because if one is absent-minded in a
large city, ones feet must pay for it dearly. (Not so,
Brother Jacob?)"[15] This is not saying that Henrici was not
able. Quite the contrary. However, he was of the true
spiritual world, as Father Rapp had been. It is true that
during his trusteeship the Society attained its greatest wealth,
but this was because of oil and coal found on their land and
the building of railroads through their property. The Indus-
trial Revolution was coming to Economy, and they had to
reach beyond their home factories to the outside world. A
business man was needed to compete in the increasingly
complicated and tough business world, where men were not
always as honest as Henrici. That the structure was about
to topple is seen by the confused finances after Henrici's
death. But this end took a long time to come.

When Father Rapp died on August 7, 1847, James
Patterson wrote:

> The founder and head of the Economy Society has
> finished his work here and gone to receive his re-
> ward in heaven for his labors of love here. The
> time has come and passed upon the Society which
> so many prophesied would be fatal to it and end it.
> How gloriously the Society has given the lie to all
> its traducers. I knew it would be so. The one
> said to be a tyrant and his people slaves! Who
> dares say so now? The Head has been removed;
> the members all left free; each to act and do for
> himself and what do you see? A band of brothers
> held together--ruled and governed now as hereto-
> fore by love![16]

This was so because the Harmonists who remained
with the founder during the Count Leon imbroglio were firm
in their conviction of a Divine Economy and Harmony.
Baker and Henrici carried on. With Baker's death in 1868,

Henrici was really the lone leader, although he had amiable
Lenz as a co-trustee. Henrici belonged to the old order of
things, which was passing into silence. As a last means to
sustain the leadership of the Harmonist spirit, Henrici asked
John S. Duss to return to Economy to teach. John had
come to Economy as a child of two in 1862, but he did not
"belong"; he was a man of the world who admired the Harmonists, but he was not truly one of them. He and the
hirelings and their families overshadowed the remaining few
Harmonists.

Finally, in 1905, the Society was dissolved by Mrs.
John S. Duss, who had become sole trustee after her husband
stepped aside for legal reasons. At that time two Harmonists
remained, Barbara Bösch and Franz Gilman. Barbara died
in 1905, and Franz in 1921 at the age of ninety-three years
and ten months.[17]

One hundred years were gone, and the dream of
Harmony and its golden rose were a memorial to a people
who lived in an age that cultivated groups who answered the
world's chaotic state with: "And I saw a new heaven and a
new earth."[18]

Notes

1.   [George Rapp] Thoughts on the Destiny of Man (Harmony:
     Harmonist Press, 1824), p. 43.

2.   William Hebert, A Visit to the Colony of Harmony in
     Indiana, in the United States of America (London:
     George Mann, 1825), p. 333.

3.   1827 Articles of Agreement, Old Economy, Frederick
     Rapp Library.

4.   Karl J. R. Arndt, George Rapp's Harmony Society,
     1785-1847 (Philadelphia: University of Pennsylvania,
     1965), p. 358.

5.   John S. Duss, The Harmonists (Harrisburg: The
     Telegraph Press, 1943), p. 77.

6.   Aaron Williams, The Harmony Society (Pittsburgh:
     W. S. Haven, 1866), p. 134.

7. Letter, R. L. Baker to Frederick Rapp, Oct. 2, 1831,
    Old Economy, Archives, Box 32.

8. Williams, Society, p. 74.

9. Document, Frederick Rapp to Consul Kahl, Jan. 17,
    1832, Old Economy, Archives, Box 32.

10. Williams, Society, p. 76.

11. Ibid., p. 77.

12. Ibid., p. 79.

13. Letter, George Rapp to Johann Bengel, Oct. 12, 1834,
    Old Economy, Archives, Box 38.

14. Letter, R. L. Baker to George Rapp, May 17, 1835,
    Old Economy, Archives, Box 39.

15. Letter, R. L. Baker to George Rapp, Sept. 25, 1835,
    Old Economy, Archives, Box 40.

16. Letter, James Patterson to Romelius Baker, Aug.
    20, 1847, Old Economy, Archives, Box 59.

17. Christiana Knoedler, The Harmony Society (New
    York: Vantage Press, Inc., 1954), p. 125.

18. Rev. 21:1.

BIBLIOGRAPHY

Arndt, Johann. Paradiesgärtlein. Philadelphia: Schäfer and Koradi, n.d.

Arndt, Karl J. R. George Rapp's Harmony Society, 1785-1847. Philadelphia: University of Pennsylvania, 1965.

_____. "Three Hungarian Travelers Visit Economy." The Pennsylvania Magazine of History and Biography, LXXIX, 2, April, 1955, pp. 197-216.

Articles of Agreement--1827. Old Economy, Frederick Rapp Library.

Bausman, Joseph H. History of Beaver Co. Penn. and Its Centennial Celebration. Vol. II. 2 vols. New York: The Knickerbocker Press, 1904.

Beck, Berton E. "Tales of the Block House." Pennsylvania Folklife. XV:2. Winter--1965-1966.

Bernhard, Karl, Duke of Saxe-Weimar Eisenach. Travels Through North America, during the years 1825 and 1826. 2 vols. in 1; Philadelphia: Carey, Lea & Carey, 1828.

Bestor, Arthur Eugene, Jr. Backwoods Utopias. London: Oxford University Press, 1950.

Bible. King James Version.

Bible. Luther Translation. Nüremberg, 1534.

Biblia Hebraica. ed. Rud. Kittel. Leipzig: J. C. Henrichs' sche Buchhandlung, 1912.

Birkbeck, Morris. Notes on a Journey in America, from the Coast of Virginia to the Territory of Illinois. London: Ridgeway and Sons, 1818.

Blair, Don. Harmonist Construction. Indianapolis: Indiana

Historical Society, 1964.

_____. The New Harmony Story.   4th ed.   New Harmony:
  Publications Committee, 1967.

_____. Building Brochure. New Harmony: Tourist Office,
  n. d.

_____. A Panorama of Rare Prints.   Tell City: News
  Publishing Co., n. d.

Blinn, H. C. "Journey to Mt. Lebanon (Ky.) in a Carriage
  in 1853." Manuscript Journal. Old Chatham, N. Y.:
  Shaker Museum.

Böhme, Jacob. Von der Menschwerdung Jesu Christi und
  von Maria der Jungfrauen. Amsterdam: 1682.

_____. Von Wahrer Busse oder Wie sich der Mensch
  im Willen und Gemüthe in sich selber erwecken müsse.
  n. p.: 1730.

Boerhaave, Herrmann. Volks-Heillehre. Stuttgart: I.
  Scheible's Buchhandlung, 1840.

Bole, J. A. The Harmony Society. Philadelphia: Americana
  Germanica Press, 1904.

Buckingham, J. S. The Eastern and Western States of
  America. Vol. II. London: Fisher, Son & Co., 1842.

Burns, Robert. The Complete Poetical Works of Robert
  Burns. Boston: Houghton Mifflin Company, 1912.

Byron, Lord. Vol. XVII of The Works of Lord Byron. Edited by Thomas Moore. 17 vols. London: John Murray,
  1840.

Cawley, A. C., ed. Everyman and Medieval Miracle Plays.
  London: J. M. Dent & Sons, Ltd., 1956.

"Charisma, " International Encyclopedia of the Social Sciences.
  1968. Vol. II.

Cobbett, William. A Year's Residence in the United States
  of America. London: Sherwood, 1819.

Duclos, V. C. "From the Diary and Recollections of Victor
Colin Duclos. Copies from the original manuscript by
Mrs. Nora C. Fretageot." Indianapolis: Indiana Historical
Collections, III, 1916.

Durant, Will and Ariel. The Age of Reason Begins. New
York: Simon and Schuster, 1961.

Duss, John S. The Harmonists. Harrisburg: The Telegraph
Press, 1943.

Evangelische Lutherische Kirche. Kleines Lutherisches Schul-
Gesangbüchlein. New York: Hardter, 1866.

Faux, William. Memorable Days in America Being a Journal
of a Tour to the United States. London: W. Simpkin and
R. Marshall, 1823.

Feurige-Kohlen. Oekonomie: Harmonists, 1826.

Fink, Gottfried W. Häusliche Andachten. Leipzig: Georg
Joachim Göschen, 1814.

Flower, George. History of the English Settlement in Edwards Co., Illinois. Chicago: Fergus Printing Co.,
1882.

Fordham, Elias Pym. Personal Narrative of Travels in
Virginia, Maryland, Pennsylvania, Ohio, Indiana, Kentucky;
and of Residence in the Illinois Territory: 1817-1818. ed.
Frederic Austin Ogg. Cleveland: Arthur H. Clark, 1906.

Gilbert, Russell Wieder. "Blooming Grove, the Dunker
Settlement of Central Pennsylvania." Pennsylvania History (January, 1953), 22-39.

"Golden Rose." The Catholic Encyclopedia. 1912. VI.

Gordon, Jean. Pageant of the Rose. Woodstock: Record
Press, 1961.

Gormly, Agnes M. Hays. Old Economy. Sewickley: George
Hays Printer, 1966.

Grebnitz, C. E. Die Besorgte Hausfrau in der Küche, Vor-
rathskammer und dem Küchengarten. Reutlingen: J. J.
Mäcken'schen, 1831.

Haas, Johann Ludwig. Repertorium für homöopathische
Heilungen und Erfahrungen. Leipzig: Ludwig Schumann,
1834.

Hall, M. P. The Secret Teachings of All Ages. California;
The Philosophical Research Society, Inc., 1959.

Harmonisches Gesangbuch. Oekonomie: the Harmonists,
1827.

"The Harmonists." The Atlantic Monthly. Vol. XVII, No.
CIII. May, 1866, pp. 529-538.

Hays, George A. The Churches of the Harmony Society.
Ambridge: Old Economy, 1964.

_____. The 1822 Harmony Wood Printing Press.
Ambridge: Old Economy, 1960.

_____. Founders of the Harmony Society. 3rd ed.
Ambridge: Old Economy, 1961.

_____. The Grotto at Old Economy. 2nd ed. Ambridge:
Old Economy, 1963.

_____. The Silk Industry and Other Crafts of the Har-
monie Society. Ambridge: Old Economy, 1964.

Heald, Henry. A Western Tour. Wilmington: J. Wilson,
Printer [1819].

Hebert, William. A visit to the Colony of Harmony in
Indiana, in the United States of America. London:
George Mann, 1825.

Herder, Johann Gottfried. Ideen zur Geschichte der
Menschheit. Wien: Johann von Müller, 1813.

_____. Werke zur Philosophie und Geschichte. Wien:
Johann von Müller, 1813.

Heuss, Theodor. Schatten Beschwörung Randfiguren der
Geschichte. Hamburg: Fischer Bücherei, 1954.

Hinds, W. A. American Communities. New York:
Corinth Books, 1961.

Hirten-Brief. Pittsburgh: L.u.W. Neeb, 1855.

History of Posey County, Indiana, illustrated. Chicago:
    The Goodspeed Publishing Co., 1886.

Hübner, J. Kinderspiegel. Hamburg: Ludwig Koch, n.d.

Jones, Rufus M. Spiritual Reformers in the 16th and 17th
    Centuries. Boston: Beacon Press, 1914.

Knoedler, Christiana. The Harmony Society. New York:
    Vantage Press Inc., 1954.

Lemmix, Elijah vs. Romulus L. Baker et al. Circuit
    Court of the United States, Western District of Pennsyl-
    vania, Pittsburgh, 1854.

Lindley, Harlow, ed. Indiana as Seen by Early Travelers.
    Indianapolis: Indiana Historical Commission, 1916.

Lockridge, R. F. The Labyrinth of New Harmony. New
    Harmony: The New Harmony Memorial Commission, 1941.

_____. The Old Fauntleroy Home. New Harmony: New
    Harmony Memorial Commission, 1939.

MacDonald, Donald. The Diaries of Donald MacDonald,
    1824-1826. Edited by Caroline Dole Snedeker.
    Indianapolis: Vol. 14--No. 2. Indiana Historical Society
    Publications, 1942.

"Martin Luther's Seal." Minneapolis: Lutheran Brother-
    hood, 1956.

Martineau, Harriet. Vol. II of Society in America. 3 vols.
    London: Saunders and Otley, 1837.

Matter, Evelyn. The Baker House. Ambridge: Old Economy,
    1968. (Mimeographed.)

Melish, John. Travels in the United States of America in the
    Years 1806-1811 and Travels Through Various Parts of
    Great Britain, Ireland, and Upper Canada. 2 vols.
    Philadelphia, 1815.

Merck Manual, The. 7th ed. Rahway: Merck & Co., Inc.,
    1940.

Milchmädchen, Das. Philadelphia: Conrad Zentler, 1818.

Montulé, Edward de. Travels in America, 1816-1817. Translated from the original French edition of 1821 by Edward D. Seeber. Bloomington: Indiana University Press, 1951.

Nachtrieb (Joshua) vs. Romelius L. Baker et al. Circuit Court of the United States, Western District of Pennsylvania, Pittsburgh, 1849.

Neues wohl eingerichtetes Koch-Buch aus mehr als fünfzehen hundert Speisen bestehend, oder Nachrichten von allem ersinnlichen Koch und Backwerk in zwei Theilen. Tübingen, 1769.

Nordhoff, Charles. The Communistic Societies of the United States. New York: Schocken Books, 1965.

Noyes, J. H. History of American Socialisms. New York: Dover Publications, Inc., 1966.

"Ora Labora" article. n. d. Old Economy, Curator's File.

Owen, Robert Dale. Threading My Way: Twenty-Seven Years of Autobiography. New York: G. W. Carleton, 1874.

Owen, William. Diary of William Owen, November 10, 1824-April 20, 1825. Edited by Joel W. Hiatt. Indianapolis: Indiana Historical Society Publications, IV, No. 1, 1906.

Passavant, William A. "A Visit to Economy in the Spring of 1840." Western Pennsylvania Historical Magazine, IV, No. 3, July, 1921, pp. 144-149.

"Patriotic German-American, A." Western Pennsylvania Historical Magazine, Vol. II, No. 2, April, 1919. pp. 107-114.

Der Psalter des Koenigs und Propheten Davids, verdeutschet von Dr. Martin Luther, gerdruckt bei Jacob Meyer für Johnson & Werner, 1812.

[Rapp, George]. Thoughts on the Destiny of Man. Harmony: Harmonist Press, 1824.

Reibel, D. B. Old Economy. Ambridge: Old Economy, 1968. (Mimeographed.)

Schoolcraft, H. R.   Travels in the Central Portions of the
    Mississippi Valley.   Comprising observations on its
    Mineral, Geography, Internal Resources and Aboriginal
    Population, Performed under Sanction of Government in
    the Year 1821.   New York: Collins and Hannay, 1825.

Shoemaker, Alfred L.   "Andreas Bernadus Smolnikar,
    God's Ambassador Extraordinary."   The Pennsylvania
    Dutchman.   March 15, 1952.

Snedeker, Caroline Dale.   The Town of the Fearless.
    Garden City: Doubleday, Doran & Co., Inc., 1931.

Stewart, Arthur I. and Veith, Loran, W.   Harmony. n. p.,
    1955.

Stotz, Charles M.   Early Architecture of Western Pennsyl-
    vania.   New York: Helburn Inc., 1936.   Re-published as
    The Architectural Heritage of Early Western Pennsylvania.
    Pittsburgh: University of Pittsburgh Press, 1966.

Stoudt, John Joseph.   Pennsylvania Folk Art.   Allentown:
    Schlechter's, 1948.

Straube, C. F.   Rise and Fall of the Harmony Society--Econ-
    omy, Pa. and Other Poems.   Pittsburgh: National Printing
    Company, 1911

Sundelin, Karl.   Taschenbuch der Arzneiformeln nach den
    Methoden der berühmtesten Ärzte.   Berlin: Th. Chr. Fr.
    Enslin, 1837.

"The Symbol of the Rose in Textile Design."   Press Release.
    New York: Scalamandré Museum of Textiles. n. d.

Thwaites, R. G.   Early Western Travels, 1748-1846.   Vol.
    X: Hulme's Journal, 1818-19; Flower's Letters from
    Lexington and the Illinois, 1819; Flower's Letters from
    the Illinois, 1820-21; Wood's Two Years' Residence, 1820-
    21:   New York: Ams Press, Inc., 1966.

Vereinigungs-Artikel der Harmonie-Gesellschaft.   Pittsburgh:
    Enrst Luft, n. d.

Vogt, Von Ogden.   Modern Worship.   New Haven: Yale
    University Press, 1927.

Weber, Max. The Theory of Social and Economic Organization. Translated by A. M. Henderson and Talcott Parsons. New York: Oxford University Press, 1947.

Wetzler, Johann Evangelist. Uber den Nutzen und Gebrauch des Püllnär Bitterwassers. Augsburg: Jos. Wolff'sche Buchhandlung, 1828.

Williams, Aaron. The Harmony Society. Pittsburgh: W. S. Haven, 1866.

Wilson, Bryan R. Sects and Society. Berkeley: University of California Press, 1961.

Wilson, John H. The Historic Town of Harmony, Butler Co. n. p., 1937.

Wilson, W. E. The Angel and the Serpent. Bloomington: University of Indiana Press, 1964.

Yelland, John Hornstein. "The Garden Grotto at Old Economy." Old Economy, 1959. (Mimeographed.)

Manuscripts

Anonymous Harmonist Article, Dec., 1818, Series 2.

"Circular," Whig Committee to R. L. Baker. Oct. 1, 1834, Box 38.

Document, Frederick Rapp to Consul Kahl, Jan. 17, 1832, Box 32.

Document for the Harmonifest, n.d., Box 7.

Folk Medicine Recipe MS, 1814, Frederick Rapp Library.

Harmonie Ode, Jan. 7, 1831, Box 29.

Receipt, E. Acker to G. Rapp, Oct. 27, 1845, Box 57.

Receipt, Inspector Adams to the Harmonists, n.d., Box 54.

Receipt, Anton Kast to the Harmony Society, Jan. 7, 1842, Box 52.

School Dictation Book, Frederick Rapp Library.

Letter: R. D. O. Templeton to the Editors, June 9, 1914.
Evansville, The Evansville Courier.

Letters: Old Economy Archives, Ambridge, Pa.

Romelius Baker to Samuel Arthur, July 6, 1848, Box 60.

R. L. Baker to John Baker, May 12, 1824, Box 4.

R. L. Baker to Jacob Henrici, Jan. 1, 1842, Box 52.

R. L. Baker to Frederick Rapp, Sept. 26, 1821, Box 3.

R. L. Baker to Frederick Rapp, April 11, 1830, Box 27.

R. L. Baker to Frederick Rapp, Oct. 2, 1831, Box 32.

R. L. Baker to George Rapp, May 17, 1835, Box 39.

R. L. Baker to George Rapp, Sept. 25, 1835, Box 40.

R. L. Baker to George Rapp, Feb. 15, 1840, Box 49.

W. P. Baum to R. L. Baker, July 29, 1847, Box 59.

John Breymaier to Lewis Pfeil, Sept. 17, 1842, Box 53.

James Cameron to R. L. Baker, Oct. 24, 1844, Box 56.

Wm. Chambers to George Rapp, Jan. 15, 1816, Box 2.

Christiana Daum to George Rapp, Sept. 13, 1841, Box 52.

Thomas Foster to Frederick Rapp, Aug. 28, 1829, Box 25.

A Friend to Daniel Lynn, Oct. 8, 1818, Box 2.

Mary Graff to Gertrude Rapp, Sept. 11, 1830, Box 28.

Harlow Heard to Frederick Rapp, Nov. 23, 1833, Box 36.

Harmonists to Lorenz Schelling, Nov. 21, 1844, Box 56.

George W. Hatch to George Rapp, April 27, 1840, Box 49.

Jacob Henrici to Romelius Baker, Dec. 8, 1937, Box 45.

Johannes Killinger to George Rapp, May 14, 1827, Box 18.

Letters re Jacob Klein, Sept. 1, 15, 1826, Box 6.

Maria Lemox to George Rapp, Nov. 16, 1844, Box 55.

Johann Maier to Georg Rapp, July 30, 1830, Box 28.

Michael Mueller to George Rapp, June 18, 1843, Box 54.

H. Muntz to R. L. Baker, July 23, 1836, Box 42.

R. T. Nevin to George Rapp, Sept. 12, 1839, Box 48.

James Patterson to Romelius Baker, Aug. 20, 1847,
Box 59.

Catherine Rapp to George Rapp, April 24, 1824, Box 4.

Frederick Rapp to J. Solms, May 11, 1824, Box 4.

Frederick Rapp to William Burtch, Oct. 8, 1830, Letterbook, 1828-1830.

Frederick Rapp to Clang, Peerson & Co., July 10, 1826,
Letterbook, 1828-1830.

Frederick Rapp to James Drake, Aug. 1, 1828, Letterbook, 1828-1830.

Frederick Rapp to John Hay, Nov. 10, 1825, Letterbook,
1825-1828.

Frederick Rapp to John D. Hay, Nov. 7, 1826, Letterbook, 1825-1828.

Frederick Rapp to John Hay, May 21, 1830, Letterbook,
1828-1830.

Frederick Reichert Rapp to George Rapp, March 27,
1804, Series 2.

George Rapp to Johann Bengel, Oct. 12, 1834, Box 38.

George Rapp to Thomas Henry, Jan. 24, 1842, Box 52.

George Rapp to Jacob Neff, April 10, 1806, Box 50.

George Rapp to Frederick Rapp, Feb. 24, 1813, Series 2.

George Rapp to Frederick Rapp, Oct. 12, 1824, Box 4.

George Rapp to Frederick Rapp, Feb. 12, 1826, Box 6.

George Rapp to Frederick Rapp, Feb. 16, 1826, Box 6.

George Rapp to Gertrude Rapp, Jan. 22, 1824, Box 4.

Gertrude Rapp to Rosina Rapp, Dec. 26, 1824, Series 2.

George Rapp et al to Maria Weber, Oct. 14, 1844, Box 56.

Johann Georg Rapp to Johann Christoph, Feb. 10, 1801, Series 2.

J. C. Reynolds to Romelius Baker, April 2, 1826, Box 42.

Gov. Joseph Ritner to George Rapp, April 16, 1838, Box 45.

John Schnee to Frederick Rapp, Oct. 27, 1819, Series 2.

Andreas Smolnikar to George Rapp, May 9, 1842, Box 53.

Letter-note, Elizabeth Solms to Gertrude Rapp, Oct. 15, 1835, Box 41.

Temperance Society to Frederick Rapp, June 16, 1829, Box 25.

Conrad Thorwarth to Georg Rapp, Aug. 12, 1832, Box 33.

C. A. Walburn to R. L. Baker, Sept. 15, 1834, Box 55.

Mary Ann Way to R. L. Baker, July 1, 1833, Box 36.

Frantz Weinberg to Joseph Bäumle, Aug. 5, 1827, Box 7.

Frantz Weinberg to George Rapp, Oct. 18, 1827, Box 7.

Z. W. Vashon to George Rapp, June 28, 1838, Box 46.

Interviews

Al-An, Mariechen Schnauz. Private interview. Evansville, Indiana, July, 1967.

Blair, Don. Private Interview. New Harmony, Indiana, July, 1967.

Elliott, (Mrs.) Josephine. Private interview, New Harmony, Indiana, July, 1967.

Ford, Fred C. Private interview. Philadelphia, Pa., May, 1966.

Haseley, (The Rev.) Leonard L. Private interview, Ambridge, Pa., August, 1967.

Henrici, Max. Private interview. Coraopolis, Pa., July, 1967.

Knoedler, Christiana. Private interview. Old Economy Village, Ambridge, Pa., August, 1967.

Lectures, Religious Thought 523: American Folk Religion, University of Pennsylvania, Autumn, 1965.

Lewis, (Mrs.) Frances. Private interview. New Harmony, Indiana, July, 1967.

May, (Mrs.) E. A. Private interview. Patterson Heights, Pa., August, 1967.

Mohn, Henry. Private interview. Leetsdale, Pa., July, 1967.

Rupp, (Mrs.) Margaret. Private interview. Zelienople, Pa., August, 1967.

Stewart, (Dr.) Arthur. Private interview. Harmony, Pa., September, 1967.

Appendix

HARMONIST PICTURES

Harmonist House, New Harmony, Indiana

Dormitory, New Harmony, Indiana

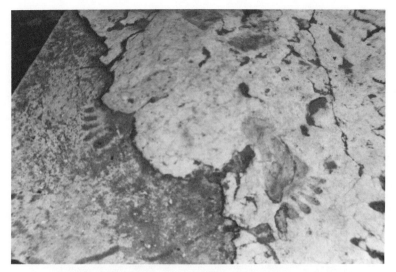

"Gabriel's Footprints," New Harmony, Indiana

Sun Dial, New Harmony, Indiana

220

The labyrinth and the grotto, New Harmony, Indiana

The orchard (the cemetery), New Harmony, Indiana

Orchards (cemeteries) at Harmony, Pa. (above)
and Economy, Pa. (below)

Fabric with rose design and ribbon
with rosettes made at Economy, Pennsylvania

Silk ribbons with rose and lily
motifs made at Economy, Pennsylvania.

Carvings by Frederick Rapp: (above) The Virgin Sophia, the
rose and the lily above doorway at Harmony, Pennsylvania;
(below) Original door of the 1822 Maltese Cross Church. The
golden rose of Micah 4:8 in both carving and glass design.
New Harmony, Indiana.

225

The golden rose of Harmony
in the Great House of Economy, Pa.

Harmonist pottery and rose design cooky
cutter for their famous ginger cookies.

Sunday dress of Harmonist ladies and men

The statue of Harmony in the garden of the Great House

From the Feast Hall, looking toward the Great House and Church
Steeple

The Feast Hall (also the School and Museum)

Left to right: The Baker House, the store, the tailor shop

The wine cellar

The classroom

233

The tailor shop

The kitchen in the Baker House

The main room in the Baker House

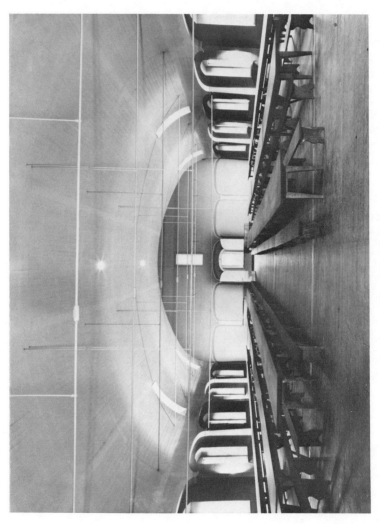

The Feast Hall

INDEX

Accounts burned 11, 15
Adam 12, 16, 17
Admission requests 34, 177
Agape 81, 85, 87
Amsterdam 4, 5
Ananias (and Sapphira) 11
Angel Gabriel 137, 219
Arndt, Johann 1
Arndt, Karl J. R. x, 4,
  71, 82, 197
Arrivals (U. S.) 5, 6
Articles of Association 24
"Atlantic" (ship) 5
Atlantic Monthly, The x
"Aurora" (ship) 6, 81

Baker, Romelius 11, 14,
  15, 26, 31-34, 53, 83,
  97, 145
Baker House 141
Band 91
Baptism 70
Beginnings 6, 7
Belief Statement of Rapp
  Group 4, 11-21
Bentel House 135
Berleburger Bible 11, 19,
  71
Bernhard, Karl of Saxe-
  Weimer x, 96, 97, 143
Bestor, Arthur E. Jr. xi
Beverages 144 ff
Biblical references:
  Acts 4:32. 11; Acts 2:44.
  45. 11; Acts 1:11. 13;
  Acts 3:20-21. 13; Acts 4:
  13. 36; Acts 4:32. 47;
  1 Cor. 7:14. 3; 1 Cor. 7:1,
  7, 8, 32. 12; Eph. IV:26.

47; Genesis 1:26-27, 12;
  Isaiah 35:1. 84; II Kings
  12:15, 22:7. 15; Luke 16:1-
  9. 173; Mark 10:13-16. 3;
  Matt. 19:12. 12; Matt. 6:6,
  7. 66; Micah 4:8 19, 41,
  49; Psalms 6, 32, 38, 51,
  102, 130, 143. 48; Rev.
  20:4, 5. 13; Rev. 17:17.
  17; Rev. 12:1. 19, 25; Rev.
  21:11. 20; Rev. 12:6, 13-
  16. 21; Rev. 21:1. 202;
  Rom. 6:3, 4. 3; Rom.
  8:19-23. 13; Song of S 2:1.
  19, 49.
Birkbeck, Morris x, 55, 139
Blair, Don 136, 141
Blockhouse 178-179
Blooming Grove (Pa.) 5
Böhme, Jakob 1, 16, 17, 18
Bole, John A. x
Buckingham, James S. x, 45,
  48, 56, 57, 81, 95, 147,
  152
Building Construction 135-136
Buildings 134
Burial 76, 78, 79
Burns, Robert (poems) 98
Business practices 169 ff
Byron, Lord (poem) 75-76

Calendric Customs 81 ff
Canonical S 48
"Canton" (ship) 4
Celibacy 6, 12, 70, 71, 137
Cemetaries 76-78, 220
Charisma 26, 27
Charitable Activities 176,
  185

237

238

239